D0521294

Sawday's

Special Places
to Stay

Dog-friendly Breaks in Britain

Front

Front	Page
A word from Alastair Sawday	**6**
Introduction	**7**
Inspections	7
What to expect	7
Map	8
Types of places to stay	8
Bedrooms	10
Bathrooms	10
Sitting rooms	10
Meals	10
Prices	10
Bookings and cancellations	10
Payment	11
Tipping	11
Arrivals and departures	11
Closed	12
Feedback	12
Complaints	12
Symbols	12
Treats	14
Membership	14
Disclaimer	14
Days out with dogs	**17-20**
Maps	**21-33**

Guide entries

Guide entries	Entry	Map
England		
Bath & N.E. Somerset	1-5	2
Cambridgeshire	6, 7	4
Cheshire	8, 9	5, 6
Cornwall	10-26	1, 2
Cumbria	27-37	5, 6
Derbyshire	38-42	6
Devon	43-61	2
Dorset	62-71	2, 3
Durham	72-74	6
Essex	75, 76	4
Gloucestershire	77-85	2, 3
Hampshire	86-89	3
Herefordshire	90-92	2
Hertfordshire	93	3
Kent	94-96	4
Lancashire	97	5
Leicestershire	98	6
Lincolnshire	99	7
Norfolk	100-107	7
Northumberland	108-112	6, 9
Oxfordshire	113, 114	3
Rutland	115, 116	6
Shropshire	117-124	2, 5, 6
Somerset	125-128	2
Suffolk	129-134	4
Sussex	135-143	3, 4
Warwickshire	144-146	3
Wiltshire	147, 148	3
Worcestershire	149-153	2
Yorkshire	154-163	6, 7

Guide entries	Entry	Map
Wales		
Anglesey	183	5
Cardiff	184	2
Carmarthenshire	185-186	2
Ceredigion	187-191	1, 2
Conwy	192	5
Gwynedd	193-198	5
Monmouthshire	199-202	2
Pembrokeshire	203, 204	1
Powys	205-209	2, 5
Scotland		
Aberdeenshire	210	9
Argyll & Bute	211-214	8, 10
Ayrshire	215	9
Dumfries & Galloway	216, 217	5, 9
Fife	218	9
Highland	219-222	8, 11
Perth & Kinross	223, 224	8
Scottish Borders	225-227	9
Stirling	228	8
Pubs-for-a-pint		
Bedfordshire	*163.1*	*3*
Brighton & Hove	*164*	*3*
Bristol	*165*	*2*
Buckinghamshire	*166, 167*	*3*
Cheshire	*168-171*	*6*
Cornwall	*172*	*1*
Gloucestershire	*173, 174*	*3*
Hertfordshire	*175*	*3*
Northamptonshire	*176*	*3*
Somerset	*177*	*2*
Staffordshire	*178*	*6*
Suffolk	*179*	*4*
Sussex	*180-182*	*4*
Wiltshire	*182.1*	*3*

Back	Page
Dog treats at a glance!	250
How to achieve a pawfect holiday...	260
Other titles from Sawday's	265
Town index for Dog-friendly Places to Stay	267
Town index for Dog-friendly Pubs	269
What's in each Special Place to Stay entry	272

Once upon a time – to the owner of a B&B, hotel or rented house – a dog was just a dog, predictable and messy or a loyal and engaging companion of their guests.

In this more nuanced, enlightened age dogs – if you like them – are sentient beings to be welcomed, pampered and talked to. Their every need is to be anticipated. A visiting dog is an essential part of the visiting team and for all of them to be happy the dog must be happy. So there may be an outside bath for dogs who have enjoyed a prolonged roll in fox poo. Candles can be lit to light their bathing. We have met dog 'decks' where the baying at the moon can be done with canine dignity and privacy. Some dogs are welcomed with a welcome pack containing biscuits and bones.

Dogs generally bring extra joy into a house, making their owners feel at home and easy in their skin. A house full of dogs often has a comfortable buzz about it, a welcome touch of chaos rather than an over-ordered self-consciousness. How can you be stiff and pompous with a terrier hauling at your new pair of socks, or a lurcher spread-eagled across you? It is well known that animals can bring joy into an old-people's home; it makes sense that the same principle is at work wherever they are, if you like them at all. But it makes sense, too, for there to be blankets to spread before the dogs take over, or for there to be a dog-free room for those who don't love them.

Em and I once stayed in a French farmhouse whose owner offered us breakfast in her engagingly bedraggled but pretty garden. We were enchanted, and couldn't move – for Em was pinned to her seat. A long-legged dog placidly rested its tummy on her knees while its feet stood squarely on the ground. She had to eat her croissant off a plate on its back. Eventually we called for help, but the moment was memorable and we plan to return. A Premier Inn just doesn't provide that sort of experience.

Alastair Sawday

Photo: Mark Bolton

It's simple. There are no rules, no boxes to tick. We choose places that we like and we are subjective in our choices. We look for comfort, originality, authenticity, and a genuine welcome. The way guests – and their pets! – are treated comes as high on our list as the setting, the atmosphere and the food.

Inspections

Our inspectors know their patch. They don't take a clipboard and they don't have a list of what is acceptable and what is not. Instead, they chat with the owner and look round – closely – and if the visit happens to be the last of the day, they stay the night. It's all very informal, but it gives us an excellent idea of who would enjoy staying there; our simple aim is to match places with guests. Once in the book, properties are re-inspected every four years so that we can keep things fresh and up to date.

What to expect

This new edition of our best-selling Dog-friendly guide contains a wonderful mix of places that welcome you and your dog (or dogs – many allow more than one). Some have specific bedrooms that are set aside for guests with a dog in tow, others welcome dogs in all their rooms. In some places dogs may sleep downstairs but not in the bedroom; do check before you book. Dogs may not, anywhere, sleep on the bed!

The 'pub' entries welcome you for a pint with your dog; the 'inn' entries have dog-friendly bedrooms too. All have bar areas that welcome dogs, and often gardens too; most pubs draw the line at allowing dogs into dining rooms (although some have a special table set aside for visitors with a dog). If you want to check the details beforehand just give them a call. Dog treats

Photo: Walcot Hall, entry 121

at the pubs and inns might include a juicy bone, homemade biscuits or even dog 'beer' and birthday cakes!

There's a fascinating mix inside these pages of B&Bs, hotels, self-catering escapes, inns, pubs and Canopy & Stars outdoor retreats. Remote and simple, or wrapped in luxury, there's something for every pooch and its owner here.

Map

If you know which region you want to stay in, our maps are your best guide. Lozenges flag up properties in colours denoting whether they are catered (red), self-catering (blue) or pubs (dark grey). The maps are the perfect starting point for planning a stay – but please don't use them for navigation.

Photo above: 8 Coastguard Cottages, entry 135
Photo right: Gamekeepers Cottage & Cross Cottage, entry 161

Types of places to stay

B&Bs

B&Bs, however grand, are people's homes, not hotels. You'll most probably have breakfast and dinner with your hosts and/or fellow guests, and the welcome will be personal. Some owners give you a front door key so you may come and go as you please; others like to have the house empty between, say, 10am and 4pm.

Do expect

- a personal welcome
- a willingness to go the extra mile
- a degree of informality, and a fascinating glimpse into someone else's way of life

Don't expect

- a lock on your bedroom door
- your room cleaned and your bed made every day
- a private table at breakfast and dinner
- an immediate response to your booking enquiry
- a TV in your room

Hotels

Those we choose generally have fewer than 50 rooms; most are family-run with friendly staff; many are in historic buildings – perhaps a castle or two; others have a boutique feel. All those in this book like dogs!

Inns

Our one-page inns entries vary from swish suites with plasma TVs to sweet simple rooms overlooking the sea. Staying in

461

a pub – above the bar or in the converted barn behind – is often great value for money.

Self-catering places

Perfect independence for couples – and families – with dogs. Cottages, farmhouses, coach houses, studios, mills, barns – each and every one has been visited by us and found to be special. We don't include places we wouldn't stay in ourselves.

Canopy & Stars

For those who love to be at one with nature, welcome to our collection of beautiful, simple, quirky (and sometimes luxurious) places to sleep under the stars. Treehouses, shepherd's huts, yurts, gypsy caravans and romantic log cabins – the choice is inspiring.

Bedrooms

We tell you if a room is a single, double, twin/double (with zip and link beds), suite (a room with space for seating), family (a double bed + single beds), or triple (three single beds).

Bathrooms

The vast majority of bedrooms in this book are en suite. Only if a bedroom has a shared or a private-but-separate bathroom do we say so.

Sitting rooms

Most hotels have one or two communal areas, while most B&Bs offer guests the family sitting room to share, or provide a sitting room just for guests.

Meals

Unless we say otherwise, breakfast is included, simple or extravagant. Some owners are fairly unbending about breakfast times, others are happy just to wait until you want it, or even bring it to you in your room.

Many B&Bs offer their guests dinner, usually an opportunity to get to know your hosts and to make new friends among the other guests. Note that meal prices are per person. Always book in advance.

Prices

Self-catering prices are mostly quoted per week. Each other entry gives a price PER ROOM per night for two. The price range covers a night in the cheapest room in low season to the most expensive in high season. Some owners charge more at certain times (during regattas and festivals, for example) and some owners ask for a minimum two nights at weekends. Others offer special deals for three-night stays. Prices quoted are those given to us for 2018 but are not guaranteed. Double-check when booking.

At many of these places dogs go free, at others where there's a charge, we say so.

Bookings and cancellations

Sometimes you will be asked to pay a deposit. Some are non-refundable; some people may charge you for the whole of the booked stay in advance; and some cancellation policies are more stringent

than others. It is also worth noting that some owners will take the money directly from your credit/debit card without contacting you to discuss it. So ask them to explain their cancellation policy clearly before booking to avoid a surprise. Always make sure you have written confirmation of all you have discussed.

Payment

All our owners take cash and UK cheques with a cheque card, and those who take credit cards have our credit card symbol. Check that your particular credit card is acceptable.

Tipping

Owners do not expect tips – but if you have been treated with extraordinary kindness, drop your hosts a line. If you are on Facebook or Twitter, you can sing their praises from our website www.sawdays.co.uk. Find their Special Place, then 'share' or 'tweet'.

Arrivals and departures

Say roughly what time you will arrive (normally after 4pm; for inns, after 6pm), as most hosts like to welcome you personally. Be on time if you have booked dinner. If, despite best efforts, you are delayed, phone to give warning.

Photo: The Lion Inn, entry 79

Closed

When given in months this means the whole of the month stated.

Feedback

The accuracy of our books depends on what you, as well as our inspectors, tell us. Your feedback is invaluable and we always act upon comments. Tell us whether your stay has been a joy or not, if the atmosphere was great or stuffy, the owners cheery or bored. Importantly, a lot of new places come to us via our readers, so keep telling us about new places you've discovered. Just visit our sites:

www.sawdays.co.uk

for hotels, inns, B&Bs and self-catering properties

www.canopyandstars.co.uk

for outdoor retreats.

Complaints

Please do not tell us if the bedside light was inadequate, the hairdryer was broken or the bedroom was cold. Tell the owner instead, and ask them to do something about it. Most owners are more than happy to correct problems and will bend over backwards to help. If you think things have gone seriously awry, do tell us.

Photo above: The Parlour & The Dairy, entry 4
Photo right: The Inn at Whitewell, entry 97

Symbols

There is an explanation of the symbols used for our Special Places to Stay on the inside back cover of the book. Use them as a guide, not as a statement of fact. However, things do change: bikes may be under repair or a new pool may have been put in. If an owner does not have the symbol that you're looking for, it's worth discussing your needs.

Note that the symbol shows places that are happy to accept children of all ages; it does not mean that they will have cots and high chairs. Many who say no to children do so not because they don't like them but because they may have a steep stair, an unfenced pond or they find balancing the needs of mixed age groups too challenging.

The symbol is given when the owners have their own pet on the premises. It may not be a cat! But it is there to warn you that you may be greeted by a dog, serenaded by a parrot, or indeed sat upon by a cat.

The symbols used at the foot of the pub entries apply to the bar and not (should the pub have them) to its bedrooms.

Treats

Dog treats provided by owners are shown on each entry and listed at the back of the book for a bit of fun. How about local sausage cooked to perfection with a splash of milk to wash it down, or a coastal walk straight from the door? Or a tour of the grounds from the resident lurchers, and a bone from the village butcher? Many dogs like to share their favourite treats and walks, and some owners are willing dog sitters so you can have a night out at a non-dog-friendly place.

Membership

Owners pay to appear in this guide. Their membership fee goes towards the costs of inspecting, publishing, marketing, and maintaining our websites. It is not possible for anyone to buy their way onto these pages as we only include places that we like. Nor is it possible for owners to write their own description. We say if the bedrooms are small, the stairs are steep or if a main road is near. We aim not to mislead you!

Photo above: The Slate Shed at Graig Wen, entry 197
Photo right: The Westleton Crown, entry 179

Disclaimer

We make no claims to pure objectivity in choosing these places. They are here simply because we like them. Our opinions and tastes are ours alone and this book is a statement of them – we do hope you will share them. We have done our utmost to get our facts right but apologise unreservedly for any mistakes that may have crept in.

You should know that we don't check such things as fire regulations, swimming pool security or any other laws with which owners of properties receiving paying guests should comply. This is the responsibility of the owners.

We hope you enjoy our dog-friendly selection – we're almost 100% sure that you and your hound will have a brilliant holiday.

CROWN
INN
The Westleton Crown
Wel
to
the
Westlet
Crow

Sawday's

'More than a bed for the night…'

Britain
France
Ireland
Italy
Portugal
Spain

www.sawdays.co.uk

Self-Catering | B&B | Hotel | Pub | Treehouses, Cabins, Yurts & More

Dogs don't appreciate cultural breaks. They want beaches, woods, puddles and fields. Here's our pick of places that welcome dogs with open paws.

ENGLAND

St Ives, Cornwall

Stride the coastal path to Zennor (six miles), on to The Gurnard's Head pub (three miles) for lunch, then bus it back to St Ives.

Bodmin Moor, Cornwall

Trek up to the two highest points in Cornwall (OS Exp 109) and look to both coasts on a clear day. The remains of an iron age hill fort reward you at the summit.

Daymer Bay, Cornwall

Lovely large sandy bay, one of the few open to dogs all year round, with proper waves.

Branscombe, Devon

Unspoilt pebble beach in pretty Branscombe where dogs can romp lead-free 50m in either direction of the car park and café. From here, a coastal walk.

Durdle Door, Dorset

Dogs on leads permitted all year round; also at Lulworth Cove and Worbarrow Bay. Dogs off-lead (except May-September) at Studland Shell Bay, a short drive east.

Camber Sands, East Sussex

When the tide is out dogs get a brilliant run on the sand. Well-managed beaches with Minnis Bay the favourite – but no dogs May-September.

Cotswold Water Park, Gloucestershire

Criss-crossed by miles of flat foot and cycle path, this massive water park has been created from dozens of quarries filled with water and linked by canals. Keep dogs on leads in the bird nesting areas, otherwise, let them bound.

Saxon Shore Way, Kent

On the long-distance footpath to the white cliffs of Dover you cross four wonderful nature reserves: Conver Creek, Harty Ferry, the village of Oare and Faversham. Dogs on leads please.

Botany Bay, Broadstairs, Kent

Big old-fashioned sandy beach with rock pools and famous chalk stacks, off limits to dogs in summer (May-September

Photo: Ben Melarickas (Millie)

10am-6pm). Dogs welcome all year on Dumpton Gap beach. And gallops on the top for drying wet dogs off.

Greenwich Park, London

A really old park (1427) stuffed full of heritage (Anglo-saxon burial mounds; the Meridian Line), with amazing views across the Thames to St Paul's. Open 6am-6pm (later in summer) for good dogs that are off-lead. Park near the Pavilion Tea House and Royal Observatory.

Groton Wood, Suffolk

Ancient woodland, enchanting walks: bluebells, nightingales, toads, newts and brimstone butterflies.

Wells-next-the-Sea, Norfolk

The Kennel Club's beacon 2014 winner is dog-friendly all year round but at nesting time dogs are on leads. Big dogs go mad for the wide open spaces of nearby Holkham; at low tide the sands reach to the horizon.

Photo: The Hayloft at Flamborough Rigg, entry 157

Worcester Woods Country Park, Worcestershire

Acres of oak woodland, wildflower meadows and two gentle, circular walks perfect for elderly pooches.

Danes Dyke, Yorkshire

A small, away-from-it-all, award-winning beach – sand, pebbles, rock pools, clean water – reached from the car park down a steep road one mile west of Flamborough Head.

Rievaulx to Byland, Yorkshire

Not one but two ruined and magnificent abbeys in the North York Moors with a beautiful and varied six-mile walk between them.

Cautley Spout, Cumbria

Take the obvious path behind the inn at Low Haygarth and walk downstream along the beck (passing the famous wild horses of the Howgill Fells) towards the magnificent 'spout'. Dogs must be under control at the top as there's a mighty drop down, and a bit of a scramble to get there. Short, wild, remote and exhilarating.

Keswick, Cumbria

Lots of wag-friendly shops, pubs and cafés in town, and fells, woodland and lakes beyond – meaning clever Keswick won the Kennel Club's 2012 Open for Dogs Awards in the Dog Friendly Town category.

St Bees, Cumbria

A great family beach three miles from Whitehaven – be sure to scoop every poop. For serious walkers, link up with the Coast to Coast Walk that runs from St Bees on the west to Robin Hood's Bay on the east – glorious.

Bamburgh, Northumberland

A vast, big skies, dog-happy beach with dunes, overlooked by magnificent Bamburgh Castle.

Attingham Park, Shropshire

Luscious parkland for dogs with a nose for the high life, at this 18th-century, National Trust mansion. A hidden gem four miles south-east of Shrewsbury, it is blessed with large parkland that borders the river. Keep dogs on leads near the deer.

Baggeridge Country Park, Staffordshire

Between Wombourne and Sedgley, a much-loved Green Flag park, created over a former colliery. There are four trails in all, from a circular Easy Access trail, perfect for wheelchairs and buggies, to a 90-minute romp through Baggeridge Wood.

WALES

Conwy Mountain, Conwy

There's walking here as adventurous as anywhere in Snowdonia – but on a smaller scale.

Elan Valley, Powys

From Rhayader to Devil's Bridge, and some of the remotest hiking south of the Cairngorms. Miles of peaty plateaus, a few sheep, wheeling red kites and five larch-lapped Victorian reservoirs with associated viaducts and dams.

Rhossili Bay, Swansea

Miles of pristine sand at the tip of the Gower Peninsula, reached via many steps. There's enough space for dogs to run free all year – and a colourful selection of kites to bark at.

St David's Head Walk, Pembrokeshire

Circular three-hour walk from Whitesands Bay, the first bit inland, the second along the wind-buffeted coastal path. Thrill to the Hats and Barrels – the rocks and reefs that still pose a threat to boats passing through these tidal races.

Usk Valley Walk, Monmouthshire

One gorgeous stretch of this 48-mile route from Brecon to Caerleon and the sea, is along the fish-rich river bank between Usk and Abergavenny. Every bit as pretty as the Wye.

Glanusk Estate, Crickhowell

Luscious acres roll as far as the eye can see – plus ancient Celtic standing stones, a bridge over the river Usk, a private chapel, farm buildings and stables, 120 different species of oak, opera (though not for the dog), and country shows galore.

Broad Haven, Bosherston, Pembs

Beautiful sheltered sand and dune bay reached via boardwalks across the famous lily ponds. Bow-wow heaven.

SCOTLAND

Culzean Castle & Country Park, Ayrshire

A 'castle in the air' perched high above the crashing waves of the Firth of Clyde, with miles of woodland walks. Leads on please for the deer park and swan pond.

Craigower, near Pitlochry, Perthshire

High-up open heathland with stunning long views, rare butterflies and scattered Scots pines. Dogs on the lead when crossing the golf course.

Hermitage, near Dunkeld, Perthshire

A woodland walk though huge Douglas firs to a folly overlooking the crashing Black Linn waterfall – best keep dogs and toddlers on leads.

Barry Mill, Carnoustie, Angus

It is a lovely walk with the dog up to Barry Mill, for the splash of the waterwheel and the smell of grinding corn: milling demos on Sundays.

Calgary Bay, Isle of Mull

Silver sands and crystal waters, exquisite on a fine day, atmospheric on a misty one. Unrestricted romps for dogs – but please think of humans too. (And the gulls and waders.)

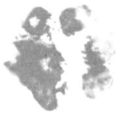

Photo: Banceithin, entry 191

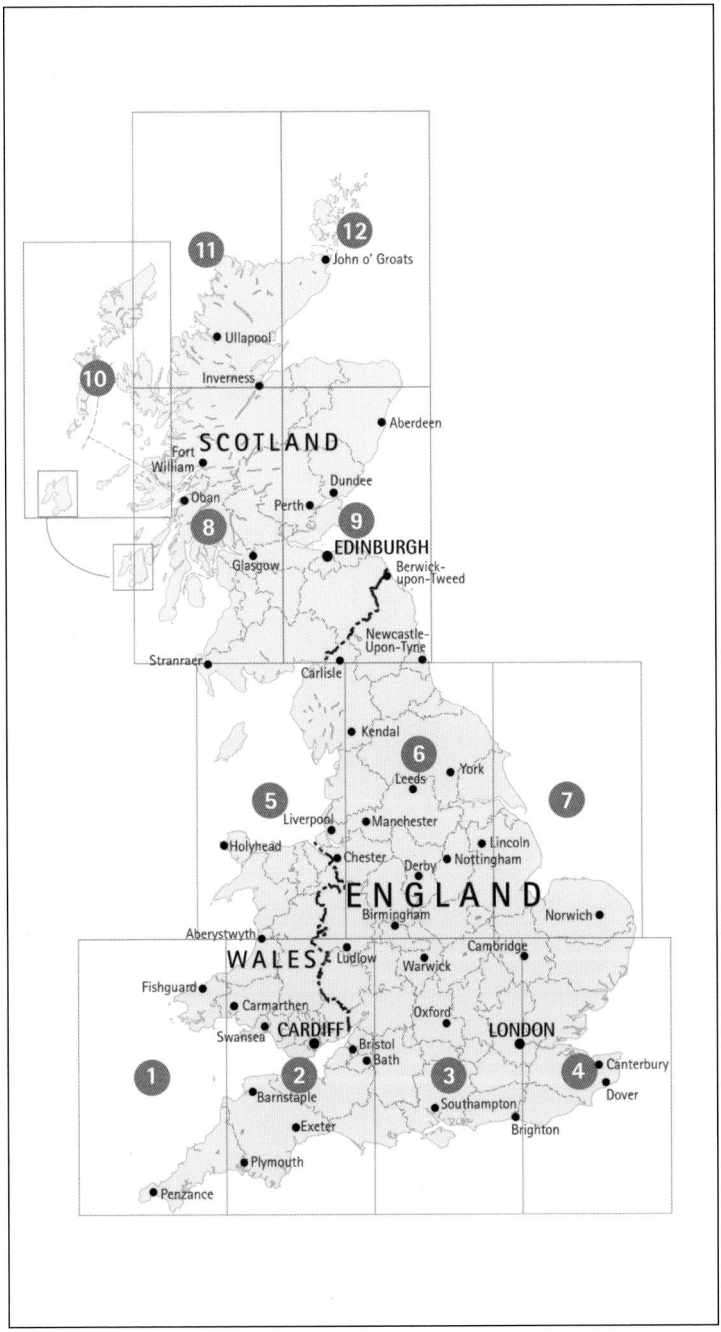

© Maidenhead Cartographic, 2018

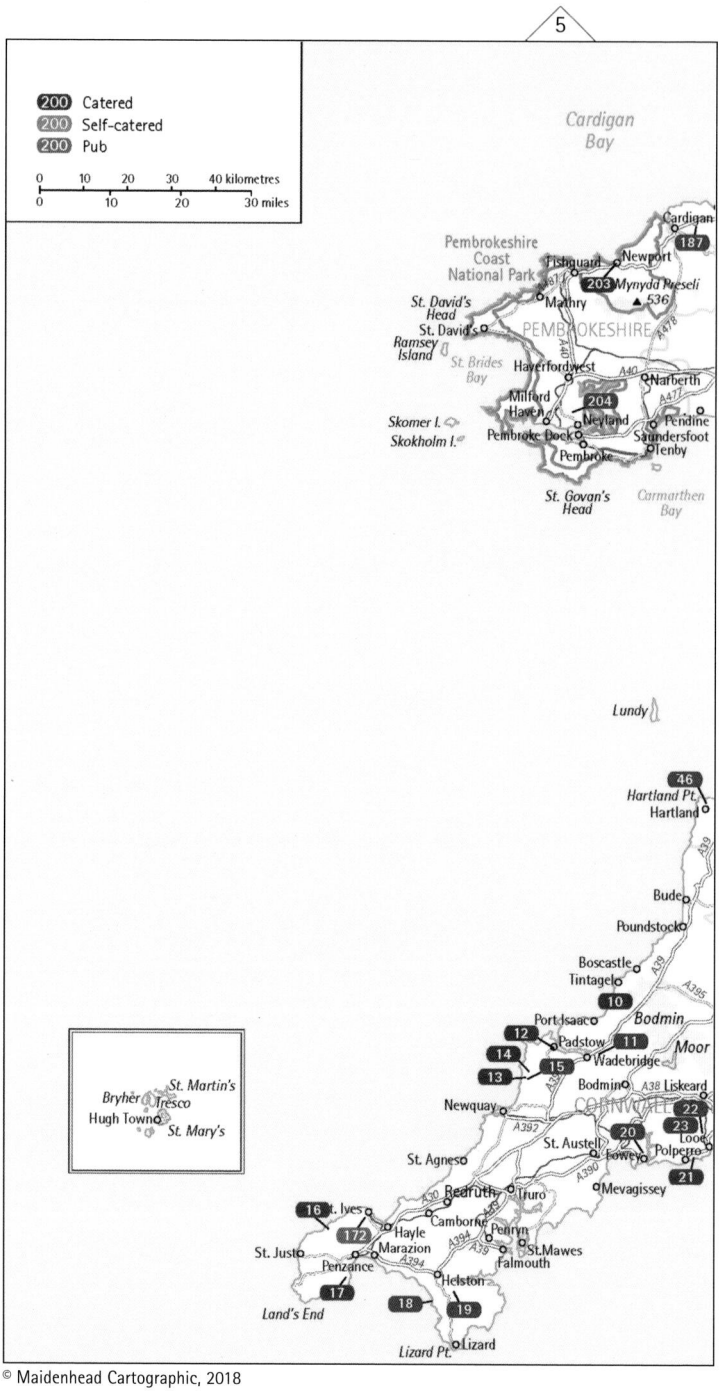

© Maidenhead Cartographic, 2018

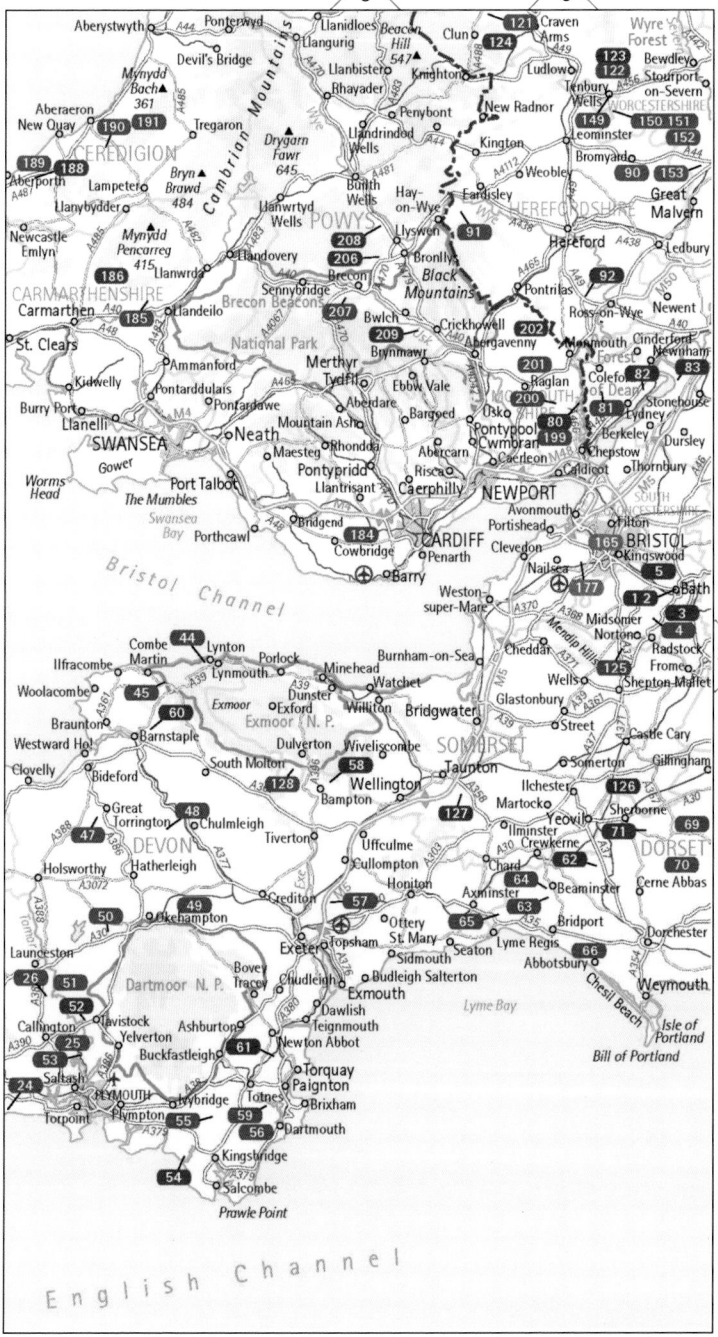

© Maidenhead Cartographic, 2018

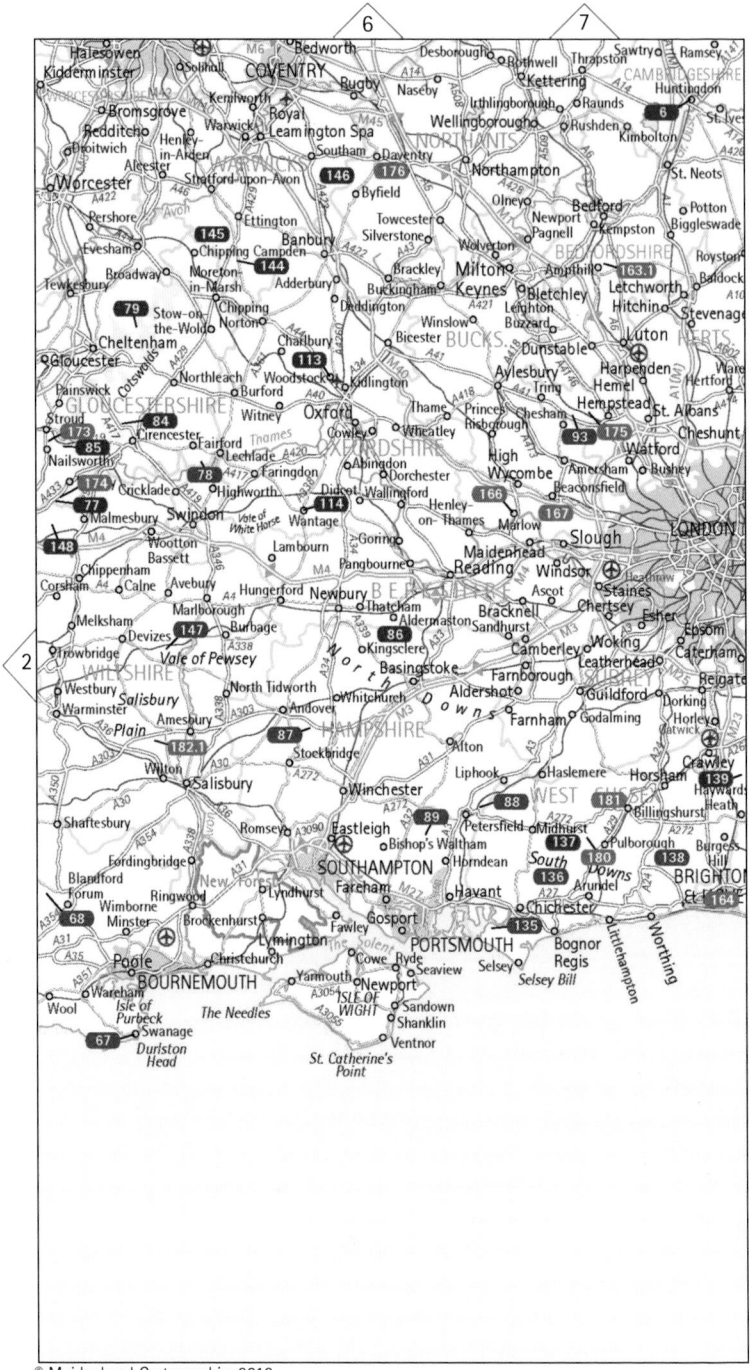

© Maidenhead Cartographic, 2018

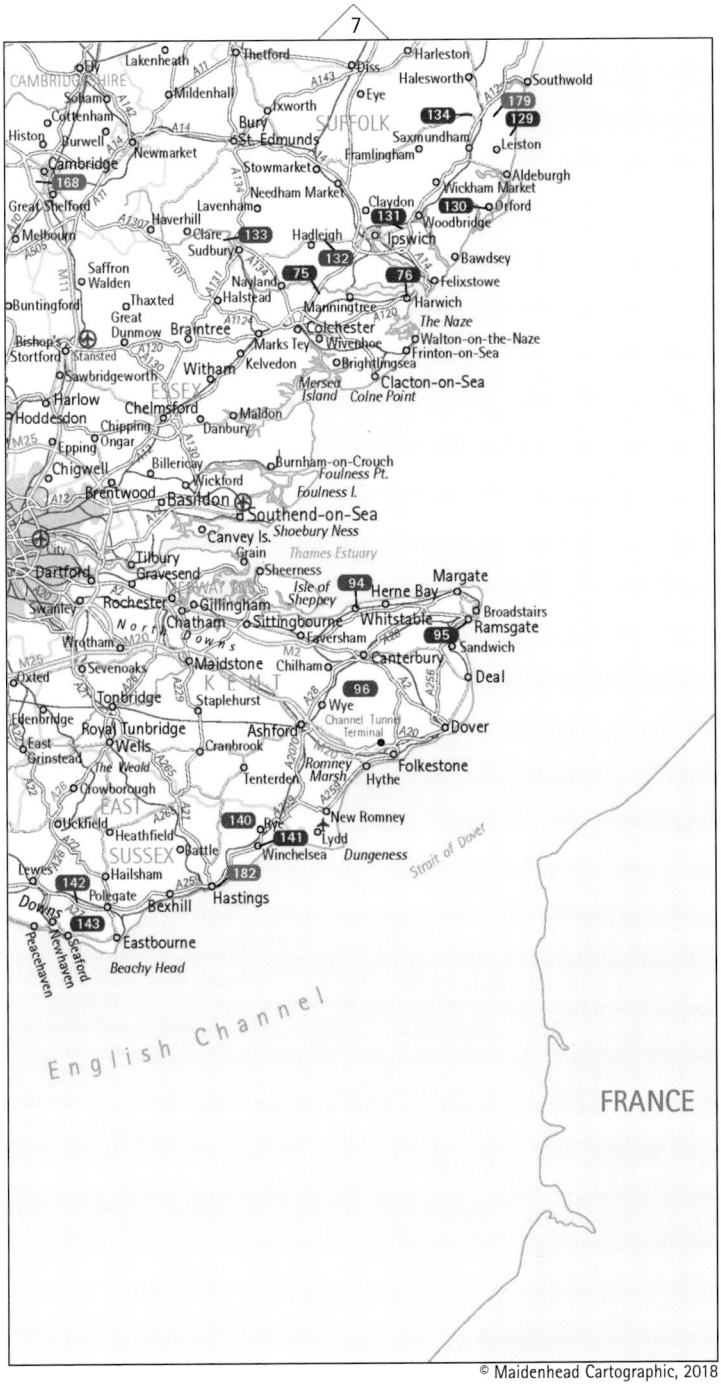

© Maidenhead Cartographic, 2018

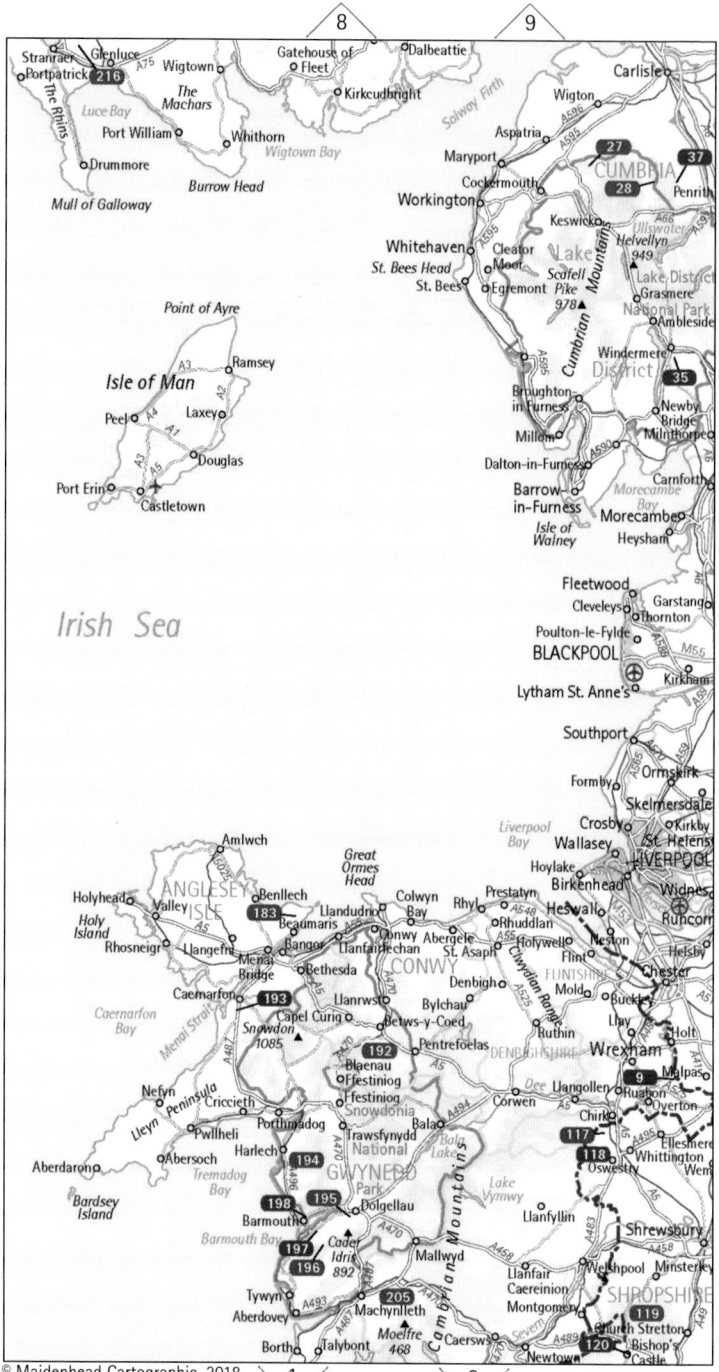

© Maidenhead Cartographic, 2018

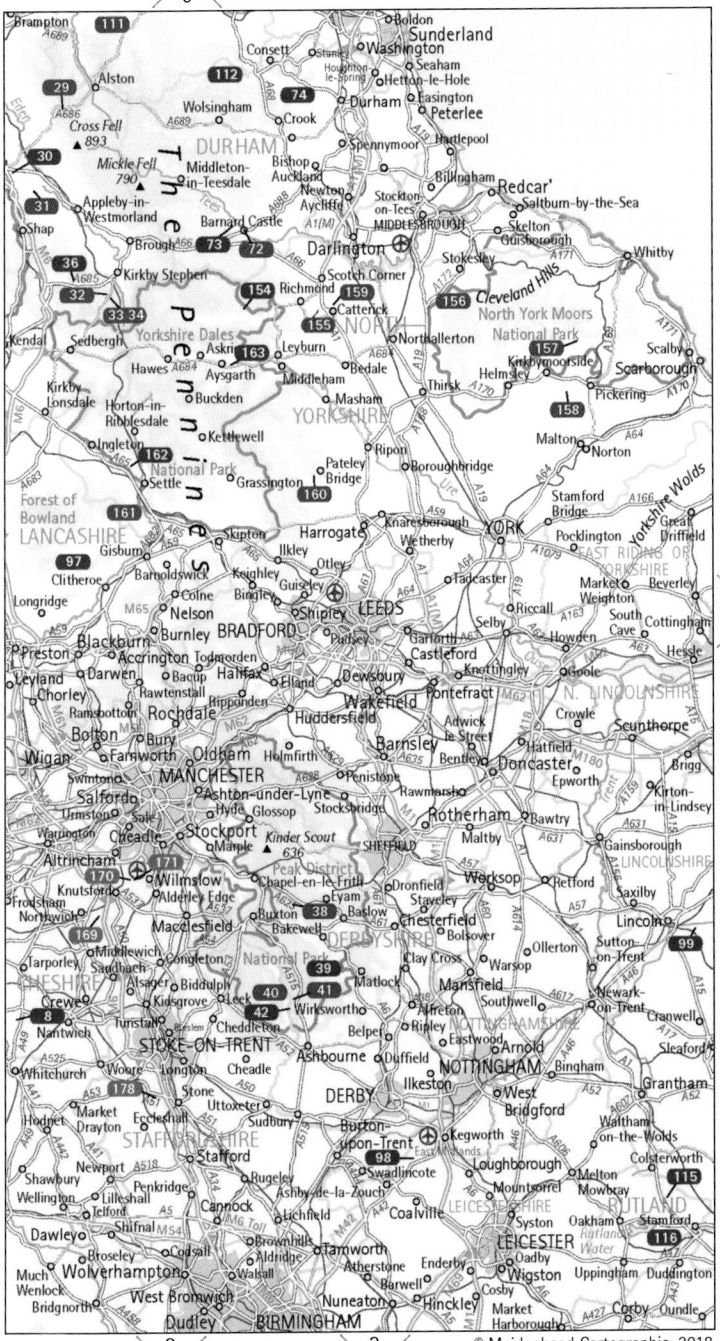
9
7
2
3
Sunderland
Washington
Seaham
Hetton-le-Hole
Easington
Peterlee
Durham
Consett
Stanley
Houghton-le-Spring
Brampton
Boldon
Alston
Wolsingham
Crook
Cross Fell
893
Mickle Fell
790
DURHAM
Spennymoor
Hartlepool
Bishop Auckland
Middleton-in-Teesdale
Newton Aycliffe
Billingham
Redcar
Saltburn-by-the-Sea
Stockton-on-Tees
MIDDLESBROUGH
Skelton
Guisborough
Appleby-in-Westmorland
Shap
Barnard Castle
Darlington
Stokesley
Whitby
Brough
Kirkby Stephen
Scotch Corner
Richmond
Catterick
Cleveland Hills
North York Moors National Park
Northallerton
Scalby
Scarborough
Kendal
Sedbergh
Yorkshire Dales National Park
Askrigg
Leyburn
Hawes
Aysgarth
Middleham
Bedale
Kirkbymoorside
Helmsley
Thirsk
Pickering
Kirkby Lonsdale
Horton-in-Ribblesdale
Buckden
Masham
YORKSHIRE
Malton
Norton
Ingleton
Kettlewell
Ripon
Boroughbridge
Settle
Grassington
Pateley Bridge
Forest of Bowland
LANCASHIRE
Skipton
Harrogate
Knaresborough
Wetherby
YORK
Stamford Bridge
Pocklington
Yorkshire Wolds
Great Driffield
Gisburn
Barnoldswick
Ilkley
Otley
Keighley
Guiseley
Tadcaster
Riccall
Market Weighton
Beverley
Clitheroe
Colne
Bingley
Longridge
Nelson
Shipley
LEEDS
Selby
South Cave
Cottingham
Burnley
BRADFORD
Pudsey
Barlborough
Howden
Hessle
Blackburn
Preston
Accrington
Todmorden
Castleford
Knottingley
Goole
Leyland
Darwen
Bacup
Halifax
Elland
Dewsbury
Chorley
Rawtenstall
Ripponden
Wakefield
Pontefract
N. LINCOLNSHIRE
Ramsbottom
Rochdale
Huddersfield
Crowle
Scunthorpe
Bolton
Bury
Adwick le Street
Hatfield
Wigan
Farnworth
Oldham
Holmfirth
Barnsley
Bentley
Doncaster
Epworth
Brigg
Swinton
MANCHESTER
Penistone
Salford
Ashton-under-Lyne
Rawmarsh
Kirton-in-Lindsey
Urmston
Sale
Hyde
Glossop
Stocksbridge
Rotherham
Bawtry
Warrington
Cheadle
Stockport
Marple
Kinder Scout
636
SHEFFIELD
Maltby
Gainsborough
Altrincham
Wilmslow
Peak District National Park
Worksop
Retford
Knutsford
Alderley Edge
Chapel-en-le-Frith
Dronfield
Eyam
Staveley
Saxilby
Frodsham
Northwich
Buxton
Bakewell
Baslow
Chesterfield
Lincoln
Macclesfield
Bolsover
Middlewich
Congleton
Clay Cross
Ollerton
Sutton-on-Trent
Tarporley
Sandbach
Alsager
Biddulph
Matlock
Warsop
Mansfield
Newark-on-Trent
Crewe
Kidsgrove
Leek
Wirksworth
Alfreton
Southwell
Nantwich
Tunstall
Cheddleton
Ripley
Cranwell
STOKE-ON-TRENT
Belper
Eastwood
Arnold
Sleaford
Whitchurch
Woore
Longton
Cheadle
Ashbourne
Duffield
NOTTINGHAM
Bingham
Grantham
Stone
Ilkeston
West Bridgford
Market Drayton
Eccleshall
Uttoxeter
Sudbury
DERBY
Hodnet
Burton-upon-Trent
Kegworth
Waltham-on-the-Wolds
Stafford
Swadlincote
Loughborough
Colsterworth
Shawbury
Newport
Rugeley
Melton Mowbray
Wellington
Lilleshall
Penkridge
Ashby-de-la-Zouch
Mountsorrel
Cannock
Lichfield
Coalville
Syston
Oakham
Stamford
Dawley
Shifnal
Brownhills
Tamworth
Oadby
Broseley
Codsall
Aldridge
Atherstone
Enderby
Much Wenlock
Wolverhampton
Walsall
Barwell
Wigston
Uppingham
Duddington
Bridgnorth
West Bromwich
Nuneaton
Hinckley
Cosby
Market Harborough
Corby
Oundle
Dudley
BIRMINGHAM
LEICESTER
RUTLAND
Rutland Water
EAST RIDING OF YORKSHIRE
LINCOLNSHIRE
DERBYSHIRE
NOTTINGHAMSHIRE
CHESHIRE
STAFFORDSHIRE
LEICESTERSHIRE
East Midlands
Trent
Ure
Ouse
Tees
Swale
Ure
Trent
Welland
Ouse
Trent
Ouse
Ouse
Great Ouse
Colne
Colne
Colne

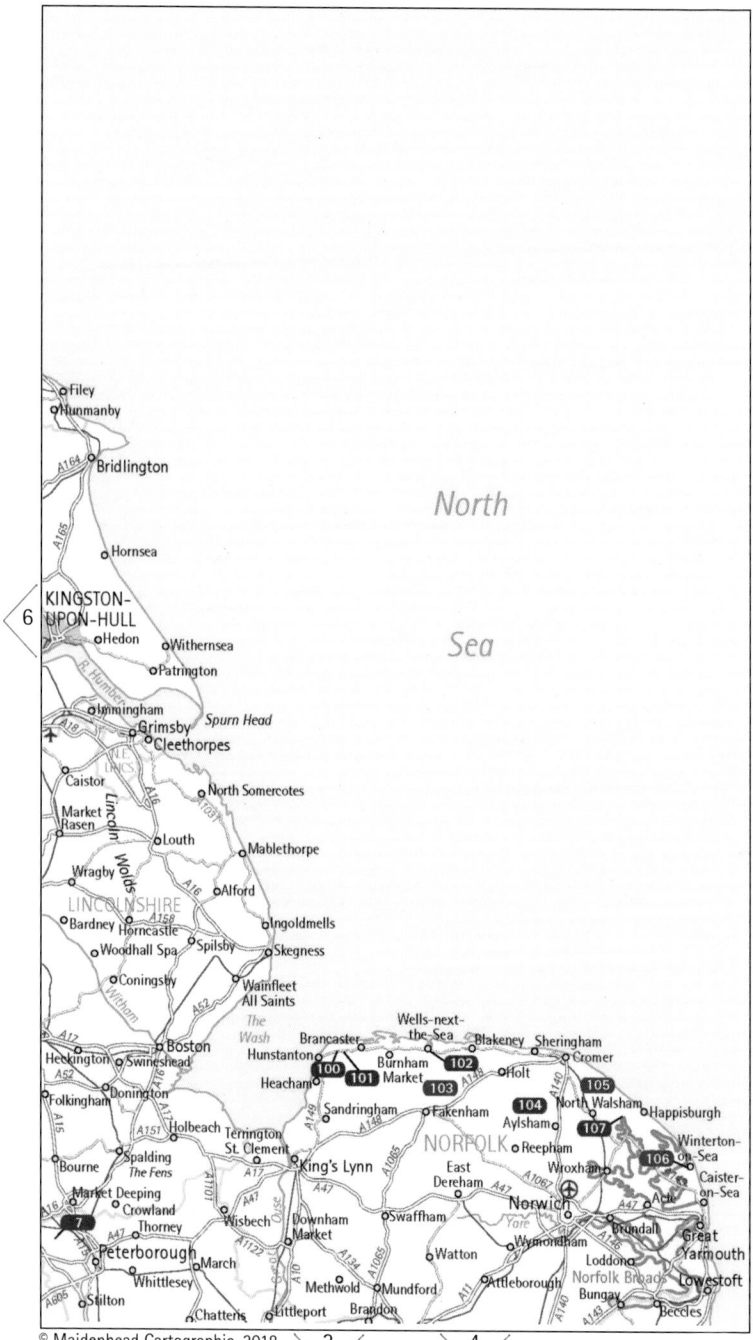

© Maidenhead Cartographic, 2018

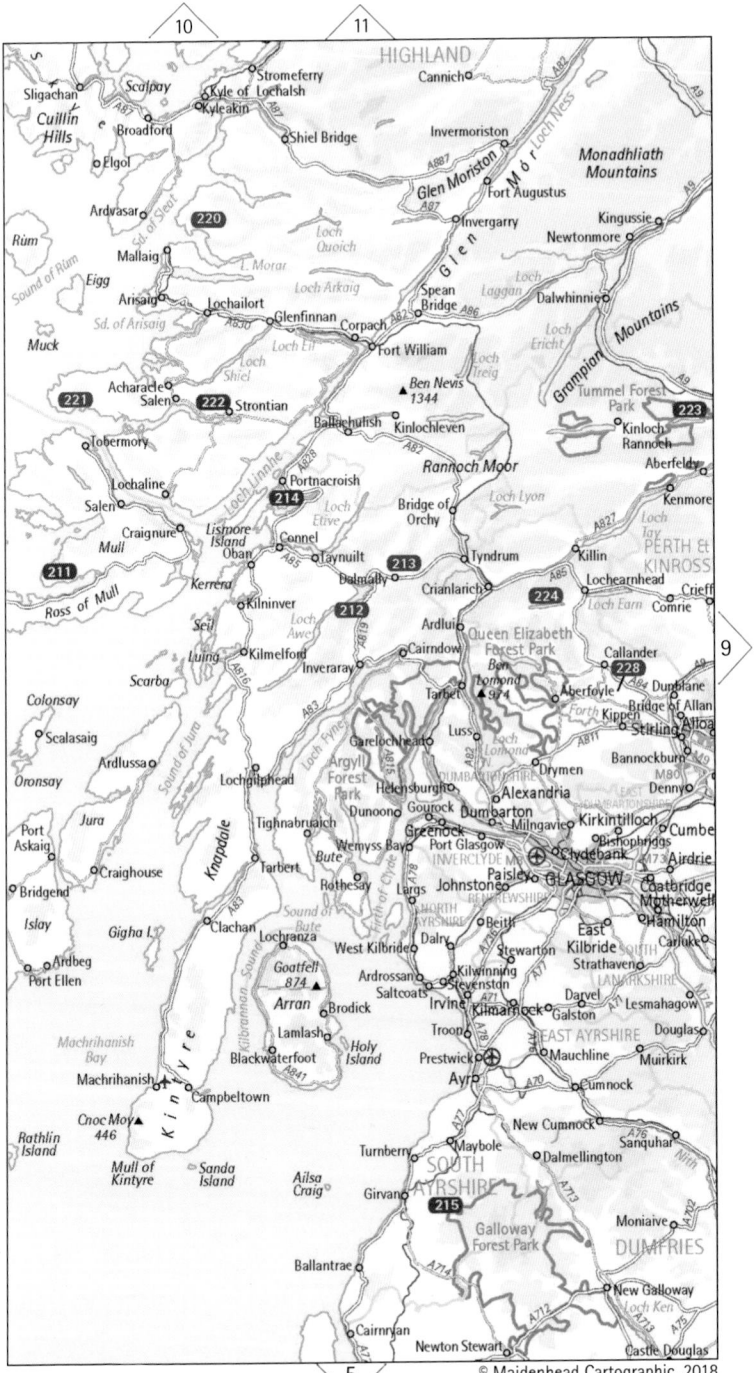

© Maidenhead Cartographic, 2018

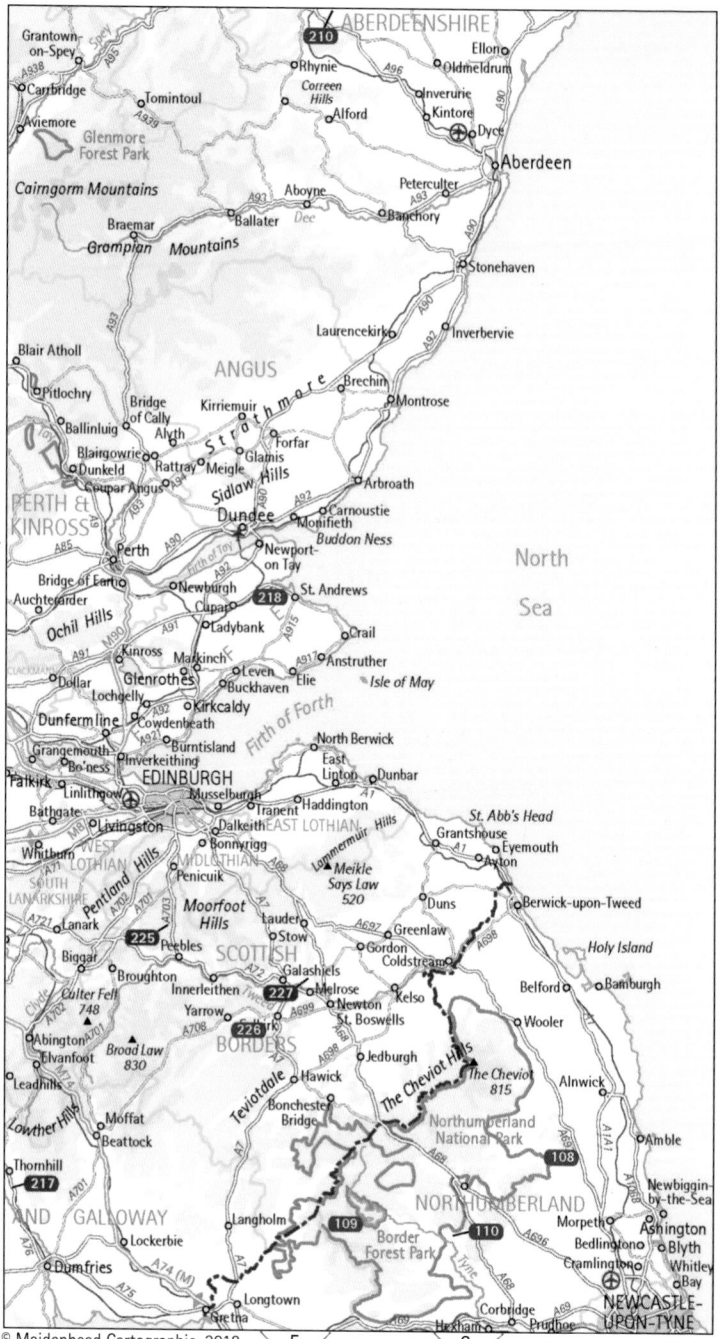

© Maidenhead Cartographic, 2018

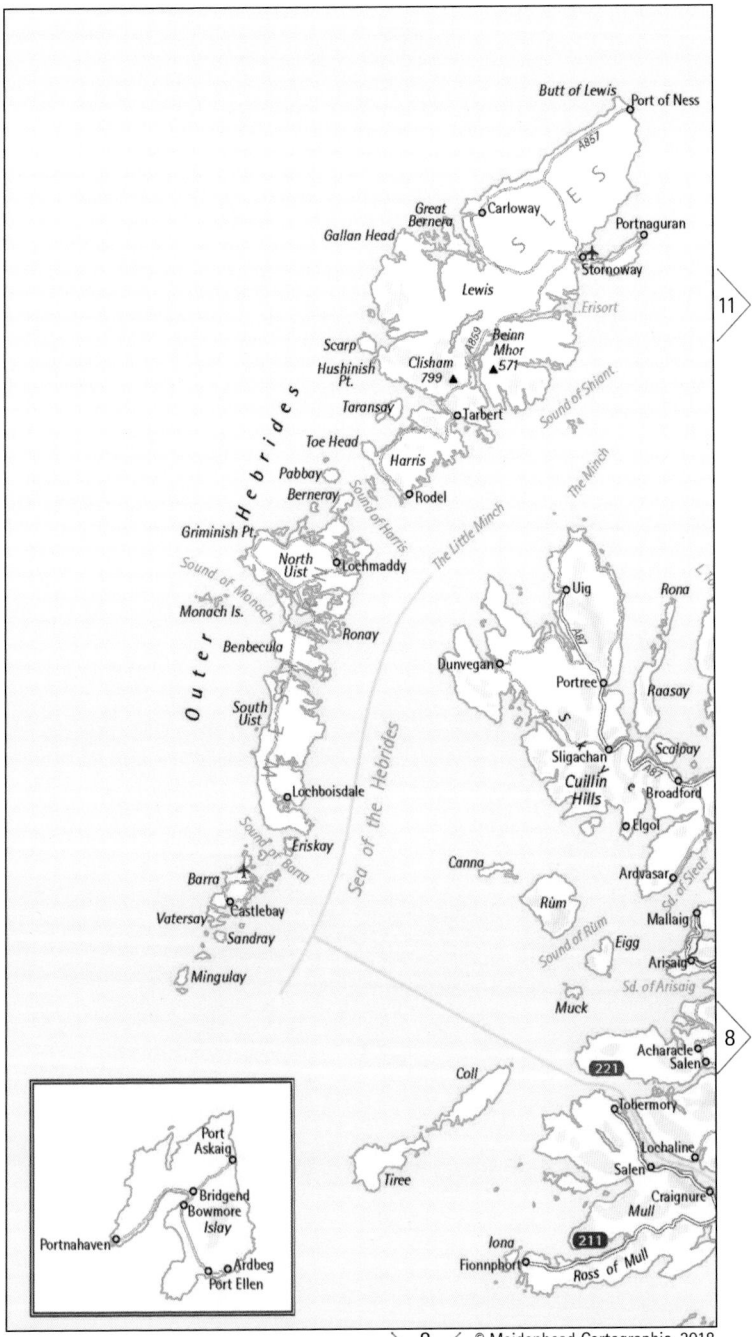

8

© Maidenhead Cartographic, 2018

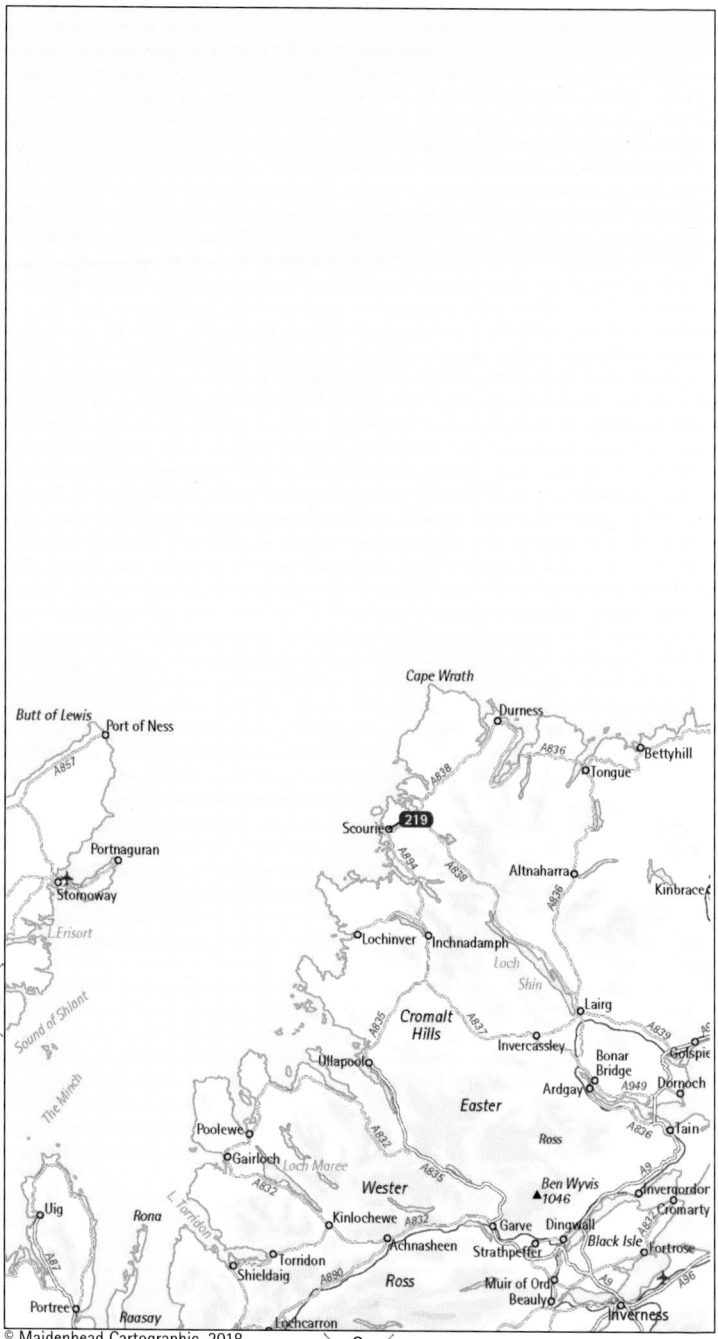

© Maidenhead Cartographic, 2018

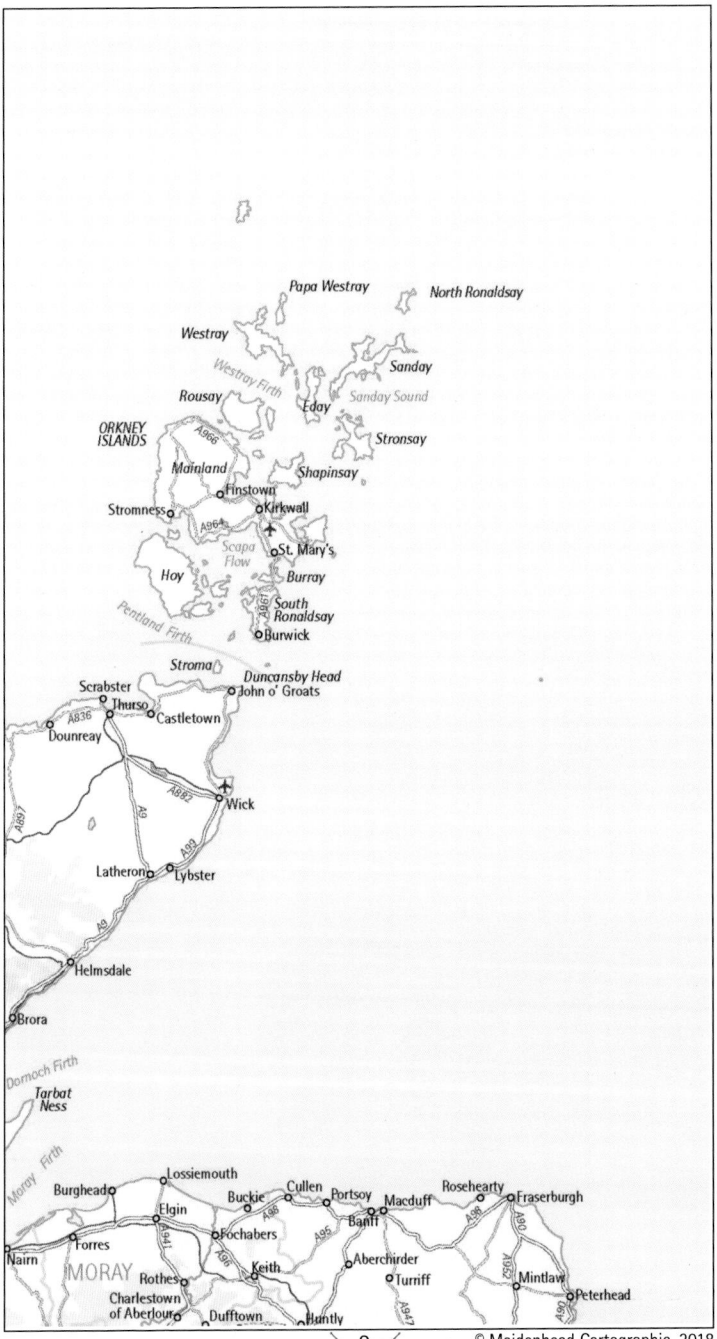

© Maidenhead Cartographic, 2018

England

Photo: istockphoto.com

No. 15 Great Pulteney

You're on the grandest street in Bath, once home to Jane Austen; the Holburne Museum of Art stands at one end, Robert Adam's famous Pulteney Bridge at the other. As for No.15, this is a quirky boutique hotel that doubles as a contemporary art gallery. You'll find collections of curios all over the place, coffee machines hidden away in dolls' houses in bigger rooms. Bedrooms are sumptuous, some smaller, others enormous, each with an original piece of art on the walls. Several have exposed plaster walls, all have Hypnos mattresses and beautiful bathrooms, perhaps a copper basin, a walk-in shower or a claw-foot bath. Vast suites flood with light courtesy of high windows, while a help-yourself larder waits on the landing for popcorn, soft drinks and ice cream. There's a sitting-room bar for coffee and cocktails, then the stylish Café 15 for Prosecco 'on the house' at breakfast, perhaps a feisty fish pie at lunch and delicious dinners from Tuesday to Saturday. The hotel is a work in progress: treatment rooms, a small garden and a car park are on the way. Good restaurants are a short stroll. Hard to beat. *Advice on walks available and there's a park very close by.*

Rooms	14 doubles: £140-£280. 8 suites for 2: £180-£400. Dogs £15 per night. Max. 2.
Meals	Lunch from £13. Dinner from £30; not Sunday to Monday. Afternoon tea £28.
Closed	Never.
	'Woof Box' with treats, bowl, Lily's Kitchen dog food, tennis ball and poo bags. Blanket provided overnight too.

Jonathan Walker
No. 15 Great Pulteney,
15 Great Pulteney Street,
Bath, BA2 4BS,
Tel +44 (0)1225 807015
Email enquiries@no15greatpulteney.co.uk
Web www.no15greatpulteney.co.uk

Entry 1 Map 2

Abbey Hotel

You're in the epicentre of Bath, just behind the abbey, in one of the prettiest quarters in town. Parade Gardens waits across the road, the river Avon pours over the weir at Pulteney Bridge, Bath rugby club stands on the far bank. As for the hotel, in summer you take to the terrace café for coffee and watch the world go by; in winter it turns into an après-ski bar for mince pies and mulled wine. Inside, the sitting room doubles as a contemporary art gallery, while wine glasses hang from the ceiling in the bar. There's lovely food in the restaurant, perhaps flame-grilled mackerel, slow-roasted venison, vanilla panna cotta with rhubarb sorbet; a pre-theatre menu is available from 5.30pm. Smart rooms upstairs have comfy beds, woollen throws and colourful headboards. Some are small, others big, all have iPads for room service, while most have stylish new bathrooms (ask for a room with one of these). Bath waits on your doorstep: rugby at the Rec, the Christmas market, the Roman Baths, Victoria Art gallery, all things thespian and plenty of Jane Austen. You're close to the station, too, so leave your car at home. *Central Bath very near park areas – easy for dog-walking.*

Rooms	46 doubles, 10 twin/doubles: £110-£475. 6 family rooms for 4: £160-£475. Dogs £15 per stay.
Meals	Lunch from £7.50. Dinner, 3 courses, £35-£45; pre-theatre menu £21.50-£27.50 (5.30pm-7pm). Sunday lunch £24-£28.
Closed	Never.
	Advice on walks and a 'Woof Box' that includes dog treats, food and a ball.

Andrew Foulkes
Abbey Hotel,
North Parade, Bath, BA1 1LF

Tel	+44 (0)1225 461603
Email	reception@abbeyhotelbath.co.uk
Web	www.abbeyhotelbath.co.uk

Entry 2 Map 1

The Wheatsheaf Combe Hay

A hidden valley, a pretty village, a gorgeous inn, three fabulous rooms. Views from the lush terraced garden – replete with veg plot and hens – stretch across to a fine ridge of trees, the manor house and church jutting out of the woods below. In summer there are barbecues, lazy lunches, horses clopping by. This is a 15th-century farmhouse with later additions – it's all but impossible to spot the join – whose exterior comes clad in Farrow & Ball creams. Outside there are Indian benches with seagrass cushions; inside, big sofas in front of the fire. Gastropub interiors have neutral colours to soak up the light, sandblasted beams, halogen spotlights and Lloyd Loom wicker dining chairs. Steps outside lead down to three deeply comfy bedrooms in a stone building. All come in contemporary rustic style with light wood furniture, flat-screen TVs, Egyptian cotton and deluge showers; there are White Company oils and bathrobes too. Climb back up for seriously good food, perhaps pork belly with quince purée, skate wing with beetroot, parmesan and capers, and Valrhona chocolate fondant. Bath is a hike across the fields. *Rooms are all ground floor and there are lots of lovely walks in the area.*

Rooms	3 doubles: £120-£150. Dogs £15.
Meals	Lunch & dinner £16.50-£26.
Closed	Rarely.
	Dog beds, dog bowls and doggy treats.

Ian & Adele Barton
The Wheatsheaf Combe Hay,
Combe Hay, Bath, BA2 7EG
Tel +44 (0)1225 833504
Email info@wheatsheafcombehay.co.uk
Web www.wheatsheafcombehay.com

Entry 3 Map 2

The Parlour & The Dairy

Find a sweet hamlet with a village green, owner Alex's house and two niftily converted old cowsheds, both with their own personality. The Dairy has a very practical, child-friendly living space with vintage Chesterfield sofa and chairs, bright cushions, a painted toy cupboard and a wood-burner; the kitchen is dressed in cheery mint green and has a cottagey feel. The Parlour is sleeker, more modern with a big linen sofa, a massive TV screen and a snazzier kitchen. Both have all the gear a happy cook may need, including recipe books to inspire. You'll sleep well in beds with Hungarian goose down and super soft cotton, a cosy wool blanket at your feet; bathrooms are spick and span with fluffy towels and Bramley soaps. Thanks to Alex's excellent eye for charming things, some modern, some upcycled, there's always something uplifting to look at in both spaces and you are left generous organic breakfasts for the first day. Each has a gravelled area with table and chairs and views over open countryside, there are excellent walks from the door and a pony trekking centre nearby. Days out to Bath and Longleat are easy. *Minimum stay: 3 nights on weekdays & high season; 2 at weekends. Serious walking country and heaven for dog owners! Countryside hazards apply (cows, horses etc.) but these are avoidable.*

Rooms	2 houses for 4: £610–£1,250 per week. 2-night stay with late check out on 3rd day, £280 (Dairy), £340 (Parlour). 3-night stay, £330 (Dairy), £405 (Parlour).
Meals	Pubs/restaurants 10-minute drive.
Closed	Never.
	Dog biscuit tin, dog bed, bowls and towels for drying.

Alexandra Jellicoe
The Parlour & The Dairy,
Carlingcott, Peasedown St. John,
Bath, BA2 8AP

Mobile	+44 (0)7739 394378
Email	alexandra.jellicoe@gmail.com
Web	36carlingcott.com

Entry 4 Map 2

The Power House

On top of Bath's highest hill lies Rikki's Bauhaus-inspired home, its glass walls making the most of a magical spot and a sensational view; on a clear day you can see the Welsh hills. In the vast open-plan living space – homely, inviting, inspiring – are treasures from a lifetime of travels: ancient Tuareg camel sacks, kitsch Art Deco pots, gorgeous Persian chests. Bedrooms in the house are airy, with doors onto a huge balcony; the snug, colourful studio room has a wood-burner and little kitchen. Rikki is an incredible chef and uses the finest ingredients from Bath's farmers' market, ten minutes away. Breakfasts are superb – good coffee too. *Self-catering available in the studio. Exceptional walks with fields, woods, streams, in short – a dog paradise.*

Rooms	1 double: £100-£120. 1 single: £70. 1 studio for 2: £100-£120. 2 further small doubles available, sharing bathrooms.
Meals	Dinner £25. Pubs/restaurants 3-minute drive.
Closed	Rarely.
	Advice on walks, a Bonio and a pat on the back.

Tiana Jacout
The Power House,
Brockham End, Lansdown,
Bath, BA1 9BY
Mobile +44 (0)7974 222666
Email tianajacout@gmail.com

Entry 5 Map 2

The Old Bridge Hotel

The Old Bridge is one of those places that mixes old-fashioned hospitality with contemporary flair, a template of excellence for others to follow. It's a big hit with the locals, who come for delicious food and exceptional wines, and it inspired the founders of Hotel du Vin, who were amazed how busy it was. Ladies lunch, businessmen chatter, kind staff weave through the throng. You can eat wherever you want: in the beautifully refurbished restaurant; on a sofa in the lounge; or sitting in a winged armchair in front of the fire in the bar. You feast on anything from homemade soup to rack of lamb (starters are available all day), while breakfast is served in a panelled morning room with Buddha in the fireplace. It's all the work of owners John and Julia Hoskins. Julia's interiors are dreamy, with style and comfort going hand in hand. Beautiful bedrooms have fresh colours, chic fabrics, crisp linen, padded bedheads. All have posh TVs and robes in excellent bathrooms, some of which overlook the river Ouse. John, a Master of Wine, has a wine shop in reception; you can taste before you buy (and you will). *In town but there are easy walks right from the hotel door.*

Rooms	18 doubles, 1 twin, 3 four-posters: £125-£230. 2 singles: £95-£125. Dinner, B&B £104-£150 per person.
Meals	Lunch & dinner £5-£35.
Closed	Never.
	Water bowls, towels for drying and dog biscuits in the room.

John & Julia Hoskins
The Old Bridge Hotel,
1 High Street, Huntingdon, PE29 3TQ
Tel +44 (0)1480 424300
Email oldbridge@huntsbridge.co.uk
Web www.huntsbridge.com

Entry 6 Map 3

The White Hart

Wash up at the White Hart and mix with the locals drawn by the lovely lived-in farmhouse feel and the big, beamy bar. The ales are good too: Oakham Jeffrey Hudson, Woodforde Wherry, Tim Taylors, Grainstore's Red Kite. Farmers gather on Fridays, the cricket team drops by on Sundays; in summer life spills onto the terrace. Flags, floorboards and a crackling fire continue the rustic feel; railway signs, wooden pitchforks and hanging station lamps add colour. You can eat simply or more grandly, anything from a ploughman's to a three-course feast, with memorably good Sunday roasts full of flavour. Walk through rooms with lovely scrubbed tables to the orangery, a glass-gabled restaurant furnished with Lloyd Loom chairs. Bedrooms (some above the bar; the rest across the way) are simple and spotless, with crisp white linen and feather pillows, free WiFi and an honest price. One is airy and lovely, with period lounge chairs and views across the fields to the church; another has a four-poster bed. This forgotten slip of England – Stamford is five miles – is prettier than most imagine. *Secure garden; the pub is surrounded by lots of good lead-free walks if dogs reliable (no main roads nearby). Sheep in neighbouring field.*

Rooms	10 doubles: £80-£130. 2 twins: £85-£120. Extra bed/sofabed available £15 per person per night. Dogs £15 per night.
Meals	Starters from £5.50. Lunch, 2 courses, £14.95. Mains £10.50-£21.95. Sunday lunch, 2 courses, £19.90.
Closed	Rarely.
	Water bowl and hose for washing off muddy paws.

Lisa Olver
The White Hart,
Main Street, Ufford, Stamford, PE9 3BH
Tel +44 (0)1780 740250
Email info@whitehartufford.co.uk
Web www.whitehartufford.co.uk

Entry 7 Map 7

The Cholmondeley Arms

As prim and proper as a Victorian schoolmistress on the outside, as stylish as Beau Brummell within: the sandblasted brick walls of this old school house rise to raftered, vaulted ceilings and large windows pull natural light into every corner. Shelves of gin hover above fat radiators, cartoons and photos nestle amongst old sporting paraphernalia, and oriental rugs sprawl beneath an auction lot of tables, pews and chairs. The glorious carved oak bar dominates the main hall and apart from the malted charms of Cholmondeley Best Bitter and other local cask ales, there are a staggering 366 varieties of ruinously good gin to discover, with the aid of a well-thumbed guide or one of the many charming staff. And when the dinner bell goes study the menus on antique blackboards or opt for sharing the amazing seafood trawler board followed by their legendary steak and kidney pie. Rooms in the old headmaster's house behind are calm and civilised with all the comfort you need. Seldom has going back to school been this much fun. *Area where a dog can exercise chasing a tennis ball. Many walks nearby: the Sandstone Trail, Cholmondeley Castle Gardens, Beeston Castle.*

Rooms	5 doubles, 1 twin: £60-£110. Dogs £10 per stay. Max. 2 per room.
Meals	Lunch & dinner £7.25-£17.95. Not Christmas Day. Sunday lunch £14.50.
Closed	Rarely.
	Biscuits on the bar, water bowls, Doggie Beer and good walks. Dog basket available for dogs staying in rooms.

Tim Moody
The Cholmondeley Arms,
Wrenbury Road, Cholmondeley,
Malpas, SY14 8HN
Tel +44 (0)1829 720300
Email info@cholmondeleyarms.co.uk
Web www.cholmondeleyarms.co.uk

Entry 8 Map 6

Mulsford Cottage

Delicious! Not just the food (Kate's a pro chef) but the sweet whitewashed cottage with its sunny conservatory and vintage interiors, and the green Cheshire countryside that bubble-wraps the place in rural peace. Chat – and laugh – the evening away over Kate's superb dinners, lounge by the fire, then sleep deeply in comfy bedrooms: cane beds, a bright red chair, a vintage desk. The double has a roll top bath, the twin a tiny shower-with-a-view. Wake for local bacon, sausages and honey and just-laid bantam eggs. Walk the 34-mile Sandstone Trail to Shropshire; Wales starts just past the hammock, at the bottom of the bird-filled garden. *Dogs can play with Raffy, our Jack Russell. Log fire to doze by. Large fenced garden, dense woodland, rivers to splash in and hours of fun to be had chasing rabbits, but watch out for sheep in fields.*

Rooms	1 double; 1 twin with separate bath/shower: £90. Singles £65. Dogs no charge. Max. 2 dogs.
Meals	Dinner from £18. Pub 1.5 miles.
Closed	Rarely.
	Dog bowls and towels.

Kate Dewhurst
Mulsford Cottage,
Mulsford, Sarn,
Malpas, SY14 7LP
Tel +44 (0)1948 770414
Email katedewhurst4@gmail.com
Web www.mulsfordcottage.co.uk

Entry 9 Map 5

Photo: Alec Studerus

The Mill House Inn

Coast down the steep winding lane to a 1760s mill house in a woodland setting. Trebarwith's spectacular beach – all surf and sand – is a ten-minute walk away. It's quite a spot. Back at the inn, the bar combines the best of Cornish old and Cornish new: big flagged floor, wooden tables, chapel chairs, two leather sofas by a wood-burning stove. The swanky dining room overlooking the burbling mill stream is light, elegant and very modern. Settle down to some rather good food: firecracker prawns; fillet of sea trout with crushed potatoes, kale, roasted banana shallot, mussel & tarragon cream; coconut panna cotta, torched pineapple, rum sponge. Bar meals are more traditional, they do great barbecues in summer and (be warned) a band often plays at the weekend. In keeping with the seaside setting, bedrooms are simple and uncluttered, with good shower rooms in the smaller standard rooms. If you stay in the little cottage be ready for a steep staircase. Coastal trails lead to Tintagel, official home of the Arthurian legends, there's biking, surfing, crabbing... you couldn't possibly be bored. *Dogs to be kept on a lead please.*

Rooms	7 doubles: £75-£130. 1 family room for 4: £75-£130. 1 cottage for 2: £120-£160. Singles £56-£97. Dinner, B&B £60-£90 per person. Extra bed/sofabed available £20 per person per night. Dogs £7.50 per night.
Meals	Lunch from £7.50. Dinner from £12. Sunday lunch, 3 courses, £17.85.
Closed	Rarely.
	Guidance on local walks. Doc Martin's dog Dodger stays here!

Mark & Kep Forbes
The Mill House Inn,
Trebarwith,
Tintagel, PL34 0HD

Tel	+44 (0)1840 770200
Email	management@themillhouseinn.co.uk
Web	www.themillhouseinn.co.uk

Entry 10 Map 1

Mill Valley

The simple joy of this sociable site and everything built on it is a perfect reflection of Lisa and Neil's approach to life. It's completely off-grid, encouraging you to escape technology and camp like you used to, exploring nature, getting generally muddy and making new friends. They have a huge commitment to sustainability and endless ingenuity. Woodland Cabin is handmade entirely from local and upcycled wood; scramble up the chunky ladder to the mezzanine double bed; stroll over to the bathing hut shared with Pixie Yurt (you have your own loo as well). Romantic Vardo cabin on wheels is tucked away behind hedges; everything from the rickety steps to the floor, walls and private compost loo have been handcrafted; step inside to wild flowers and bohemian furnishings. The Yurt is a unique handmade creation too; pop the kettle on the wood-burner for tea and get something sizzling over the campfire for dinner. The Cornish coast is your playground, with magical woodland walks, coastal paths and beaches to explore as well as good country pubs in hidden villages. Resident dogs are happy to play with yours. *Babies welcome in cabin & yurt. Big secure garden; woodland & riverside walks with heaps of swimming opportunities. Farmland, so beware of livestock. Dog-sitting service.*

Rooms	Cabin for 2: from £90. Wagon for 2: from £80. Yurt for 4: from £80. Prices per night. Max. 6 dogs.
Meals	Self-catering.
Closed	Never.

Jar of Mera Dog pure goody snacks. The Cabin has a 'mud room' for drying off; Pixie Yurt has space for lots of dog beds.

Canopy & Stars
Mill Valley,
Egloshayle, Wadebridge, PL27 6JQ
Tel +44 (0)117 204 7830
Email enquiries@canopyandstars.co.uk
Web www.canopyandstars.co.uk/millvalley

Entry 11 Map 1

The Seafood Restaurant

In 1975 a young chef called Rick Stein opened a restaurant in Padstow. These days he has four more as well as a deli, a pâtisserie, a seafood cookery school and 40 beautiful bedrooms. Despite this success, his homespun philosophy has never wavered: buy the freshest seafood from fisherman on the quay, then cook it simply and eat it with friends. It is a viewpoint half the country seems to share – the Seafood Restaurant is now a place of pilgrimage – so come to discover the Cornish coast, walk on the cliffs, paddle in the estuary, then drop into this lively restaurant for a fabulous meal, perhaps black risotto with Cornish cuttlefish, grilled Padstow lobster with fine herbs, hot chocolate fondant with toasted marshmallow ice cream. Book in for the night and a table in the restaurant is yours, though flawless bedrooms are hard to leave. They are scattered about town, some above the restaurant, others at the bistro or just around the corner at St Petroc's House. All are immaculate. Expect the best fabrics, Vi-Spring mattresses, stunning bathrooms, the odd terrace with estuary views. *Minimum stay: 2 nights at weekends. Walks along Camel Trail by Camel estuary, or across harbour and on to beautiful North Cornwall coast paths.*

Rooms	32 doubles, 8 twin/doubles: £120-£315. Dogs £20 for 1st night, £5 thereafter, per dog. Max. as many as can comfortably fit.
Meals	Lunch £38.50. Dinner £58.50.
Closed	25-26 December.

Fleecy Chalky's pal blanket, guide to dog walks in Cornwall, personal dog bowls, and 100% natural dog treats from Green & Wilds with selected breaks.

Jill & Rick Stein
The Seafood Restaurant,
Riverside, Padstow, PL28 8BY

Tel	+44 (0)1841 532700
Email	reservations@rickstein.com
Web	www.rickstein.com/stay

Entry 12 Map 1

Bedruthan Hotel & Spa

Bedruthan has the lot – stunning sea views, a couple of swimming pools, a spa with treatment rooms, then sitting rooms and restaurants galore. The most recent addition is a sensory spa garden offering seven steps to heaven: a salt scrub; a sauna; a cold bucket shower; a dip in the hot tub; a wet scrub; a visit to the sky garden; a second bite at the hot tub. Adults get the run of the place in school time, then children come in the holidays and slide down zip wires or sign up to surf school. Qualified staff look after younger children, who can paint, play, or jump into a cage of coloured balls while their parents snooze on sunbeds by the pool. There's a wood burner in the quiet sitting room, a cocktail bar that opens onto a terrace, then stylish bedrooms with retro colours and sparkling bathrooms. Some have separate rooms for children, others have terraces or sea views, a few overlook the car park. Younger children have early suppers, adults return later for a slap-up meal, perhaps guinea fowl, whole lemon sole, chilled strawberry soup with prosecco sorbet. The beach is a short stroll. *Easy access to the coast path; Mawgan Porth beach below allows dogs year round and has a shallow river.*

Rooms	38 twin/doubles: £135-£270. 27 suites for 4: £205-£490. 30 family rooms for 4: £175-£305. 6 singles: £75-£125. Dinner, B&B from £95 p.p. Well behaved dogs welcomed, £12 per night. Maximum: 5 dogs.
Meals	Lunch from £6. Dinner £27.50-£32.50. Sunday lunch £13-£24.50.
Closed	3 weeks in January.
	Biscuits, bedding and bowls.

Janie White
Bedruthan Hotel & Spa,
Mawgan Porth, Newquay, TR8 4BU
Tel +44 (0)1637 860860
Email stay@bedruthan.com
Web www.bedruthan.com

Entry 13 Map 1

The Scarlet

The Scarlet does what few others can – this may be a super-cool design hotel with one of the loveliest spas in the land, but the service here is fantastic: friendly, attentive, ready to help. As for the hotel, it sits above the sea with a vast wall of glass in reception to frame the view. Outside, you'll find a hot tub in the garden from which you can stargaze at night; inside, there's a stylish restaurant that opens onto a decked terrace, where you scoff delicious Cornish food while gazing out to sea. Elsewhere, an open fire in the sitting room, a pool table in the library, then a cool bar for Cornish wines and ales. Exceptional bedrooms all have sea views, then balconies or terraces, private gardens or viewing pods. Expect organic cotton, oak floors from sustainable forests, perhaps a free-standing bath or a huge walk-in shower. As for the spa, you get tented treatment rooms, chill-out pods that hang from the ceiling, and then a couple of swimming pools flanked by sunbeds. Finally, the hotel is green to its core, with a biomass boiler, solar panels and state-of-the-art insulation. *Minimum stay: 2 nights at weekends. Easy access to South West Coast Path. Mawgan Porth beach, just below, open to dogs all year round; a small shallow stream runs down one side.*

Rooms	21 doubles, 8 twin/doubles: £195-£405. 8 suites for 2: £270-£460. Dinner, B&B £140-£280 per person. Dogs £15. Max. depends on breed and size (check with hotel).
Meals	Lunch, 3 courses, £24.50. Dinner, 3 courses, £45.50.
Closed	Rarely.
	Bowls, water, biscuits and an information leaflet about dogs at the hotel.

Meeche Hudd
The Scarlet,
Tredragon Road,
Mawgan Porth, TR8 4DQ
Tel +44 (0)1637 861800
Email stay@scarlethotel.co.uk
Web www.scarlethotel.co.uk

Entry 14 Map 1

5 & 6 Porth Farm Cottages

The beach is a ten-minute stroll, the cliff path crosses the National Trust coastline, the quiet village has a surf school, shop and fish 'n' chips: all the ingredients for a terrific seaside holiday. The cottages are part of a horseshoe of stone barns with communal gardens, swings and zip wire, all tucked into a hillside with views over the Vale of Lanherne and out to sea. The conversions are impressive, with underfloor heating, elm floorboards and wonderful woodwork. No. 5's staircase spirals up to a gallery landing and comfy bedrooms. Soak in a roll top bath; blast away sand under a huge shower head. Downstairs: cosy up by the fire in an open-plan living room; the kitchen and dining table catch the morning sun. Outside: watch the sunset over the bay with an evening drink and gaze up at the 'living roof' of flowers. It's a short drive to the Eden Project or St Ives, but mostly you can leave the car behind. The coastal path stretches to Newquay, Watergate Bay and Padstow (good bus service, too) and there's a friendly farm shop down the valley on your way to the ancient village of St Mawgan. *Minimum stay: 3 nights; 7 nights in high season.*

Rooms	1 cottage for 4, 1 cottage for 6: £400-£1,310 per week. 3-night stay £400. Dogs £20 per stay. Max. 2.
Meals	Self-catering.
Closed	Rarely.
	Underfloor heating, advice on walks and dog poo bags by the door.

Carol & Peter Misch
5 & 6 Porth Farm Cottages,
Mawgan Porth, Newquay, TR8 4BP
Mobile +44 (0)7779 659838
Email 5and6pfmanagementgroup@gmail.com

The Gurnard's Head

This quirky inn is one of the best, the sort of place you'd hope to find at the end of the road. Outside, the wild west coast weaves up to St Ives; secret beaches appear at low tide, cliffs tumble down to the water, wild flowers streak the land pink in summer. Inside, it's earthy, warm, stylish and friendly, with rustic interiors, colour-washed walls, stripped wooden floors and fires at both ends of the bar. Logs are piled high in an alcove, maps and art hang on the walls, books fill every shelf; if you pick one up and don't finish it, take it home and post it back. Cosy rooms have warm colours and the odd antique, then Vi-Spring mattresses, crisp white linen, colourful throws and Roberts radios. Downstairs, you can scoff delicious food in the bar, the restaurant or out in the garden in good weather. Tasty snacks wait – pork pies, crab claws, half a pint of Atlantic prawns – as does more substantial fare, maybe grilled sardines, Cornish lamb with root vegetables, roasted apples and pears. Picnics can be arranged, there's bluegrass folk music in the bar most weeks. *Large back garden. Beautiful coastal path, and a sandy beach as well if you time the tides right.*

Rooms	3 doubles, 4 twin/doubles: £120-£185. Dinner, B&B £170-£235 (based on double occupancy). Camp bed available for children, £25 per night for children 5+ years, free for under 5's.
Meals	Lunch from £12. Dinner, 3 courses, £25-£35. Sunday lunch from £13.
Closed	Christmas.
	Dog biscuits, blanket, towels, advice on walks, poo bags and dog bowls. Very friendly staff too.

Charles & Edmund Inkin
The Gurnard's Head,
Zennor,
St Ives, TR26 3DE
Tel +44 (0)1736 796928
Email enquiries@gurnardshead.co.uk
Web www.gurnardshead.co.uk

Entry 16 Map 1

The Old Coastguard

The Old Coastguard stands on the water in one of Cornwall's loveliest coastal villages. It's a super spot and rather peaceful – very little has happened here since the Spanish sacked the place in 1595. It's owned by Edmund and Charles Inkin, brothers who are past masters at running lovely small hotels; warm colours, attractive prices, great food and kind staff are their hallmarks. Downstairs, the airy bar and the dining room come together as one, the open plan informality creating a great space to hang out. You get smart rustic tables, earthy colours, local ales and local art, then wooden floors and a crackling fire. Drop down a few steps to find a bank of sofas and a wall of glass framing sea views; in summer, doors open onto a decked terrace, a lush lawn, then the coastal path weaving down to the small harbour. Bedrooms hit the spot: warm colours, excellent beds, robes in fine bathrooms, books everywhere. Most have the view, eight have balconies. Don't miss dinner: salt and pepper monkfish, fish stew with mussels, chocolate mousse with tonka bean ice cream. *Secure garden with sea views. Pebbled beach a stone's throw away and plenty of walks nearby.*

Rooms	10 doubles, 3 twin/doubles: £140-£225. 1 suite for 2: £180-£225. 1 family room for 4: £180-£195. Dinner, B&B £192.50-£277.50 (based on double occupancy).
Meals	Lunch from £6. Dinner, 3 courses, about £30. Sunday lunch from £12.50.
Closed	1 week in early Jan.
	Dog biscuits, blanket, towels, advice on walks, poo bags and dog bowls. Very friendly staff too.

Charles & Edmund Inkin
The Old Coastguard,
The Parade, Mousehole,
Penzance, TR19 6PR
Tel +44 (0)1736 731222
Email bookings@oldcoastguardhotel.co.uk
Web www.oldcoastguardhotel.co.uk

Entry 17 Map 1

Halzephron Cabin

Up the hill from the village, behind Lucy and Roger's landmark B&B (you won't miss the white crenellations) and across the walled garden, you'll find your snug, seaside hideaway. An unassuming white shack on the outside, the compact interior has been given a full, contemporary makeover. There's a romantic wood-burner for the cooler evenings as well as electric radiators throughout, and a mini kitchen with oak breakfast bar and views of the bay – when it's too dark to admire them you can just turn to the flat screen TV. The bathroom has a beautiful double-ended bath and a nautical porthole window that reminds you of your coastal surroundings, although with the faint sound of the waves lapping below as you drift off, you probably won't have forgotten. French windows open onto the lawn, and if you go for a little wander you'll find the secret garden overlooking the cove below. From here you can see all the way to St Michael's Mount on a clear day! For more sea and golden sand, Halzephron is a perfect launch pad for miles of secluded beaches and a selection of local fishing villages that offer delicious, fresh seafood. *Secure walled garden. Right on coastal path, by the beach; 2 all year dog-friendly beaches within 10 minutes.*

Rooms	Cabin for 2: from £75 per night. Max. 1 dog.
Meals	Self-catering.
Closed	Never.

Advice on walks, river to swim in, coastal path walks, year-round dog-friendly beaches 5-10 min walk, and lovely dog-friendly pub 5-min walk.

Canopy & Stars
Halzephron Cabin,
Gunwalloe, Helston, TR12 7QD

Tel	+44 (0)117 204 7830
Email	enquiries@canopyandstars.co.uk
Web	www.canopyandstars.co.uk/halzephroncabin

Entry 18 Map 1

Trelowarren

'A jewel in the palm of your hand', wrote Daphne du Maurier of Trelowarren. It remains one of Cornwall's finest estates. The entrance drive brings you in past a long row of evergreen Holm oaks that emerge from an ancient Cornish 'hedge'. The main house, 500 years old, belongs to the Vyvyan family and is at the heart of this vast project. There's a gorgeous swimming pool, spa treatment centre, courtyard restaurant and a pop-up pizza house in the old stables; the whole place is yours to explore. These old estate houses have been handsomely restored to be as modern as possible inside, and they are just around the corner from the courtyard and the newly-converted restaurant. (Here you might linger all day, so exquisite and cosy is it.) The estate is a wonderful place for families – deep in the great outdoors yet so close to much else. The lush south coast is nearby, the Helford River too; the Lizard wraps around Trelowarren, and Penzance is a short drive away. Neither adults nor children can fail to enjoy themselves here; it is a paradise for those who love Cornwall. *Minimum stay: 2 nights on weekdays; 3 nights at weekends; 7 nights in high season. A thousand acres of woodland walks.*

Rooms	1 cottage for 4, 6 cottages for 6, 1 cottage for 8: £595-£2,595 per week. Max. 2 dogs.
Meals	Lunch from £6.95. Dinner, 3 courses, from £22.95. Wine from £15.50.
Closed	Never.
	Dog-friendly beach map – there are lots of beaches and walks all year round.

Kerenza Cooksey
Trelowarren,
Mawgan, Helston, TR12 6AF
Tel +44 (0)1326 221224
Email info@trelowarren.com
Web www.trelowarren.com

Entry 19 Map 1

Coriander Cottages

No shortage of natural entertainment here: a gaggle of waddling ducks, a buzzard hovering overhead, a night-time display by bats, a terrace for a ringside view: for a deep-country setting, these converted farm buildings are surprisingly lively! Both cottages combine ultra-green credentials with rustic luxury. Solar panels and geothermal heat ensure energy is renewable, rainwater is harvested, and natural textiles create harmony. Open-plan living spaces are sleek with limestone flooring, wooden beams and stone walls; there are comfortable leather sofas, rugs, leafy plants and toasty wood-burning stove; super kitchens are well-equipped; bedrooms are cosy and inviting; bathrooms are fabulous with TVs, candles and aromatherapy oils. Balconies and terraces have valley views to Fowey, a gentle mile downhill, and charming owner Colin, who lives next door, will drive you if you're not happily mobile. Beaches, the Coast Path and Saint's Way are close, the Eden Project and Lostwithiel are not much further. Superb. *Please see website for availability. Pets welcome in White Willow only. Due to local wildlife dogs to be kept on lead within the grounds.*

Rooms	2 cottages for 2: £600-£840 per week. Max. 2 dogs.
Meals	Self-catering.
Closed	Rarely.
	Coastal, country lane and riverbank walks.

Colin King
Coriander Cottages,
Penventinue Lane, Fowey, PL23 1JT
Tel +44 (0)1726 834998
Email stay@coriandercottages.co.uk
Web www.foweyaccommodation.co.uk

Entry 20 Map 1

Talland Bay Hotel

The position here is magical. First you plunge down rollercoaster lanes leaving the world behind, then you arrive at this lovely hotel and find a rather good view – a vast carpet of sea that shoots off to the horizon. Pine trees stand guard on one side, an old church crowns a hill on the other, then two acres of lawns roll down to a ha-ha before the land tumbles down to the bay. In summer, loungers and croquet hoops appear on the lawn, and you can nip down to a beach café for lunch by the water. Back at the hotel there's a conservatory brasserie, a sitting room bar and a roaring fire in the half-panelled dining room. You'll find art on the walls, polished flagstones, a terrace for afternoon tea. Follow the coastal path over the hill, then return for a good dinner, perhaps roasted scallops with caramelised orange, loin of venison with chestnut purée, lemongrass panna cotta with peach sorbet. Bedrooms have warm colours, vast beds, beautiful linen, the odd panelled wall. One has a balcony, a couple open onto terraces, all have lovely bathrooms. Gardens, beaches and the coastal path wait. *Garden, beach and coastal walks.*

Rooms	15 twin/doubles: £120-£240. 4 suites for 2: £200-£280. 3 cottages for 2: £160-£240. Dinner, B&B £95-£180 per person. Dogs £10.
Meals	Lunch from £5.50. Dinner: brasserie from £12.95; restaurant £36-£42. Sunday lunch £21.50-£25. Afternoon tea from £6.
Closed	Never.
	Biscuits and blanket.

Stephen Waite
Talland Bay Hotel
Porthallow, Looe, PL13 2JB
Tel +44 (0)1503 272667
Email info@tallandbayhotel.com
Web www.tallandbayhotel.co.uk

Entry 21 Map 1

Treworgey

A rural idyll within easy reach of coastal treasures. A place to come with the young, the old, with friends or family; children can play, nature lovers ramble, animal lovers get a fix of farming life. Wooden floors, rugs, fires, kitchens well-equipped for big meals, comfy beds, lovely fabrics and, often, a gorgeous view of the Looe Valley and, beyond, the sea. Lois is a one-bedroom cottage, cosy and enveloping with a slipper bath and fresh flowers; Trelawney is one of the larger cottages with those views, a grandfather clock, a four poster bed and oak kitchen. The Farmhouse is grander, perfect for a large gathering with its Aga-warmed kitchen, sash windows and flagstone floors; Jasmine has a sweet conservatory for meals with views. All are toasty warm thanks to a Biomass boiler. You'll find a summer house where you can borrow the computer, a walker's map or a DVD, a games room, a heated pool with spa and sauna, tennis court and an honesty fridge filled with produce. There's a private riding school, too, and home-cooked meals can be delivered. *Short breaks Nov-April. Private secure garden for each cottage. Dog-tie up area with water, shelter & beds (near pool area while you swim). Farm & woodland walks; 3 miles from dog-friendly beaches.*

Rooms	1 cottage for 2, 1 cottage for 4, 1 cottage for 6: £412-£2852. 1 house for 11: £1,263-£3,927. Prices per week. Dogs £23 per stay. Dogs £23 per week or part week. Max. 2.
Meals	Self-catering.
Closed	Never.
	Dog treats, bowls, towel and a collar tag with postcode and phone number. Outside hose for washing dogs off.

Holly Wright & Andy Kyte
Treworgey,
Duloe, Looe, PL14 4PP
Tel +44 (0)1503 262730
Email stay@treworgeycottages.co.uk
Web www.treworgeycottages.co.uk

Entry 22 Map 1

Treworgey Farm

The shepherd's huts at Treworgey Farm are a wonderful way to explore a fabulous area of Cornwall. The farm is Holly and Andy's family business, spread over 150 acres overlooking the Looe river valley. It's a lively place, with a riding school on site that runs on weekdays and a few holiday cottages dotted about. The Hideaway Hut sits in its own corner of the farm and The Lambing Hut is on the west with uninterrupted views. Both come with a private shower and loo twenty metres off. From here you can hit the coastal path or ramble down in the woodlands, but you're more than welcome to use the games room, the pool, and the tennis court, which you'll share with the cottages. Tea and cake, light suppers or Cornish cream teas can be delivered to your door. There's a wood-burner in the hut to keep you warm and a gas hob for cooking along with all the basics, but why not hike out to the local (forty minutes uphill on the way out) and try their sparkling cider and some good pub food. The beach is only a few minutes by car and the many attractions of Cornwall await. *Secure private garden. Bluebell woods, open fields and riverside walks from the door. Great dog-friendly pub nearby.*

Rooms	2 shepherd's huts for 2 (space for 2 in tent alongside hut): from £76 per night. Dogs £15 per dog per stay. Max. 1.
Meals	Self-catering.
Closed	December/January.

Private fenced garden for dog to play in; empty field for running free off lead. Throws for furniture. Advice & maps for fantastic dog walks, dog-friendly beaches, pubs and days out.

Canopy & Stars
Treworgey Farm
Duloe, Liskeard, PL14 4PP
Tel +44 (0)117 204 7830
Email enquiries@canopyandstars.co.uk
Web www.canopyandstars.co.uk/treworgeyfarm

Entry 23 Map 1

The Old Coach House at Windsworth

Ditch the gadgets – this wonderful place is strictly for those who want to experience sustainability and it won't suit seekers of glitz. Getting here is fun: along winding lanes, through leafy glades, down the track… to arrive at an old coach house surrounded by much wildlife and incredible views over the sea. These totally private acres include woodlands and fields, a labyrinth, a shower and loo for campers (if you want to add friends) and a steep path that drops down to the seashore. Caroline is enthusiastic, charming, near enough to be on hand. This is her off-grid adventure: wood-burners for cooking and heating; solar panels for lights, shower, fridge; a Kelly kettle – and no WiFi. There are, though, flushing loos, an LPG gas hob and a charger for mobiles. You have a lofty living room off the kitchen with guitars, African drums and games for kids, a simple bedroom with a big bed, a sleeping platform in the attic and (an optional extra) a self-contained studio up outside steps. Stroll to the veggie café at the Monkey Sanctuary, walk the coastal path to the fishing port of Looe. Slow heaven for close friends or families. *Unusual bedroom layout – check on owner's website before booking. Dog-friendly beach; paths through woods. Free-ranging chickens, as well as sheep, goats, ponies so dogs on a lead please.*

Rooms	1 house for 8: £335-£1,500 per week. Short breaks available from £245. Dogs £20 per stay.
Meals	Pubs/restaurants 1 mile.
Closed	Never.

Cosy dog blanket, water bowl and towels.

Caroline Petherick
The Old Coach House at Windsworth,
Looe, PL13 1NZ
Tel +44 (0)1503 262671
Email stay@windsworth.org.uk
Web www.windsworth.org.uk

Entry 24 Map 2

Okel Tor Mine

It's not often you sleep in a World Heritage Site in an AONB, where flora and fauna – badgers, kingfishers, otters, rare mosses – also mark it as an SSSI. The two cottages – converted buildings of a former Victorian copper and tin mine – sit in a fairytale landscape of ivy-clad chimneys and tree-covered hillsides. Totally hidden, even from each other, with sweeping views over the river Tamar, their small but thoughtful layouts are perfect for a romantic retreat. Open-plan living areas are country-cottage cosy with wood-burning stoves, deep red sofas, rugs on flagstone floors and a table by the window for those views. A simple kitchen and, for wet-weather days, books, games and DVDs. Bedrooms are fresh and unfussy country-pine, with equally neat shower rooms with handmade soaps. Stroll to the village shop and pubs in Calstock, walk along the river to the National Trust's Cotehele House, enjoy walks on the Bere Peninsula or visit Morewell Ham Quay port and copper mine. Within 30 minutes you could be enjoying Dartmoor, Bodmin Moor or Whitsand Bay. Return to your private decking, birdsong, watery views and serenity. *Minimum stay: 2 nights; 7 in high season. River to swim in, woodland and heathland walks from door, far from any roads. Short walk from 2 dog-friendly pubs.*

Rooms	2 cottages for 2: £349-£699 per week. Extra bed/sofabed available at no charge.
Meals	Self-catering.
Closed	Never.
	Throws provided, doggy towels available and wonderful country walks.

Greg Smith
Okel Tor Mine,
Calstock, PL18 9SQ
Mobile +44 (0)7976 799663
Email greg1971@mac.com
Web www.tinmine.com

Spring Park

The five wagons, tabernacle and cabin at Spring Park each have an individual charm (owners Kitty and Paddy used to own two vintage boutiques, so this is right up their street!) and almost all have their own private wood-fired hot tub to soak in. There's Duke, a classic 1940's showman's wagon, with bright vibrant paintwork on the outside and interior furnishings to match. Next, Maiden, a restored railway wagon has been paired up with a large modern cabin, Wisteria Cottage. Then there's Pip, a sturdy 1930's steam roller living van with spacious cabin alongside. Next is The Duchess, bright blue with bathroom in the hut next door. Hercules, a large cedar living van, holds an eclectic mix of antique finds. St Agnes is a Scandinavian-inspired tabernacle where the nic-nacs take a turn for the ecclesiastical. Finally, The Old Potting Shed is a cosy cottage for four, a far cry from its dusty origins. Each has its own kitchen and a fifth of an acre of private garden, perfect for just lying back and daydreaming in the Cornish countryside. If you do want to go adventuring, head down to the beach for surfing, scale the Dartmoor peaks or wander through the local villages and markets. *In the Tamar Valley – an AONB with loads of walks and rivers.*

Rooms	4 wagons for 2: from £72. 1 wagon for 2-4: from £71. 1 tabernacle for 2: from £72. 1 cabin for 4: from £70. Prices per night. Hot tub £30 per stay. Dogs £20 per dog per stay. Max. 2.
Meals	Self-catering.
Closed	Never.
	Treats, biodegradable poo bags, towels and advice on some of our favourite walks.

Canopy & Stars
Spring Park,
Rezare, Launceston, PL15 9NX

Tel	+44 (0)117 204 7830
Email	enquiries@canopyandstars.co.uk
Web	www.canopyandstars.co.uk/springpark

Entry 26 Map 2

High Houses

Tucked away at the quieter end of the Lake District National Park is this beguiling 17th-century hilltop house – all lime-plastered walls, rustic beams, open fires and original flagstones. Its delightful owners, who live in the house's other half, have resisted smoothing out the rough edges; 1920s graffiti still adorns the stable dividers. The hardships of country living have, however, been banished: find lovely new pink and soft-green 'pineapple' covers on sitting room chairs, delicious bed linen and towels, hand-made soaps and piping hot radiators. Bedrooms may prompt some tough decisions – do you choose the room with the roll top bath (semi en suite) and the cockloft for kids, or the four-poster with the sofabed and the log fire? The farmhouse kitchen is cosy with Aga, big fridge and gadgets aplenty, but reluctant cooks can book Jill's homemade meals in advance. Beautiful views reach out from every fine sash window to wildlife-rich farmland beyond – 350 private acres, yours to explore. Venture further and you reach the Lakes and the Solway Plain. Heaven for sybarites and walkers. *Great place for walking with your dog: totally surrounded by fields, bridlepath right behind house and no traffic.*

Rooms	1 house for 6: £700-£900 per week. £550 for a 3-night stay at weekends in low season or a 4-night stay on weekdays. Max. 3 dogs.
Meals	Self-catering.
Closed	Never.
	Water bowl and perfect walks from the door.

Jill Green
High Houses
Snittlegarth, Ireby, Carlisle, CA7 1HE
Tel +44 (0)1697 371549
Mobile +44 (0)7929 397273
Email enquiries@highhouses.co.uk
Web www.highhouses.co.uk

Entry 27 Map 5

Scales Plantation

High in the wilds of the North Lakes, in the woods around Scales Farm, Tabitha and Rob Wilson have created a selection of fabulous boltholes. Three shepherd's hut camps with timber kitchens are set in semicircular clearings on the edge of the trees; there's a family safari tent, a bell tent and cabin camp too. The sites are sheltered and peaceful, with views out towards Bowscale Fell and Mount Skiddaw. As part of the regeneration of the woodland, the once thick canopy has been thinned to allow wildlife such as the resident red squirrels to flourish. The camps have already come to feel like natural extensions of the Lake District, with beautiful walks across the fells on your doorstep. You can get trail advice or hire bikes just down the road and head into the hills, then come back to the rustic comfort of the hut and your toasty wood-burner. Groceries can even be supplied by your hosts: simply choose from the list of supplies in advance and they'll be waiting on your arrival. *The whole of the Lake District on the doorstep for dogs to drag their owners around! Keep dogs on leads when sheep are about.*

Rooms	3 shepherd's huts for 4: from £70. 1 safari tent for 6: from £108. Camp for 4: from £90. Prices per night. Max. 2 dogs.
Meals	Self-catering.
Closed	Never.
	Advice on walks and dog-friendly activities and nearby pubs.

Canopy & Stars
Scales Plantation,
Scales Farm, Berrier, Penrith, CA11 0XE

Tel	+44 (0)117 204 7830
Email	enquiries@canopyandstars.co.uk
Web	www.canopyandstars.co.uk/scalesplantation

Entry 28 Map 5

The Lodge

Splendidly located on a wide bend of the river Eamont, The Lodge is frontier living at its finest. While the exterior of this timber log cabin blends perfectly into its natural surroundings, the interior comes as a surprise: simple and homely, but beautifully furnished with several stylish touches. From the upstairs 'master' bedroom – with views that make the most of the spot – a wrought-iron spiral staircase drops down into the centre of the well-equipped kitchen/sitting room. Find comfy armchairs around a wood-burner and sliding doors that open to a veranda and summer breezes; occasionally deer come to the river bank for a drink. You can catch trout for your supper, then cook up a storm on the four-hob gas oven, followed by a soak in the hot tub. Edenhall estate offers plenty of scope for hiking and cycling as well as private stretches of river fantastic for salmon, and you're also on the very edge of the Lake District. You can arrange for your supper to be waiting in the oven, book a full hamper before you arrive, or arrange a massage to ease away hiker's pains. *Very secluded area with no traffic. Riverside & lots of other walks from the door and further afield: great yomping territory for you & your dog.*

Rooms	Cabin for 6: from £264 per night. No charge for 1 dog, £15 per dog per stay for 2+.
Meals	Self-catering.
Closed	Never.
	Outdoor bed, blanket, water bowl and dog lead.

Canopy & Stars
The Lodge,
Eden Hall,
Penrith, CA11 8ST

Tel	+44 (0)117 204 7830
Email	enquiries@canopyandstars.co.uk
Web	www.canopyandstars.co.uk/thelodge

Entry 29 Map 6

George and Dragon

Charlie Lowther has found a chef who does perfect justice to the slow-grow breeds of beef, pork and lamb produced on the Lowther Estate – and you'll find lovely wines to match, 16 by the glass. Ales and cheeses are local, berries and mushrooms are foraged, vegetables are home-grown and his signature starter, twice-baked cheese soufflé with a hint of spinach is divine. As for the long low coaching inn, it's been beautifully restored by craftsmen using wood, slate and stone, and painted in colours in tune with the period. Stripped wooden tables, comfy sofas, intimate alcoves and crackling fires make this a delightful place to dine and unwind; old prints and archive images tell stories of the 800-year-old estate's history. Outside is plenty of seating and a lawned play area beneath fruit trees. Upstairs are 11 bedrooms of varying sizes (some small, some large and some above the bar), perfectly decorated in classic country style. Carpeting is Cumbrian wool, beds are new, ornaments come with Lowther history, showers are walk-in, baths (there are two) are roll top, and breakfast is fresh and delicious. *Dogs welcome in the bar dining area and bedrooms (not the main restaurant).*

Rooms	11 twin/doubles: £100-£160. Singles £85-£119. Extra bed/sofabed available £25 per person per night. Dogs £10 per stay. Max. 3.
Meals	Lunch & dinner from £12. Sunday lunch from £12.95.
Closed	26 December.
	Doggy welcome pack including treat, map of local walks and doggy bag.

Charlie Lowther
George and Dragon,
Clifton,
Penrith, CA10 2ER
Tel +44 (0)1768 865381
Email enquiries@georgeanddragonclifton.co.uk
Web www.georgeanddragonclifton.co.uk

Entry 30 Map 6

Steele's Mill

There's been a working grain mill here since 1327; this one was built in the 1800s. Fragments of the past remain: staircases and floors of oak grown on the estate, grinding stones set into the floor, and the old apple-wood cogs encased in glass. There's a lovely approach to this stunning conversion, a hugely comfortable retreat for four, with the master bedroom positioned grandly at the top, and below the tiny twin. Cook just-caught brown trout from the river Lyvennet on a shiny black Rangemaster, dine at a handmade oak table furnished with welcoming flowers and a bottle of wine, lounge on a leather sofa by the gas wood-burner, idle with a book on the balcony. By day, venture out on the snaking road past fields of cattle to King's Meaburn village, to Appleby for delis, pubs and a country fair in summer, to Lowther Castle for those seeking gothic revival grandeur. Nature is embraced indoors, too: the mill has a hidden bat loft with an aperture only accessible to the pipistrelle! Colours are cream and duck-egg blue melting into pale oak, mattresses are superb, shower heads drench you and the peace is supreme. *Minimum stay: 3 nights; 7 nights in high season. Secure garden, woodland walks and safe rivers.*

Rooms	1 house for 4: £600-£920 per week. Dogs 1 free; 2nd £30 per stay. Max. 3.
Meals	Self-catering.
Closed	Never.
	Advice on walks.

Karen Addison
Steele's Mill,
King's Meaburn, Penrith, CA10 3BU
Tel +44 (0)1931 714017
Mobile +44 (0)7831 865749
Email karenaddison@karenaddison.co.uk
Web www.steelesmill.co.uk

Entry 31 Map 6

The Burton

Selina's gorgeous showman's wagon dates back to 1940 and was originally pulled by four horses. These days it sits behind the farmhouse with views up Clouds Fell and a fire pit in the garden for starry nights. It's a brilliant feat of interior engineering with a Nordic, chalet feel. You get everything you need wrapped up in oodles of rustic chic: rugs on wood floors, chairs at a pretty table and a wood-burner to keep you cosy. Find books and flowers too, and a welcoming tipple waiting for you. A sweet little kitchen bar comes with a microwave and a hob, and a tiny shower room does the trick in style. The bed is fabulous: lovely linen, a good mattress and drawers below. There's a decked terrace at the front, then a drying room, a fridge/freezer and piles of logs in the shed behind, home to the boiler that assures hot showers. Selina is happy to take delivery of supplies before you arrive, but she also manages a lovely local inn, so a slap-up meal is on hand if you don't want to cook. Great walking to be had straight from the door; return to your romantic space, get yourself a cup of tea and be glad you're here. *Surrounded by livestock so advise dogs on leads, but many different walks all within a 4-mile radius: woodland, riverside and fells.*

Rooms	Wagon for 2: from £98 per night. Dogs £10 per dog per stay. Max. 1.
Meals	Self-catering.
Closed	Never.

Wonderful walks from the doorstep up and onto the Cumbrian fells.

Canopy & Stars
The Burton,
Stennerskeugh, Ravenstonedale,
Kirkby Stephen, CA17 4LL

Tel	+44 (0)117 204 7830
Email	enquiries@canopyandstars.co.uk
Web	www.canopyandstars.co.uk/theburton

Entry 32 Map 6

The Farmhouse at A Corner of Eden

A lovely Georgian farmhouse in a glorious valley with infinite sky and distant Cumbrian hills. The wood, the stone, the honesty of the structure create an enveloping, peaceful retreat. Layered on to this lovely house is deep comfort and more than a touch of luxury. The hunting lodge-style sitting room has a log fire, antlers, sofas and the beautiful beamed dining room has seating for a small crowd. Bedrooms sport original fireplaces, too, and have polished wooden floors, gorgeous wallpapers and spoiling fabrics. Both bathrooms are super stylish. Richard and Debbie are the loveliest hosts – they live in an adjacent barn and have thought of everything, generously leaving fluffy robes, thick towels, Barbours and wellies to borrow, drinks in the honesty bar in the dairy and a welcome basket bursting with local goodies and champagne. The large range cooker will excite keen cooks and the not so keen can easily find their way to the pub across the fields or just ask Debbie to arrange for caterers to whip something up. Simply heaven. Take Angel Barn and Shepherd's Cottage, too, and come with 16 friends. *Minimum stay: 3 nights at weekends. Dogs welcome downstairs. Walled garden, paths from the door; river, woods & open access land (sheep). Maps with walks highlighted. 3 pubs allow dogs in bar when eating.*

Rooms	1 cottage for 8: £995-£1,495 per week. £750-£935 for a 3-night weekend or 4-night mid-week stay. Dogs £20 per dog per stay.
Meals	Self-catering. Pub 1 mile.
Closed	Never.
	Welcome dog biscuit, water bowl and spare dog towels.

Debbie & Richard Greaves
Low Stennerskeugh, Ravenstonedale,
Kirkby Stephen, CA17 4LL

Tel	+44 (0)1539 623370
Mobile	+44 (0)7759 469059
Email	enquiries@acornerofeden.co.uk
Web	www.acornerofeden.co.uk/the-farmhouse/

Entry 33 Map 6

Shepherd's Cottage

A heavenly hideaway for couples in a glorious corner of the world, coddled between the Lakes and the Dales. You approach through a charming walled garden, then straight into the kitchen with its flagged floor, red Aga, lovely beams and glorious view. Snuggle by the wood-burner (logs on the house) in the beamed sitting room with your very generous welcome basket: champagne, locally made chocolates, homemade bread and cake, all you need for breakfast, and a mini honesty bar with beers, wines and spirits. Upstairs to your oak beamed bedroom and bathroom: the handmade king-size bed is spoiling (with choice of feather or fibre pillows), so too the bathroom with ruby red roll top, thick white towels, robes and large shower. Debbie's creative flair makes the whole place sparkle, and outside you get *another* red roll top, front and back gardens to follow the sunshine. Walk across fields to the pub for supper, head back for a cosy night in. Great for romantic couples who want privacy, but you can also take other properties – The Shepherd's Cottage and The Farmhouse are attached, Angel Barn and helpful owners are nearby. *Walled garden, paths from the door; river, woods & open access land (sheep). Maps with walks highlighted. 3 pubs allow dogs in bar when eating*

Rooms	1 cottage for 2: £600-£945 per week. £465-£580 for 3-night weekend or 4-night mid-week break. Children under 10 years can stay in the 'Little Room', £25 for z-bed, no charge for travel cot and high chair. Dogs welcome downstairs. Dogs £20 per dog per stay.
Meals	Self-catering. Pub 1 mile.
Closed	Never.
	Welcome dog biscuit, water bowl and spare dog towels.

Debbie & Richard Greaves
Shepherd's Cottage, Low Stennerskeugh, Ravestonedale, Kirkby Stephen, CA17 4LL
Tel +44 (0)1539 623370
Mobile +44 (0)7759 469059
Email enquiries@acornerofeden.co.uk
Web www.acornerofeden.co.uk/shepherds-cottage/

Entry 34 Map 6

Linthwaite House

It's not just the view that makes Linthwaite so special, though Windermere sparkling half a mile below with a chain of peaks rising beyond does grab your attention. There's loads to enjoy here – 14 acres of gardens and grounds, a fantastic terrace for sunny days and interiors that go out of their way to pamper your pleasure receptors. The house itself is beautiful, one of those grand Lakeland Arts & Crafts wonders, with original woodwork and windows in all the right places. Logs are piled high by the front door, fires smoulder, sofas wait in the conservatory sitting room, where big views loom. Country-house bedrooms are coolly uncluttered with warm colours, chic fabrics, hi-tech gadgetry, fabulous bathrooms. Those at the front have lake views, a couple have hot tubs, you can stargaze from one of the suites. Downstairs, ambrosial food waits in the dining rooms (one is decorated with nothing but mirrors), perhaps seared tuna with pickled ginger, chargrilled pigeon with beetroot purée, caramelised banana tart with peanut butter ice cream. Sunbeds wait on the terrace. Fabulous. *Minimum stay: 2 nights at weekends. The dog-friendly rooms have private external access; 14 acres of grounds for walks. Dogs not allowed in main hotel building; kennel in the grounds.*

Rooms	21 doubles, 5 twin/doubles: £306-£454. 4 suites for 2: £492-£684. Price includes dinner for 2. Dogs £10. Max. 1 medium size or 2 small.
Meals	Lunch, 3 courses, from £24.95. Dinner included; non-residents, £58.
Closed	Rarely.
	Dog treats, toy, bowls, mat and bed.

Nic Crow
Linthwaite House,
Crook Road, Bowness-on-Windermere,
Windermere, LA23 3JA
Tel +44 (0)15394 88600
Email stay@linthwaitehouse.com
Web www.linthwaitehouse.com

Entry 35 Map 6

Brownber Hall

Peter and Amanda, London escapees keen on cycling and walking, have stylishly restored this big old house, adding contemporary touches and all the comforts. The atmosphere is relaxed and sociable, there's an honesty bar with local craft beers and excellent wines, plenty of space to chill, and heaps of bedrooms with deeply comfortable beds to choose from. The rooms at the front have the views. Breakfast tables have white cloths and wild flower posies; wake to homemade granola, sausages, bacon, sourdough toast and great coffee. Join the Coast to Coast path by foot or bike, hop on the wonderfully scenic Settle to Carlisle railway. *Lots of glorious dog walks straight from the front door. 2 dog-friendly rooms, 1 downstairs.*

Rooms	4 doubles, 2 twin/doubles: £90-£130. 1 suite for 2: £110-£140. 1 single: £50-£60. Cot available, £10. Extra bed £15 per night with breakfast included. Dogs £5 per stay.
Meals	Dinner for walkers by arrangement. Pub/restaurants 5 miles.
Closed	Christmas.
	Water bowls and towels for cleaning off muddy dogs.

Peter & Amanda
Brownber Hall, Newbiggin-on-Lune,
Kirkby Stephen, CA17 4NX
Tel +44 (0)1539 623208
Mobile +44 (0)7412 504765
Email peter@brownberhall.co.uk
Web www.brownberhall.co.uk

Entry 36 Map 6

Johnby Hall

You are ensconced in the quieter part of the Lakes and have independence in this Elizabethan manor. Once a fortified Pele tower, it's a fascinating historic house yet very much a lived-in family home with a wonderful atmosphere. The airy suites have a sitting room each with books, children's videos, squashy sofas, pretty fabrics and whitewashed walls. Beds have patchwork quilts, windows have stone mullions and all is peaceful. Henry gives you sturdy breakfasts, and you can join him and Anna for convivial home-grown suppers by a roaring fire in the great hall. Children will have fun: hens and pigs to feed, garden toys galore and woods to roam. *Please keep dogs who aren't trustworthy with chickens under control within in the garden; sheep fields nearby too.*

Rooms	1 twin/double, with sitting room; 1 family room for 4: £125. Singles £87.50. Extra bed/sofabed £20 per person per night. Children £15 per night. Under 5s free.
Meals	Supper, 2 courses, £22.50. Pub 1 mile.
Closed	Rarely.
	Acres of garden and woodland sniffs; 1 room has an enclosed garden that's dog-proof for most breeds!

Henry & Anna Howard
Johnby Hall,
Johnby, Penrith, CA11 0UU
Tel +44 (0)1768 483257
Email bookings@johnbyhall.co.uk
Web www.johnbyhall.co.uk

Entry 37 Map 5

The Corner House

A delightful 18th-century cottage opposite Tideswell church – the 'Cathedral of the Peak'. Bells ring in the hour while voices from the Tideswell Male Voice Choir drift blissfully over the garden. Oak beams and flagstone floors recall the cottage's fascinating past, while John and Nikki have introduced modern comforts from an Aga to White Company towels, Laura Ashley bed linen and country antique furniture. A generous welcome hamper including tea, coffee, local handmade sausages, chutney, bread and a Tidza pud awaits in the kitchen, which has a sociable table for six. Plump sofas surround a wood-burner stocked with logs in the cosy sitting room. Head up the wide, carpeted staircase to sleep in peaceful bedrooms; doubles have comfy king-size or super king-size beds, while the twin overlooks the church. There's a big bathroom on the first floor and a small shower room up the next flight of stairs. In sunny weather, you can breakfast al fresco in the pretty garden alongside the churchyard. Stroll to pubs and cafés from the front door, or put on your walking boots to explore the Peak District. *Minimum stay: 3 nights; 7 in high season. See website for availability. Separate garden that is partly walled and gated to path. Keep dogs on leads as lane has occasional passing cars.*

Rooms	1 cottage for 6: £560-£1,125 per week. Max. 2 dogs.
Meals	Pubs/restaurants 5-minute walk.
Closed	Rarely.

Dog bed, bowls and treats, towels for drying and poo bags. Advice on local dog-friendly cafés, pubs and walks.

Nikki Turton
The Corner House,
1 Pursglove Road, Tideswell,
Buxton, SK17 8LG
Mobile +44 (0)7876 763730
Email info@thecornerhousetideswell.co.uk
Web www.thecornerhousetideswell.co.uk

Entry 38 Map 6

The Peacock at Rowsley

The Peacock sits between two fine houses, Haddon Hall and Chatsworth House. You can follow rivers up to each – the Derwent to Chatsworth, the Wye to the Hall – both a stroll through beautiful parkland. As for the hotel, it was built in 1652 and was home to the steward of Haddon. Inside, old and new mix gracefully: mullioned windows, hessian rugs, aristocratic art, then striking colours that give a contemporary feel. You'll find Mouseman tables and chairs in the restaurant, where French windows open onto the terrace. Elsewhere, a fire smoulders in the bar every day, the daily papers wait in the sitting room, the garden lawn runs down to the river. Stylish bedrooms have crisp linen, good beds, Farrow & Ball colours, the odd antique; one has a bed from Belvoir Castle. Good food waits in the restaurant, with meat and game from the estate, perhaps venison terrine, roast partridge, Bakewell Tart with buttermilk ice cream. There's afternoon tea in the garden in summer and you can fish both rivers, with day tickets available from reception. Guests also receive a discount on entry to Haddon Hall. *Minimum stay: 2 nights at weekends. Lots of walking in woodland and fields. Peak Park area – follow countryside code. Derwent &Wye rivers.*

Rooms	10 doubles, 2 four-posters: £205-£310. 1 suite for 2: £250-£310. 2 singles: £130-£145. Dogs £10 per dog per night. Max. 2.
Meals	Lunch from £4.50. Dinner £60. Sunday lunch £22.50-£29.50.
Closed	Rarely.

Dog biscuits at turndown, towels and lots of walking information.

Laura Ball
The Peacock at Rowsley,
Bakewell Road, Rowsley,
Matlock, DE4 2EB

Tel	+44 (0)1629 733518
Email	reception@thepeacockatrowsley.com
Web	www.thepeacockatrowsley.com

Entry 39 Map 6

Fern Cottage

Up a steep, bumpy road, with no sign of habitation… a mystery tour? Then a sturdy, limestone cottage, with deep-set windows and handsome proportions appears. Turn around, and you'll stagger at the views over the Staffordshire/Derbyshire hills. There's even a wall seat from which to enjoy them. Originally the mine manager's house for nearby copper workings, and then the owners' family home, it's been thoughtfully updated without losing authentic charm. Window seats, alcove cupboards and original fireplaces mix with pale colours, cottagey furnishings and a sprinkling of well-chosen antiques to create a calm, tranquil atmosphere. Pale-painted floorboards lend an airy feel to the small, well-kitted kitchen. A window seat plump with cushions and a wood-burning stove make the sitting room cosy while a sunny conservatory extension cleverly doubles as a dining space. Large, light-filled bedrooms and bathroom are comfortably pretty yet unfussy, with wake-you-up views. Go walking and cycling; explore Chatsworth and local industrial heritage. The biggest joy is the secret corners in the terraced gardens, perfect for reading and dreaming. *Minimum stay: 4 nights on weekdays; 3 at weekends & high season. Enclosed garden; walks from the door.*

Rooms	1 cottage for 4: £650-£790 per week. Dogs £15 per dog. Max. 3.
Meals	Restaurants 3 miles.
Closed	Rarely.
	Dog treats, bowls and poo bags.

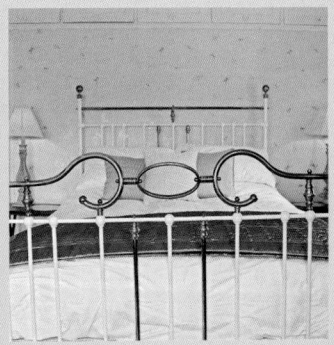

Robert & Jo Wood
Fern Cottage,
Ecton, Ashbourne, DE6 2AH
Tel +44 (0)1335 310393
Email stay@alstonefieldmanor.com
Web www.alstonefieldholidaycottages.com/fern-cottage/

Entry 40 Map 6

Wisteria Cottage

Heavenly walks start from the door – then it's back to a cosy wood-burner, and bathrooms made for lingering. High in the hills above Dovedale is a handsome 19th-century cottage swathed in wisteria, a former blacksmith's workshop. There's a walled garden at the back (lawns, shrubs, trees, French tables and chairs), a stylish New England feel within. The space has been beautifully designed, with open-plan living downstairs, a bathroom and a twin, and a dreamy bedroom with a big shower up the runner'd stair. From the porch you enter the boot room (handy!), then the dove-grey kitchen, a chef's delight, and the sitting room, charming and immaculate, with a leather sofa and tartan wool cushions, a renovated stone fireplace and logs on the house. Bedrooms are fresh and sophisticated, with a quirky dash of vintage. The added bonus? The George lies across the road, a village inn where the rooms are timeless and the chefs get creative with seasonal produce. Charming. *Minimum stay: 3 nights at weekends & in high season; 4 nights on weekdays. Enclosed garden, walks from the door; boot room.*

Rooms	1 cottage for 4: £710-£870 per week. Dogs £15 per dog. Max. 2.
Meals	Self-catering. Pub across the road.
Closed	Rarely.

Dog treats, water and food bowls and poo bags.

Robert & Jo Wood
Wisteria Cottage,
Alstonefield, Ashbourne, DE6 2FX
Tel +44 (0)1335 310393
Email stay@alstonefieldmanor.com
Web www.alstonefieldholidaycottages.com/wisteria-cottage/

Entry 41 Map 6

Derbyshire

B&B

Casterne Hall

Wind up the steep drive and be rewarded by the vista of this Georgian manor and a 360ª panorama. A fascinating house owned by the Hurt family since 1480, it's been a film set many times. Your elegant top floor suite has a huge convivial sitting/dining room with a log fire; comfortable bedrooms with beautiful linen; games, books, art, antiques and family pieces. Breakfast is in the majestic hall: Caroline's feast of home-laid eggs with local bacon, black pudding, artisan bread; delicious dinners too. Charles (author of mapped walks) has all the local tips: footpaths from the door, market towns, Carsington Water, period homes. *Top floor suite for 2-8. Minimum stay: 2 nights at weekends. Parking on-site. Fabulous walks right from the front door, and all dogs love the river and stepping stones at Dovedale. (Please note: chickens, sheep and cows.)*

Rooms 2 doubles, let to same party only; 2 twins, let to same party only: £140. Singles £70. All 4 rooms booked together: £482.
Dogs £10 per dog, and bring as many as you like!

Meals Pubs/restaurants 4 miles.

Closed Rarely.

Water bowls, towels on request and a hose for washing paws.

Charles & Caroline Hurt
Casterne Hall,
Ilam, Ashbourne, Derby, DE6 2BA
Tel +44 (0)1335 310489
Email shuter1@me.com
Web www.casterne.co.uk

Entry 42 Map 6

Doggyshire

Barking Mansion

Bow WOW! Here's a place for the more discerning of our canine companions, the most classy of pedigree chums! But why are we confining this treat to posh pooches? This is surely a place any of us would stay if only we had the right lineage! A glorious, wisteria-clad folly built by Palladio during a little-known trip to London in 1545 and complete with er, wood-burner, this place is no doghouse. Owner Bertie is sure to regale you with tales (tails?) of an earlier life when he was a member of the racy Kennel Club on Barkley Square. Dinner is served in a silver bowl in the splendid gardens where all high-end hounds gather to do their business. You'll have a ball! (A nice, shiny red one).

Rooms 1 suite with outdoor bathroom.

Meals A dog's dinner.

Closed Only to non-pedigree types.

That shiny red ball is all yours.

Bertie Woofter
Barking Mansion,
Hide Park
Upper Growling W00 FK9
Tel Dog 'n' bone is ex-directory
Web www.bedandbarkiewithbertie.com

Entry 43 Map 00

Garden Studio

A cosy apartment overlooking the sea that sits close to Exmoor's coast path where it sweeps dramatically into the Valley of the Rocks. There's a collection of guest houses on the North Walk promenade which crosses – near the top – the funicular linking Lynmouth and Lynton. The Downings have transformed theirs into a calm retreat, with self-catering space on the ground floor. Inside is sweet, fresh and simple. The walls are white, the shower room bedecked in gleaming red tiles. The bedroom sits behind a wooden half wall, brightened cheerfully in blushing pink, a happy contrast with the dark brass bed. Living and kitchen spaces come together, one corner stocked with all the white goods you could need, the other has a sofabed, stacks of books and a library of walking maps. Wind-blasted wanderers can return to privacy, take a drink on the sheltered terrace or get cosy with a DVD. In the morning you may choose to seek out Sarah and Ian's fabulous local and organic breakfasts in the B&B above (your hosts are relaxed and charming). There are miles of coast, wood and moorland to explore; pubs and tea rooms along the way. *Minimum stay: 4 nights on weekdays; 3 nights at weekends. Lovely walks – join the coastal path.*

Rooms	1 apartment for 2: £325-£410 per week. Dogs £5 per night per stay. Max. 2.
Meals	Self-catering.
Closed	Rarely.

Dog biscuits, water bowl, towel, throw for furniture and outside tap with hose.

Ian & Sarah Downing
Garden Studio,
North Walk House, North Walk,
Lynton, EX35 6HJ

Tel	+44 (0)1598 753372
Email	walk@northwalkhouse.co.uk
Web	www.northwalkhouse.co.uk

Entry 44 Map 2

Longlands

The five Longlands lodge tents jut impressively out of the hillside on raised wooden decks, in a wide open field near the North Devon coast. They're the perfect haven for big family escapes, sleeping six each. The lodge tents are beautifully made, with a king-sized bed, two single beds and a cabin double, all with thick duvets, spare blankets and hot water bottles. Each has a fully equipped kitchen, private loos and showers and a spacious living area. Tire the little ones out on beach excursions or coastal walks, or the games room full of games and other treasures. The on-site honesty shop can take care of the basics, you can have meals organised for arrival or those occasional lazy evenings and the games room has plenty to offer in any weather. Book out the hot tub for a private session and soak up the stunning views, or there are even two boats on the lake for racing round the island! The area is packed full of every kind of adventure; outdoor sports on Exmoor, coastal villages and towns full of galleries. *Dogs on leads except in wood please. Details of dog-friendly beaches and pubs given. Dog-sitting service available.*

Rooms	5 safari tents for 6: from £124 per night. Dogs £25 per dog per stay, payable on departure. Max. 2.
Meals	Self-catering.
Closed	November – March.
	Towels, beds, bowls, treats, poo bags and Dirty Dog shampoo. Also hose and poo bin under the lodges.

Canopy & Stars
Longlands,
Coulsworthy,
Combe Martin, EX34 0PD

Tel	+44 (0)117 204 7830
Email	enquiries@canopyandstars.co.uk
Web	www.canopyandstars.co.uk/longlands

Entry 45 Map 2

Loveland Farm

On the border of Devon and Cornwall – beautifully remote yet close to surfing and dog-friendly beaches, and the wildly dramatic south west coast path – Loveland Farm is a place that celebrates modern simplicity and, thanks to Jeff's tree planting, is carbon neutral. It's home to chickens, pigs, ducks, a pair of Asian Water buffaloes, Karina and Jeff's original creation Loveland Pod and now four more bubble-shaped pods with clear sides for the moon and stars to shine through at night, shiny copper rain showers, ghost chairs, and cashmere blankets. The Griffins' world travels with their fashion line inspired the ingenious, stylishly quirky design here and two of their domes welcome dogs. Welcombe Pod has space too for four humans – with a four-poster and sofa bed, and two wooden huts out on the elevated deck for the kitchenette, shower and eco loo. Hartland Pod sleeps six in a double and two sofabeds, it has space to sit and stare and suspended from its strong steel skeleton, mini chill out tents for children! People love to unwind here with woodland, river and meadow views by day, star-gazey skies by night. *The perfect place to bring your dog: fields for running and local dog-friendly beaches only a mile away.*

Rooms	1 geodome for 2-4: from £120. 1 geodome for 2-6: from £120. Extra bed/sofa bed £20 per person. Prices per night. Dogs £30 per dog per stay. Max. 1.
Meals	Self-catering.
Closed	Rarely.
	Pig's ears, and advice on dog walks and local dog-friendly beaches.

Canopy & Stars
Loveland Farm,
Hartland, EX39 6AT

Tel	+44 (0)117 204 7830
Email	enquiries@canopyandstars.co.uk
Web	www.canopyandstars.co.uk/lovelandfarm

Entry 46 Map 1

The Woodland Retreat

From the welcome cream tea to the moment you leave, you'll find The Woodland Retreat fits its name perfectly. The shack is one of our wilder retreats, small and rustic, with a big double bed and bunks occupying each wall. The wood-burner in the middle does its best to keep out the chill, but don't forget your chunky jumper if you're going in spring or autumn. A few steps away is a converted wood-panelled bus with optional extra sleeping space. The kitchen and shower are outdoor but covered, and the terrace with its sofas and table acts as a lounge and dining room. The bell tent is an extra day space, perfect for taking yourself off to read or nap. Owners Lydia and Alex have a long history in the arts and their record label is run from the on-site recording suite which you can hire if you book their other cabin too, Candyland Studios. They built this 8-person cabin themselves with timber from the woodland, straw bales from the land and a reclaimed tin roof. If you don't feel like making music, head out to the coast at nearby Bude or rack up some miles hiking the stunning surrounding scenery. *Four acres of woodland to explore.*

Rooms	Cabin for 6: from £85 per night. Cabin for 8: from £175 per night. Max. 2 dogs in Candyland Studios, 4 in Woodland Retreat.
Meals	Self-catering.
Closed	November – March.
	Blankets and dog biscuits.

Canopy & Stars
Stapleton Farm, Langtree,
Torrington, EX38 8NP

Tel	+44 (0)117 204 7830
Email	enquiries@canopyandstars.co.uk
Web	www.canopyandstars.co.uk/woodlandretreat

Entry 47 Map 2

Horry Mill

In deepest Devon where the birds chirrup, the river flows and the stars shine brightly at night is the much-loved Horry Mill. Here, award-winning mixed woodland is carefully managed, bees, birds and bluebells are encouraged, and a small herd of beef cattle, pigs, ducks and hens merrily thrive. The guardians of this special place are Sonia and Simon, welcoming hosts both, who live in the Millhouse and are on hand should you need them. Inside the miller's cottage is all you need: an inviting dining room with a creamy Rayburn, a vintage iron bedstead up wide oak stairs, a wonderful old fireplace with limitless logs. There are plenty of books and games and a flat-screen TV too, so holing up in bad weather is sheer pleasure here. A pretty window seat upstairs overlooks the cottage garden – secluded and south-facing, with a barbecue for summer meals. If you're feeling lively you can hot-foot it to Winkleigh (three shops, two pubs); if you're not, you can discover the gardens at Rosemoor, or plan a delicious lunch in Chagford. Your hosts know all the best places. *Minimum stay: 7 nights in high season. Woodland for walks. Chickens and ducks wander freely into your garden, and garden not secure.*

Rooms	1 cottage for 4: £345-£650 per week. Overseas payments must be made in sterling. Max. 2 dogs.
Meals	Self-catering.
Closed	Never.
	Woodland walks, maps and dog towels.

Simon & Sonia Hodgson
Horry Mill,
Hollocombe, Chulmleigh, EX18 7QH
Tel +44 (0)1769 520266
Email horrymill@aol.com
Web www.horrymill.com

Entry 48 Map 2

Fairfield

Chris and Tracey know a thing or two about how to set up a home. For years they lived in a house Chris built on his father's land; then they came to Acorn Farm where they converted the chicken house that they still call home. So, it's no surprise that when it came to creating this shepherd's hut camp, they were in their element. The old pagan tree circle at the centre of a field seemed the perfect magical spot. Step in to find two double bunk beds and a single sofabed, a dining table on one side and kitchen on the other. A second hut houses the shower and compost loo and despite the seclusion of the site, there's hot running water and even a phone charging point. After Chris had built all the functional stuff, Tracey got creative. A retro theme spans the 50s and 60s, from cutlery and taps, to radio and old sewing machine; she also filled trunks with rugs, hampers, and indoor and outdoor games. You're greeted with wine and cheese, there's a barbecue spot with lanterns hung round the circle. There's a big meadow and friendly farm animals too. A private paradise on the edge of Dartmoor. *Fencing around hut; 45 acres of fields & woodland; local footpaths. Shower hut dog-friendly or cold hose! Lots of sheep on farm so take care; local pub dog-friendly. Please bring own dog bed.*

Rooms	Shepherd's hut for 5: from £95 per night. Extra camping spaces available. Horses welcome at £25 per night. Dogs £25 per dog per stay. Max. 2.
Meals	Self-catering.
Closed	Never.
	Doggy box with towel, blanket, bowls, treats, toys and spare leads.

Canopy & Stars
Fairfield,
Acorn Farm, Spreyton, EX17 5AL

Tel	+44 (0)117 204 7830
Email	enquiries@canopyandstars.co.uk
Web	www.canopyandstars.co.uk/fairfield

Entry 49 Map 2

Eversfield Safari Tents

Complete canvas comfort in a quiet wildlife-filled valley. A double room, twin room and a double cabin bed in each tent means plenty of space for families or groups of friends. There's a sofa, dining table, a blanket box full of games, and a wood-burning stove in the kitchen but, being pitched on a big wooden deck, you can cook outside on the barbecue too and make the most of the lovely views across lake. Owners Anna and Jon have a farm shop which sells delicious organic stuff. No need to tramp through the fields either as each tent has its own en suite shower pod and separate loo – just stoke the wood-fired boiler to heat up your water. Eversfield sits on the edge of Dartmoor National Park, and is the perfect base for walkers who want to discover this famously wild wilderness. At home there's also plenty on offer – row the boat around the lake or try your hand at fly fishing. If you catch rainbow trout you can cook it for your campfire supper while spotting constellations. If the wind blows in a certain direction you may hear a faint noise from the road but otherwise you'll likely forget all about 'life outside'. *Dartmoor National Park on doorstep, forests & sandy beaches for walks. Organic farm with sheep, pigs & cattle in fields so dogs need to be kept on leads.*

Rooms	2 safari tents for 6: from £125 per night. Dogs £20 per dog per stay. Max. 2.
Meals	Self-catering.
Closed	November – February.
	Advice on walks.

Canopy & Stars
Eversfield Safari Tents,
Water Meadow, Ellacott Barton,
Bratton Clovelly, EX20 4LB
Tel +44 (0)117 204 7830
Email enquiries@canopyandstars.co.uk
Web www.canopyandstars.co.uk/eversfield

Entry 50 Map 2

Devon Yurt

This organic farm is as wholesome as they come! Build a fire, wild swim, pick flowers… Owners Julia and Andrew restored farm house and barns, created veg gardens, dug ponds, planted trees, and stocked the fields with their much-loved rare breed sheep, ponies and good-looking chickens. Great Links is the more remote of the two yurts; it's a whopping 21-foot diameter space with room for kitchen and dining, emperor-size sleigh bed and extra futons for friends and children. Watch the sun set over the moors and tors from your private barbecue area. Little Links is lovely for couples, and young families may like being closer to the farm. Both are snug with rugs, sheepskins and wood-burner. Find an impressive walk-in shower in the shared bathroom nearby; great wood-fired outdoor bathtub too – soak under the stars lit by tea lights and lanterns. Amazing trails all around and Julia knows the best wild swimming spots. Take a day trip to the Eden Project, walk in the tree tops at Tree Surfers or explore the carved gorge in Lydford. And if it rains… rumour has it Julia whips out a fresh banana loaf to soften the blow. *Dogs over 9 months welcome. Great Links has a secure garden. Dogs on leads if unused to animals. Walks from the door; watery fun in Tamar Valley, river Tavy, Dartmoor streams.*

Rooms	1 Yurt for 2-6: from £95 per night. 1 Yurt for 2-4: from £90 per night. Dogs £25 per dog per stay (£35 for week-long stays). Max. 1.
Meals	Self-catering.
Closed	October – March.
	Bowls, blanket, towels and doggy treats.

Canopy & Stars
Devon Yurt,
Borough Farm,
Kelly, PL16 0HJ
Tel +44 (0)117 204 7830
Email enquiries@canopyandstars.co.uk

Entry 51 Map 2

The Horn of Plenty

The Horn of Plenty is one of those clever hotels that has survived the test of time by constantly improving itself. This latest addition is six gorgeous new rooms, four of which have terraces or balconies that give 40-mile views over the Tamar Valley. Potter about outside and find six acres of gardens, then a path that leads down through bluebell woods to the river. Inside, beautiful simplicity abounds: stripped floors, gilt mirrors, fine art, fresh flowers everywhere. Bedrooms in the main house come in country-house style, those in the garden have a contemporary feel. All have smart colours, big comfy beds, perhaps a claw-foot bath or a ceiling open to the rafters; ten have a terrace or a balcony. Despite all this, the food remains the big draw, so come to eat well, perhaps beetroot mousse with goat's cheese parfait, grilled duck with chicory and orange, chocolate cannelloni with banana sorbet; views of the Tamar snaking through the hills are included in the price. Afternoon tea is served on the patio in summer. Tavistock, Dartmoor and The Eden Project are close. *The Tamar Valley (2 minutes) provides woodland and rivers. Dartmoor (10-minute drive) offers everything a dog dreams of!*

Rooms	16 twin/doubles: £120-£265. Singles £110-£255. Dinner, B&B £100-£172 per person. Extra bed/sofabed available £25 per person per night. Dogs £10 per night.
Meals	Lunch from £19.50. Dinner, 3 courses, £49.50. Tasting menu £65.
Closed	Never.
	Dog snacks, 5-acre gardens, loads of great local walks.

Julie Leivers & Damien Pease
The Horn of Plenty,
Gulworthy, Tavistock, PL19 8JD

Tel	+44 (0)1822 832528
Email	enquiries@thehornofplenty.co.uk
Web	www.thehornofplenty.co.uk

Entry 52 Map 2

South Hooe Count House

It's lovely here, so peaceful in your own private cottage perched above the Tamar; the views over the river are glorious and steep steps lead to the shore and a little jetty – borrow a canoe and paddle up stream. Rowers, geese and herons glide by on misty mornings; the woodland garden is full of spring bulbs, vegetables you can pick, free-range hens, chatting guinea fowl and Arabella and Willow the donkeys. Settle on the cushioned window seat in the pretty sitting room with toasty wood-burner, books, art and family photos; copper urns and pewter jugs on a deep slate sill brim with flowers. The cosy kitchen has a lived-in, charming feel with old pine, pretty china, coffee grinder, Belfast sink and cosy Rayburn. Sip coffee on the sheltered terrace that catches the morning sun. The light-filled bedroom has a comfortable bed, thick curtains and that view to wake to; the double ended rolltop bath is a treat. Delightful Trish can give you routes for good walks, lend you a map and suggest places to visit, boat trips to take. Nearby Tavistock has independent shops, galleries and a lively Saturday market. Live by the tide and emerge refreshed. *Babes in arms very welcome. Lovely woodland walks with no sheep. Tamar river below: lots of fun.*

Rooms	1 house for 3: £595 per week. Short breaks of 3 nights or more. Max. 2 dogs.
Meals	Self-catering.
Closed	Rarely.
	Towels, bowls and advice on walks. A river to swim in and resident wonder dog Rags to entertain.

Trish Dugmore
South Hooe Count House,
South Hooe Mine, Hole's Hole, Bere
Alston, Yelverton, PL20 7BW
Tel +44 (0)1822 840329
Email southhooecounthouse@gmail.com
Web www.southhooecounthouse.com/booking

Entry 53 Map 2

The Henley Hotel

A small house above the sea with fabulous views, super bedrooms and some of the loveliest food in Devon. Despite these credentials, it's Martyn and Petra who shine most brightly, their kind, generous approach making this a memorable place to stay. Warm interiors have wooden floors, Lloyd Loom furniture, the odd potted palm, then big windows to frame the view. Below, the Avon estuary slips gracefully out to sea. At high tide surfers ride the waves, at low tide you can walk on the sands. There's a pretty garden with a path tumbling down to the beach, binoculars in each room, a wood-burner in the snug and good books everywhere. Bedrooms are a steal (one is huge). Expect warm colours, crisp linen, tongue-and-groove panelling and robes in super little bathrooms. As for Martyn's table d'hôte dinners, expect to eat very well. Fish comes daily from Kingsbridge market, you might find grilled figs with goat's cheese and Parma ham, roast monkfish with a lobster sauce, then hot chocolate soufflé with fresh raspberries. Gorgeous Devon is all around. Better than the Ritz! *German spoken. Minimum stay: 2 nights at weekends. Beach right below for swimming and playing (only minor restrictions during summer months). South West Coast Path just outside, garden to relax in.*

Rooms	2 doubles, 2 twin/doubles: £120-£137. 1 suite for 2: £150. Singles from £85. Dinner, B&B £87-£97 per person (2 night minimum). Dogs £5 per night. Max. 2 per room.
Meals	Dinner £36.
Closed	November – March.

Maps and advice on walks, towels on request, entertainment and company from resident Labrador Kasper.

Martyn Scarterfield & Petra Lampe
The Henley Hotel,
Folly Hill, Bigbury-on-Sea,
Kingsbridge, TQ7 4AR

Tel	+44 (0)1548 810240
Email	thehenleyhotel@btconnect.com
Web	www.thehenleyhotel.co.uk

Entry 54 Map 2

The Batman's Summerhouse

The 1930's Batman's Summerhouse at Riverleigh has been beautifully restored with natural materials – wood, cotton, glass – in a clean yet comfy Scandinavian style. Find a snuggly double on a mezzanine up steep steps and a bunk room for three downstairs. With one wall of glass looking out to the spectacular riverbank setting, the open-plan living area has a super kitchen with gas hobs and store cupboard staples. Stacks of well-thumbed cookbooks give you a clue to the owner: Miranda is a food writer and can have supper waiting for you when you arrive. You're 10 metres from the main house so quite independent. Fling open the double doors to bring in the countryside, catch salmon and trout in the river. You're nestled in woodland in the Avon valley of South Devon; home to dippers, wagtails, buzzards, otters, deer, hares and the greater horseshoe bat. Fetch morning croissants from the garden centre, a pleasant stroll along the river bank; there are great local pubs, and lovely beaches nearby – Bigbury on Sea, Blackpool Sands, and Bantham for surfing are all a short drive. *Miles of beautiful riverside walks, 8 acres of private woodland. Dog-friendly beaches nearby – even in summer months.*

Rooms	Cabin for 5: from £120 per night. Dogs £25 per dog per stay. Max. 2.
Meals	Self-catering.
Closed	Never.

Organic dog biscuits, dog towels, and acres of private woodland for walks in your pyjamas and wellies.

Canopy & Stars
The Batman's Summerhouse,
Riverleigh,
Kingsbridge, TQ7 4DR
Tel +44 (0)117 204 7830
Email enquiries@canopyandstars.co.uk
Web www.canopyandstars.co.uk/batmans

Entry 55 Map 2

Big Barn

Perfect for family celebrations or big groups, this versatile barn sits by a lake deep in beautiful South Hams farmland. Inside a long dining table for 12 spans the vast vaulted, open-plan living space; oak beams soar above. The interiors are impressive: a mix of antique and modern furniture, a sleek granite kitchen, big relaxing sofas, oak floors, a state-of-the-art wood-burner and a silent eco-friendly heat recovery system. There are four smart bedrooms downstairs, with sumptuous pillows and bed linen on huge Louis XVI and Victorian ironwork beds, all have lake views and dark slate en suite bath/wet rooms. The Crows' Nest, a romantic mezzanine up spiral stairs, is the fifth. You're tucked away down a private drive (plenty of parking) with a fantastic outside space: barbecue terrace, games room and an enclosed baby and toddler play area. Owner Caroline (in the farmhouse) has created a stylish yet practical place for get-togethers. Dartmoor and the coast of the South Devon peninsula are minutes away. *Short breaks available. Glorious walks on South Devon coast path and Dartmoor.*

Rooms	1 barn for 10: £1,600-£3,500 per week. 2 night stays: £1,200-£1,600; 3 night stays: £1,400-£1,800. Dogs £25 per dog per stay. Max. usually 2.
Meals	Self-catering.
Closed	Rarely
	Dog blanket, towels and a welcome treat when booking through Sawday's.

Caroline Murray
Big Barn,
Larcombe Farm, East Allington,
Totnes, TQ9 7QB
Tel +44 (0)1548 521670
Email info@bigbarndevon.co.uk
Web www.bigbarndevon.co.uk

Entry 56 Map 2

Scorlinch Shepherd's Hut

Your adventure begins with a farm buggy ride through the hay field and straight to your door. The cosy eco-hut is powered by a mini wind/solar-power station and almost everything inside is locally made, from the wool insulation in the walls to the woolly sheep-print curtains. The private decking is all yours, complete with a gazebo to protect you from the elements, a barbecue and a stunning view. A breakfast basket can be delivered, including homemade butter, jams and bread, local bacon and home-laid eggs. Explore the 20-acre farm – meet the sheep, chickens, turkeys and guinea fowl, and perhaps spot the odd peregrine falcon or stoat; you're welcome to collect eggs and feed sheep. There's a footpath to the local village with a lunch stop at the Five Bells Pub on the way. Or you can 'walk the plank' for a shortcut across the river. Dartmoor with its wonderful, wild walks is an easy 40-minute drive. There's very little noise here, beyond that of nature, and the stars are fantastic on a clear night. *Babies welcome. Fenced (sheep-free) field but dogs can escape under gate. Great dog walks; river Clyst which dogs love to paddle in! Working sheep farm: dogs need up-to-date worming and to be on lead in fields.*

Rooms	Shepherd's hut for 2: from £80 per night. Dogs £15 per dog per stay. Max. 1.
Meals	Self-catering.
Closed	November – March.

Welcome dog treat on arrival and dog towels can be provided.

Canopy & Stars
Scorlinch Shepherd's Hut,
Scorlinch Farm,
Cullompton, EX15 2NJ

Tel	+44 (0)117 204 7830
Email	enquiries@canopyandstars.co.uk
Web	www.canopyandstars.co.uk/scorlinch

Entry 57 Map 2

Loyton Lodge

You get the impression the tiny lanes that wrap around this small estate act as a sort of fortification, one designed to confuse invaders and protect this patch of heaven. And heaven it is – 280 acres of rolling hills and ancient woodland, with wild flowers, pristine rivers, strutting pheasants and the odd red deer commuting across the fields. It's England circa 1964 with nothing but birdsong to break the peace, and glorious walks that start at the front door. As for Loyton, it's a great little base for a night or two deep in the hills. It mixes contemporary interiors with an old-school feel – roaring fires, comfy sofas, wonderful art, even a snooker room. Bedrooms have warm colours and smart fabrics, perhaps a sleigh bed or a claw-foot bath, then books and robes and crisp white linen. Breakfast is a treat – bacon and sausages from home-reared pigs, eggs from estate hens – and there's dinner by arrangement, perhaps local asparagus, lemon sole, walnut and fruit crumble. Take the whole house and bring the family or come for the odd night of live jazz. Exmoor waits, as do good local restaurants. *Woodland, extensive lawns and streams to discover. Farmland beyond with livestock so leads on dogs encouraged.*

Rooms	7 doubles, 2 twin/doubles, 1 twin: £95-£130. Singles from £80. Extra beds £20 (under 12s free). Max. 3 dogs.
Meals	Dinner, 3 courses, about £30 by arrangement.
Closed	Rarely.
	Towels, water bowl, bedding, dog treats and lovely walks from the door.

Isobel, Sally & Angus Barnes
Loyton Lodge,
Morebath, Tiverton, EX16 9AS
Tel +44 (0)1398 331051
Email thelodge@loyton.com
Web www.loyton.com

Entry 58 Map 2

Fingals Barn

Unusual, quirky and fun. Loyal fans return year after year for Fingals' laid-back charm. In a rolling green valley half a mile from the river Dart, all you need is here: the house has snooker, grass tennis, croquet and a pool. You can self-cater in the oak-framed barn where your kitchen is simple, or (sometimes) eat convivially in the atmospheric restaurant. Reached from an outside stair, your huge private space has massive beams and floor-to-ceiling windows overlooking the gardens. Polished oak floors with faded oriental rugs, well-snuggled-in sofas, a rocking horse, grand piano and books and games will suit families and friends. The main bedroom, with pine bed and Indian throw, sloping roof and skylight windows, hides behind a sliding Japanese screen; the second bedroom is much smaller; the bathroom has a green-footed roll top tub. Children can knock a ball about, swim, make friends, as you order your favourite tipple and loll on a steamer chair. Golfers can golf (ask Richard about discount at the local club), and everyone can head off to the beach, the river, the pub… the area is a treat to discover. *Minimum stay: 3 nights; 7 in high season. Secure garden, woodland and river. Goats, ducks and chickens in walled garden so please keep dogs under control.*

Rooms	1 barn for 6: £560-£1,395 per week. Short breaks £390-£975. Dogs £5 per dog per night. Max. 3.
Meals	Self-catering. Restaurant occasionally open. Pub 1 mile.
Closed	Never.
	Advice on walks, dog towels, resident friendly lurchers to play with – and plenty of love and attention!

Richard & Sheila Johnston
Fingals Barn,
Old Coombe, Dittisham,
Dartmouth, TQ6 0JA
Tel +44 (0)1803 722398
Email info@fingals.co.uk
Web www.fingalsapart.co.uk

Entry 59 Map 2

Coombe Farm

Easy-going, foodie, country-lovers fit right in here. Lisa and Matt, passionate about real food, cook home-grown dinners; charcuterie a speciality. Their fine old Devon long house sits in a green fold of farmland and you're free to wander the garden, chat to the pigs, plunge in the invigorating pool. The dramatic Blue Room has a fab bathroom; the smaller, equally comfy Cloud Room, eponymous wallpaper; inviting Green Room has a wood-burner; find a quirky mix of family and brocante finds. There's a snug sitting room full of art; continental breakfast can be in your room if you want. No. 3 cycle route close by; Exmoor walks and coast 20 minutes. *Minimum stay: 2 nights at weekends and in high season. Public footpath running through the property and into the woods. Cattle, sheep, pigs and chickens so dogs must be reliable or on a lead.*

Rooms	1 double, 2 twin/doubles: £75-£90. Dinner, B&B £60-£70 per person. Max. 2 dogs.
Meals	Dinner from £25. Restaurants 15 minutes walk.
Closed	Rarely.

Hose to wash muddy paws, stream running through the garden to splash in. Dog towels on request.

Matthew Eckford
Coombe Farm,
Goodleigh, Barnstaple, EX32 7NB
Tel +44 (0)1271 324919
Mobile +44 (0)7775 941031
Email info@coombefarmgoodleigh.co.uk
Web www.coombefarmgoodleigh.co.uk

Entry 60 Map 2

Bulleigh Barton Manor

Tea and scones will be waiting. Find long, leafy views to wake up to, a pool for lazy summer days, ponds and a big colourful garden with a summerhouse. Liz and Mark have restored their house with care, uncovering beams and lovely bits of old wood and filling it with original art and books. Bedrooms are inviting: sink-into beds, china pieces on white window sills, a pot of garden flowers, local fudge and homemade cake. They are keen on sourcing the best local produce and their host of hens lay your breakfast eggs. Dartmoor and the south coast are at your feet; return to a friendly hello from Zennor the dog by the fire. *Over 16s welcome. Large garden, alpacas in paddock, sheep in neighbouring fields. Lots of walks nearby. Information on walks & dog-friendly pubs & beaches; guide to Dartmoor provided. Garden Suite has direct access to garden.*

Rooms	2 doubles: £86-£135. 1 suite for 2 with kitchenette: £96-£130. Singles £77-£120. Dogs £7.50 per dog per night. Max. 2 in suite, 1 in Brooking Room.
Meals	Pubs/restaurants 0.5 miles.
Closed	Rarely.

Devon-made food, handmade treats; towels, blanket, poo bags, shampoo. Identity tag with local contact details.

Liz & Mark Lamport
Bulleigh Barton Manor,
Ipplepen,
Newton Abbot, TQ12 5UA
Tel +44 (0)1803 873411
Email liz.lamport@btopenworld.com
Web www.bulleighbartonmanor.co.uk

Entry 61 Map 2

The Acorn Inn

Perfect Evershot and rolling countryside lie at the door of this 400-year-old gem in Thomas Hardy country. New owners Natalie and Richard took the reins to revive its fortunes, with head chef Guy Horley cooking hearty food. It's very much a traditional inn; locals sup pints of Otter Ale in the long flagstoned bar and guests sample good food sourced within 25 miles. In the dining room, the atmosphere changes to rural country house with smartly laid tables, terracotta tiles, soft lighting and elegant fireplaces. Good gastropub fare is taken seriously, be it an Acorn Inn homemade burger, or open lasagne of confit rabbit followed by twice cooked pork belly, and a warm sticky toffee pudding. Little ones have their own menu, and stacks of colouring books and crayons to keep them busy while they wait. Service is helpful and friendly. Bedrooms creak with age and style; there are antiques and fabric wall-coverings, super little bathrooms, perhaps a wonky floor or a lovely four-poster. It's worth splashing out on a larger room if you want space. *Footpath through 900-acre parkland in village, and countless other footpaths in all directions. Coastal path within 20-minute drive.*

Rooms	4 doubles, 2 twin/doubles, 3 four-posters: £99-£160. 1 suite for 3: £160-£205. Singles £89-£205. Extra bed £20 p.p.p.n. Dinner, B&B £80-£133 per person. Dogs £12.
Meals	Lunch & dinner £5.25-£22.95. Bar meals from £4.95.
Closed	Rarely.
	Dog-friendly guide to the area, water bowl, towel and treats. Walking map and dog treats in the bar too.

Natalie & Richard Legg
The Acorn Inn,
Evershot, Dorchester, DT2 0JW
Tel +44 (0)1935 83228
Email nread@rchmail.com
Web www.acorn-inn.co.uk

Entry 62 Map 2

Camping Coach

The quirky train carriage gleams inside and out. Turn the chunky brass handle on the door of this ancient London Brighton & South Coast Railway carriage and enter another era. Find original fittings (luggage racks, rounded windows, leather straps and brasswork), but the tradition gives way slightly in the presence of a fully equipped kitchen and adjoining loo and shower at one end. In the main saloon there is a long bench seat that converts into a double bed and at the other end there is a wonderful antique French stove to keep you warm. Of course, you could spend your days in the living van a few steps from the coach, which is gaily decorated and equally comfortable. The van's seating can also convert into two single beds (ideal for children), so you can sleep four people in the whole camp together and then invite each other over for tea! There are pubs and restaurants, markets and teashops where you can explore the area's varied produce. You're a fossil's throw from the Jurassic Coast for some lovely beach walks and surrounded by endless fields and hills. *Children over 5 welcome. Fabulous walking area.*

Rooms	Train carriage for 4: from £100 per night. Max. 1 well-behaved dog.
Meals	Self-catering.
Closed	Never.
	Towels and advice on walks.

Canopy & Stars
Camping Coach, High Cross Cottage,
Whitecross, Netherbury, DT6 5NH

Tel	+44 (0)117 204 7830
Email	enquiries@canopyandstars.co.uk
Web	www.canopyandstars.co.uk/campingcoach

Entry 63 Map 2

Laverstock Farm

Laverstock is a family estate where Everdene and Herdwick huts have found quiet stretches of the Woodland Walk to settle down. You are perfectly positioned for trips to Lyme Regis, long hikes up Dorset's highest hills, Lewesdon and Pilsdon; go to the top of the Jurassic Coast's loftiest cliff, then return to your cosy shepherd's hut for a campfire supper in the woodland. Inside each you'll find a comfy double bed, table and chairs and a wood-burner. A camp kitchen is under the awning outside with gas hobs and a big solid sideboard for prepping and cooking. The hot shower and flushing loo are about 100 metres away in the shared washroom. There's no electricity in the huts but you'll be given some lanterns which you can recharge in the communal games room, where you'll also find a fridge. There's a welcome pack of Laverstock's own apple juice, freshly baked cake and some eggs, if the chickens have been on form, and you can order a farmhouse breakfast. From then on, you can simply relax into the gentle countryside, or head out seeking adventure. *Babies welcome. Woodland & grounds with stream to cool off in; info pack including dog safety around the farm & surrounding countryside. Lots of dog-friendly walks, pubs & restaurants nearby.*

Rooms	2 shepherd's huts for 2: from £75 per night. Dogs £20 per dog per stay. Max. 2.
Meals	Self-catering.
Closed	Never.
	Dog bowls, homemade dog biscuits (flour, oil, free-range egg, banana, herbs and peppermint oil). Towels are available & hose pipe for muddy dogs.

Canopy & Stars
Laverstock Farm,
Laverstock House, Laverstock,
Bridport, DT6 5PE

Tel	+44 (0)117 204 7830
Email	enquiries@canopyandstars.co.uk
Web	www.canopyandstars.co.uk/laverstock

Entry 64 Map 2

The Wellhouse & Wellhayes Barn

Trundle along a bumpy track to a tranquil lake enjoyed by dragonflies and ducks – tall trees and acres of woodland and pasture surround you. Choose between the light-filled house or the newly-completed barn – both have been loved into life by furniture designer James who has done much of the work himself. In the house there are floor to ceiling windows, a striking open-plan living space, James's wonderful furniture, interesting art, a bathroom for each bedroom and a cosy wood-burner. The barn is just as light, warm and comfortable with a wheelchair-friendly downstairs bedroom and wet room, an open-plan living room and a stonker of a bedroom upstairs with views and a log-burner. Both kitchens are modern, sleek and have all the stuff you need including a hamper of local food, but catering can be arranged if you want a break. Grand romps are yours in ten acres of woodland, the young at heart will adore splashing around the lake in the boat, you're just a few miles from the Jurassic coast for picnics and fossil hunting, the coastal path for puffing up and down, Lyme for shops and restaurants. *Minimum stay: 3 nights; 7 nights in high season. A great base for dog walking – explore the footpaths through woods and fields that start and finish at the door.*

Rooms	1 barn for 4: £900-£1,550 per week. 1 house for 6: £2,500 per week. Extra bed/sofabed available at no charge. House & barn can be booked together to sleep up to 12.
Meals	Restaurants 10-minute walk.
Closed	Never.
	Surprise dog treats in the welcome hamper.

James Verner
The Wellhouse & Wellhayes Barn,
Wellhayes, Harcombe,
Lyme Regis, DT7 3RN
Mobile +44 (0)7796 991606
Email stay@wellhayes.com
Web www.wellhayes.com

Entry 65 Map 2

Short House Chesil Beach

Drive through swaying pampas grass and umbrella pines to this newly-restored Purbeck stone and pink rendered cottage: the deep blue sea shimmers in the distance and a solemn terracotta warrior stands guard. Sheep graze the surrounding National Trust farmland and you've only an unspoilt meadow between you and Chesil Beach. Charming owners Andrew and Julie, live in the 18th-century house next door and stock up the cottage with wine and local Dorset delights from the farm shop. Find a large, sociable, open plan kitchen dining and sitting room with high ceilings, bright kilims, oak floors and purple doors. Julie's bold canvases hang on the walls, there's comfortable furniture, piles of books and DVDs, even an excellent Bose sound system. The two double bedrooms have finely dressed beds in feather and down, glorious watery views and smart bathrooms with roll tops and travertine stone walls. Both open onto a west-facing terrace overlooking the garden and sea. You can play tennis, hop on a horse from the riding stables, visit Abbotsbury Gardens or ancient Swannery by foot, or tackle wonderful coastal walks from the door. *Minimum stay: 3 nights; 7 in high season. Secluded location, no main roads nearby. 400-metre walk to the beach across the field.*

Rooms	1 house for 4: £800-£1,470 per week. Extra bed/sofabed available at no charge.
Meals	Pubs/restaurants 1 mile.
Closed	Never.
	Beach runs and towels for drying after splashing in the sea.

Andrew Wadsworth
Short House Chesil Beach,
Labour-in-Vain Lane,
West Bexington, DT2 9DE
Tel +44 (0)1305 871600
Mobile +44 (0)7836 262222
Web www.short-house.co.uk

Entry 66 Map 2

The Mount

A very English scene with rolling green hills tumbling down to long sandy beaches and The Mount which sits apart from the hustle and bustle of Swanage in quieter Durlston. Here lovely local owners Elaine and Carl know exactly what makes a great get-together and have thought of everything – a pool table disguised as a dining table, an 'arty stuff' drawer for budding painters, musical instruments for prodigies and a secret attic for the kids. Cooks will love the big colourful kitchen and there are long, fire-lit evenings to be spent crashed out on leather chesterfields heaped with velvet cushions. Bedrooms at the front are elegant with sea views (one en-suite) but you won't feel hard done by in the servants' quarters, smaller but with iron beds and pretty curtains. There are two family bathrooms and a charming garden surrounds all – grab a colourful deckchair from the wall and relax on the lawn with a book. For days out there's Swanage town with some great up-and-coming eateries, a steam train for littlies, or if you just want to get away from it all the coastal path is at hand for walking and wild swimming. *Minimum stay: 3 nights; 7 in high season. Secure garden. Walks minutes from the door. Dog-friendly cafés.*

Rooms	1 house for 14: £1,800-£4,100 per week.
Meals	Restaurants 10-minute walk. Caterer available.
Closed	Never.

A little something in the welcome pack and towels for drying.

Elaine Pearson & Carl Styants
The Mount,
16 Durlston Road,
Swanage, BH19 2HX
Mobile +44 (0)7849 854875
Email stay@themountswanage.co.uk
Web www.themountswanage.co.uk

Entry 67 Map 3

53 Durweston

Rural chic at its best! A thatched 18th-century cottage bursting with character and clutter-free style. Dreamy window seats, an inglenook fireplace, oak floorboards and latch doors, exposed beams, cob walls, wood-burners, a rustic antique dining table, a vintage leather armchair... fresh flowers, soft furnishings, candles and contemporary artwork complete the picture. Picasso line drawings dot the kitchen – a long, narrow Victorian addition with stone flooring, a painted dresser and all you'll need. Up the cottagey stairs to the two oh-so-pretty bedrooms, light and luxuriously carpeted with views of church, water meadows and woods beyond. Both have king-size, French style, cream iron beds, crisp white cotton and chests of drawers; the larger gets a buttonback chair, the smaller, a cast-iron fireplace, and the big bathroom between them has sumptuous towels and toiletries. All this, and a herb and flower-planted garden, in the quietest part of a beautiful Dorset village. Fantastic for cycling and chalk ridge walks, and a ten-minute drive from Georgian Blandford. It'll be hard to leave. *Secure garden and miles of beautiful country walks right on the doorstep.*

Rooms	1 cottage for 4: £590–£1,450 per week. Dogs £10 per dog per stay. Max. 2.
Meals	Self-catering.
Closed	Never.
	Water bowl, food bowl and a dog treat.

Emma Perry
53 Durweston,
Blandford Forum, DT11 0QA
Mobile +44 (0)7966 490836
Email emmaperry_uk@yahoo.co.uk
Web www.53durweston.com

Entry 68 Map 3

Colber Farm

The Happy Hare and The Pleasant Pheasant shepherd's huts on this peaceful farm are surrounded by miles of footpaths. Arrive to a cream tea or cake and settle in to a slice of cosy, quiet rural heaven. Each hut has a comfy bed, ample storage, a cunning en suite bathroom and wonderful green views of the open countryside. Sit in bed and watch the sunrise… Essentials are provided along with marshmallows, fresh herbs are planted around the huts and breakfast hampers are available on request: bread, sausages, bacon, mushrooms, eggs, butter, homemade jam. Whip up coffee and cook on your gas hob; or there's the hot plate on the wood-burner and a tripod for the fire bowl if you love the smell of wood smoke and fancy being outside. Rambles start from your door, the river Stour runs through the farm and you can spot swans and herons. As well as hearing the cows go back and forth, you'll meet the resident pheasants and perhaps the eponymous hares. It's a 20-minute walk to the pubs and shops of Sturminster Newton – have a long, starry soak in your own private hot tub when you get back. *Babies welcome. Miles of walks; maps with marked walks; dog-friendly pubs & cafés within walking distance. Working farm so dogs to be kept under control / on tether.*

Rooms	2 shepherd's huts for 2: from £75 per night. Dogs £10 per dog per stay. Max. 1 medium/large or 2 small.
Meals	Self-catering
Closed	Never.

Dog treats or pig's ears, doggy wash-down kit with towels & 'pet head' shampoo, poo bags. Long tether so owners can enjoy the hot tub without their dog running off!

Canopy & Stars
Colber Farm,
Stalbridge Lane,
Sturminster Newton, DT10 2JQ

Tel	+44 (0)117 204 7830
Email	enquiries@canopyandstars.co.uk
Web	www.canopyandstars.co.uk/colberfarm

Entry 69 Map 2

Stock Gaylard

Down a farm track, just above the small stream and just around the corner from the deer park you'll find heaps to choose from: yurts, woodsman's wagon and shepherd's hut or doubledecker bus and cabin. Each camp has its own spot, and the whole site faces west so whether you're lying in bed or toasting marshmallows over the fire, you'll get the best of the sun setting below the horizon. Owners Andy and Josie had the yurts built (using the estate's very own ash) by a local joiner, who also made all the bespoke furniture. You'll find cosy rugs and comfy beds with compost loo and outdoor shower just on the edge of the deck, and a wood fire-heated bath under the stars (flushing toilet and electric shower up at the farm buildings too). Cosy Sawpit Wagon and hut have uninterrupted views; Parsons Camp bus has an alfresco dining top deck. Fry up some venison sausages from the estate on the campfire or walk to the local pub for supper. There are 1,800 acres of land to explore, with beautiful mixed woodland. Head out for fishing, archery, llama trekking and paintballing. *Lots of woodland walks on the estate and surrounding area. Animals in nearby fields so keep dogs on leads when out walking.*

Rooms	1 camp for 14 : from £150. 1 camp for 10: from £128. 1 camp for 11: from £138. 1 wagon for 2-4: from £80. Prices per night. Extra space available in bell tent or sleeping in own tents. Max. 1 dog.
Meals	Self-catering.
Closed	October – March.
	Advice on walks.

Canopy & Stars
Stock Gaylard,
Sturminster Newton, DT10 2BG

Tel	+44 (0)117 204 7830
Email	enquiries@canopyandstars.co.uk
Web	www.canopyandstars.co.uk/stockgaylard

Entry 70 Map 2

Munden House

A super B&B – run with great warmth by Annie and Colin, who love to pamper guests. You stay in the independent garden cottages; all have luxurious beds, vintage pieces, colourful throws or rugs and kitchen areas; one has a galleried bedroom above a snug sitting room. Continental breakfasts are delivered each day: homemade muesli, granola and jams, garden compotes, eggs if the hens are laying and bread from the 100-year-old bakery next door. The garden is a treat too: sweeping lawns, herbaceous borders, orchard, wildlife ponds and tucked away seating spots for soaking up the sublime far-reaching views over the Dorset countryside *Dogs welcome in Garden Cottage and Dairy Cottage. Dogs are welcome to use the garden and there are footpaths and plenty of excellent walking nearby.*

Rooms	Dairy Cottage for 2: £95-£115. Garden Cottage for 2: £115-£125. The Summer House for 2: £115-£130. Dogs £10 per stay. Max. 2 per cottage.
Meals	Pub 2 miles.
Closed	Christmas.

Dog treats, towels and comfy bed.

Annie & Colin Fletcher
Munden House,
Mundens Lane, Alweston,
Sherborne, DT9 5HU
Tel +44 (0)1963 23150
Email stay@mundenhouse.co.uk
Web www.mundenhouse.co.uk

Entry 71 Map 2

Photo: Quentin Craven

Nether Westwick

Teesdale is timeless – all dry stone walls and wildflower-spangled meadows rising into stark fells… then it's home to warm limbs by the wood-burning stove. All four rooms of this threshing barn turned cottage exude character and craftsmanship. The sitting room has an arched door with stone surround and a cat's cradle of naked beams; the kitchen, well-equipped and beautifully fitted, has a wooden sprung bench above the radiator; and if you have any parts left to warm, the impressive wet room has a heated marble seat beneath its rainfall shower. Couples will love the old iron bedstead (with a modern mattress) in a cute bedroom with rustic furnishings and reclaimed oak floor; kids or extra guests have a sofabed in the sitting room. Sally stocks a welcome basket with locally sourced products, wine, and herbs from the secluded south-facing garden. Follow the river Tees a mile west to Barnard Castle, a market town with Norman ruins, antique shops and Bowes Museum, one of northern England's cultural gems. *Weekends (Fri-Sun) & mid-week (Mon-Thurs) breaks. Secure courtyard garden. Lots of varied walks: ancient, walled green lanes where dogs can run free, woodland, moorland and riverside.*

Rooms	1 cottage for 2: £380-£480. Extra bed/sofabed available at no charge. Max. up to 3 dogs, depending on size.
Meals	Self-catering.
Closed	Rarely.
	Homemade edible treats and towels.

Sally Davies
Nether Westwick,
Westwick,
Barnard Castle, DL12 8UP
Tel +44 (0)1833 695692
Email enquiries@netherwestwick.co.uk
Web www.netherwestwick.co.uk

Entry 72 Map 6

Rose & Crown

Romaldkirk is one of those lovely villages where little has changed in 200 years. It sits peacefully in the north Pennines, lost to the world and without great need of it. As for the Rose & Crown, it dates to 1733 and stands on the village green next to a Saxon church. Roses ramble across stone walls at the front, so grab a pint of local ale, then sit in the sun and watch life pass by. Inside, you can roast away in front of a fire in the wonderfully old-school bar while reading the paper. There's a peaceful sitting room for afternoon tea, then a panelled restaurant for excellent food, perhaps honey-glazed goats' cheese with apple and hazelnut, shoulder of pork wrapped in Parma ham, banana Bakewell tart. Thomas and Cheryl bought the place in 2012 and have been improving it ever since: it has never looked better. Stylish rooms – some in the main house, others out back, a couple in a cottage next door – have warm colours, comfy beds, Bose sound systems and super bathrooms. Don't miss High Force waterfall, the magnificent Bowes Museum or the sausage sandwich at lunch. *Great walks from the door, village green next to the inn and river nearby.*

Rooms	7 doubles, 3 twins: £115-£160. 2 suites for 2: £180-£200. 1 cottage for 4: £115-£200. Singles £95. Dinner, B&B from £79 per person. Max. 2 dogs.
Meals	Lunch from £10.50. Dinner, 3 courses, from £27. Sunday lunch £19.50.
Closed	23-27 December; 1 week in January.
	Dog beds, towels for drying and locally made dog treats.

Thomas & Cheryl Robinson
Rose & Crown,
Romaldkirk, Barnard Castle, DL12 9EB
Tel +44 (0)1833 650213
Email hotel@rose-and-crown.co.uk
Web www.rose-and-crown.co.uk

Entry 73 Map 6

Burnhopeside Hall

It's peaceful, traditional, pristine, and nothing is too much trouble for Christine. Welcome to a listed Georgian house on a 475-acre estate near Durham, its elegant sitting rooms furnished with pictures and photos, log fires and big sofas, billiards table and a baby grand, and great sash windows with garden and woodland views. Resident springer spaniel Max loves all dogs, so bring yours; stroll the magnificent lawns, cycle alongside the river. Breakfast? Eggs from the hens, bacon from the pigs, honey and fruits from the walled garden: a perfect start to the day. Enormous beds, luxurious linen and fresh flowers await your return. *Lots of river and woodland walks, with a safe garden well away from the road (off-lead is no problem).*

Rooms	4 doubles: £85-£120. 1 apartment for 4: £100-£150. Singles £70-£85.
Meals	Pubs/restaurants 4 miles.
Closed	Rarely.

Acres of dog-friendly garden and farmland to explore.

Christine Hewitt
Burnhopeside Hall,
Durham Road, Lanchester, DH7 0TL
Tel +44 (0)1207 520222
Email harmerchristine@hotmail.com
Web www.burnhopeside-hall.co.uk

Entry 74 Map 6

Maison Talbooth

The outdoor swimming pool is heated to 29°C every day, a chauffeur is on hand to whisk you down to the hotel's riverside restaurant, a grand piano waits in the sitting room, where guests gather for a legendary afternoon tea. They don't do things by halves at Maison Talbooth, a small-scale pleasure dome with long views across Constable country. The house, an old rectory, stands in three acres of manicured grounds; the pool house is a big draw with its open fire, honesty bar, beautiful art and treatment rooms. Interiors are equally impressive. There are no rooms, only suites, each divine. Some on the ground floor have doors onto terraces where hot tubs wait, but all pamper you rotten with flawless bathrooms, fabulous beds, cool colours and hi-tech excess. At dinner you're chauffeured to the family's restaurants (both within half a mile): Milsoms for bistro food served informally; Le Talbooth on the river Stour for more serious fare, perhaps poached lobster with orange and fennel, saddle of venison with plums and bitter chocolate, pineapple and coconut soufflé with piña colada ice cream. A great escape. *Lots of walks nearby, through woods and by river. Livestock around part of the year on some walks.*

Rooms	12 suites for 4: £210-£420. Singles from £170.
Meals	Dinner at Milsoms £25; at Le Talbooth £35-£50.
Closed	Never.
	Biscuits, blankets, towels and dog walks.

Paul & Geraldine Milsom
Maison Talbooth,
Stratford Road, Dedham,
Colchester, CO7 6HN
Tel +44 (0)1206 322367
Email maison@milsomhotels.com
Web www.milsomhotels.com

Entry 75 Map 4

The Pier at Harwich

They don't do things by halves at the Pier – a cool £1.5 million has recently been spent on a 21st-century makeover for this iconic coastal hotel. It sits on the harbourside with views of town and water, its front terrace a big draw in good weather. Inside, a cool new look captivates. A chic warehouse feel waits in the bar – stripped walls, hanging lamps, leather bar stools, big windows to frame the view. You get craft beers and cask ales, a gin library and Prosecco cocktails, then small plates of Nordic design if you fancy a light bite. Hungry souls fly upstairs to the famous first-floor brasserie, where mirrored booths and leather banquettes now come as standard, and doors open onto a balcony, where you can tuck into your lobster Thermidor while gazing out onto the estuary. Bedrooms – some above, others next door in a former inn – have fancy bedheads, seaside colours, crisp white linen and super bathrooms; the suite, with its vast window, has a telescope with which to scan the high seas. Coastal walks and blue flag beaches wait, as does the Electric Palace, the second oldest cinema in Britain. *Beach and promenade to walk on, sea to swim in.*

Rooms	10 doubles, 3 twins: £120-£170. 1 suite for 2: £200-£230. Singles from £95. Dinner, B&B from £100 p.p.
Meals	Lunch from £6.50. Dinner à la carte £25-£40. Sunday lunch from £19.50.
Closed	Never.
	Blankets, towels, advice on walks, doggy dinners, water bowls and treat.

Paul & Geraldine Milsom
The Pier at Harwich,
The Quay,
Harwich, CO12 3HH
Tel +44 (0)1255 241212
Email pier@milsomhotels.com
Web www.milsomhotels.com

Entry 76 Map 4

The King's Arms

Next to the main road in Didmarton, close to Tetbury and the Badminton Estate, is this recently refurbished inn – a perfect place in the Cotswolds. Expect beams and stone-flagged floors, inviting dark green walls adorned with antlers, fat candles on dining tables, lovely painted settles, and photos showcasing local history. There's a big old fireplace for winter, darts and dominoes in the bar, a lovely walled garden and a wood-fired pizza oven that's doing brisk business. Blackboard menus on the walls are chalked up daily. Pop in for a deli pizza with cured and spiced meats, the King's burger with cheese and chorizo, or sautéed mixed nut and herb polenta with cherry tomatoes and basil – you won't go home disappointed. Wash your food down with a fine wine or a local tipple – Bath Gem, Uley Bitter, perhaps one of their guest beers. If you fancy staying, rooms upstairs are cosy and stylish, with comfy beds, crisp linen, down duvets and spotless shower rooms. A couple of cottages suitable for larger groups await in the coaching stable. *Resident celebrity dog, Spoof, and a large enclosed garden where dogs can run off leads.*

Rooms	4 doubles, 1 twin/double: £95-£140. 1 single: £60-£65. 1 cottage for 4, 1 cottage for 6: £120-£250. Dogs £15 per dog per night.
Meals	Light lunch from £6.50. Mains from £12.95. Wood-fired pizzas, £9.50 (summer only).
Closed	Never.
	Dog beds, bowls and treats. Love and fuss for every dog. Snuffle dog beer too!

Mark Birchall
The King's Arms,
The Street, Didmarton,
Badminton, GL9 1DT
Tel +44 (0)1454 238 245
Email enquiries@kingsarmsdidmarton.co.uk
Web www.kingsarmsdidmarton.co.uk

Entry 77 Map 3

Great Farm

Wind your way along the leafy path through the trees and cross the narrow footbridge over the river – young-at-heart adventurers will find it idyllic. Otter Camp, Nightingale Camp and Barn Owl Camp are close together but secluded with a private clearing. Cross the water again and you'll have The Island at Great Farm all to yourself. Otter and Nightingale are intimate and off-grid, though the swish bathrooms are a step above camping. The river Coln forms a boundary to the front, there's woodland to the rear, and sheep and cattle nearby. Each spot has its own campfire, kitchen with gas hob (some outdoors), flushing loo and shower – and many thoughtful touches. Leonie can provide a hamper of local ingredients for breakfast and picnics; dinner can be delivered too. If the river is too chilly, Otter, Nightingale and The Island have their own hot tubs. You're on a family-run working farm in the rural heart of the Cotswolds, with pretty villages and pubs galore and great walks. Go down river to Lechlade, or the Cotswold Water Park – Leonie will give you a map. If you're lucky, you'll spot an otter... *Great walks, river to play in. Dogs need to be on a lead near farm livestock.*

Rooms	Cabin for 2: from £105. Shepherd's hut for 2 (+ space for 2/own tent): from £95. Camp of 2 gypsy wagons for 4-6 (+ space for 10/own tents): from £105. Train carriage for 2 (+ space for own travel cot): from £95. Prices per night. Dogs £20 per dog per stay. Max. 2.
Meals	Self-catering.
Closed	October – March.
	Advice on walks.

Canopy & Stars
Great Farm,
Whelford, Fairford, GL7 4EA
Tel +44 (0)117 204 7830
Email enquiries@canopyandstars.co.uk
Web www.canopyandstars.co.uk/greatfarm

Entry 78 Map 3

The Lion Inn

The determination to restore this old inn's charms has been a joyous success. Push open the heavy oak door to reveal a beautiful main bar: rugs on pale-painted floors, candles at mullioned windows, rough stone walls, and a log fire crackling in a 15th-century inglenook. Jugs of fresh flowers, battered leather armchairs and grand gilt-framed paintings enhance the authentic feel. Peruse the papers over a pint of real ale, play scrabble, cards or one of the selection of games. Order from the seasonal menu: perhaps slow roast pork belly with creamed potatoes, savoy cabbage, red wine jus and prunes, followed by honey and almond panna cotta. Country-chic rooms upstairs – one with its own small balcony, one above the lively snug bar – are toasty-warm and TV-free, with inviting beds and soothing colours, upholstered armchairs and antique furniture. Bathrooms are just as good, with Bramley products and en-suite showers. Winchcombe is on the Cotswold Way; Chipping Campden, Broadway and Cheltenham are a short drive. *Garden, river and lake a short walk away.*

Rooms	7 doubles: £110-£185. 1 suite for 3: £150-£195. Extra bed/sofabed £25 per child per night. Dogs £15 per dog per night. Max. 2 dogs per room.
Meals	Lunch from £12. Dinner, 3 courses, £28.
Closed	Never.
	Dog beds in bedrooms, treats and biscuits on request. Towels, water in the gardens and lots of walking maps of the Cotswold Way.

Sue Chalmers
The Lion Inn,
North Street, Winchcombe,
Cheltenham, GL54 5PS
Tel +44 (0)1242 603300
Email reception@thelionwinchcombe.co.uk
Web www.thelionwinchcombe.co.uk

Entry 79 Map 3

Tudor Farmhouse Hotel

A gorgeous small hotel, one of the best. It sits on the edge of the Forest of Dean, a magical world of woodland walks, medieval castles, meandering rivers and bleating sheep. You're in the middle of a tiny village with country views all around. Step inside to find sparkling interiors – Colin and Hari have spent a small fortune turning their realm into something very special indeed. An airy elegance mixes with golden stone walls and original timber frames, the house bearing testament to its Tudor roots. Big or small, bedrooms are divine – stylishly uncluttered with smart fabrics, robes in fine bathrooms and super-comfy beds. Those in the main house have ancient beamed ceilings, those in the old barns have original stone walls. The bigger rooms are faultless: the best beds, claw-foot baths, enormous showers, the lap of luxury. Lovely local food awaits, perhaps cider-cured salmon, haunch of venison, rhubarb Bakewell tart; there are home-laid eggs for breakfast, too. You can kayak on the Wye, forage in the forest, take to cycle tracks. Don't miss Puzzlewood or Clearwell Caves. *Minimum stay: 2 nights on weekends. Fourteen acres of secure land; the whole of the Forest of Dean and Wye Valley to explore with a number of printed walks.*

Rooms	10 doubles, 3 twins, 2 four-posters: £100-£230. 5 suites for 2: £180-£230. Singles £90-£220. Extra bed/sofabed available £25 per person per night. Dogs £10 per night. Max. 1 per room.
Meals	Lunch from £6.95. Dinner, 3 courses, £30-£40. Sunday lunch from £14.50.
Closed	Never.
	Bag of dog biscuits, a collapsible travel dog bowl, a rope toy, mini dog shampoo and a pack of poo bags.

Colin & Hari Fell
Tudor Farmhouse Hotel,
High Street,
Clearwell, GL16 8JS
Tel +44 (0)1594 833046
Email info@tudorfarmhousehotel.co.uk
Web www.tudorfarmhousehotel.co.uk

Entry 80 Map 3

Up^

Your spirits lift arriving at Up^ and climbing the 20 steps to the broad, raised deck among the trees… hence the name. Light streams through the glass front and into every room and the views of the Wye Valley are amazing. Watch the sunset from the comfort of your big double bed, before picking fresh herbs from the indoor herb wall and cooking up a fragrant feast on the barbecue. When night sets in, a clear sky can be enjoyed with the powerful telescope or the naked eye, and naked everything else, from the outdoor bathtub on the deck (private despite the nearby minor road). During the day, the cabin has plenty to keep you busy. Brush up on your piano skills on the baby grand, put some LPs on the record player if you remember how, lounge on the suntrap deck, or use the complimentary yeast and flour to try out owner Jill's open-fire bread recipe. It'd be a shame not to head out and hike, bike or canoe your way around this AONB on your doorstep, but when you're somewhere this relaxing, it can just be too hard getting Up^ in the morning. *Enclosed garden, but not dog proof. Walks from the door and to dog-friendly pub; list of dog-welcoming pubs that can be combined with a walk. No dogs on furniture and must have up to date flea control.*

Rooms	Cabin for 2: from £100 per night. Dogs £15 per dog per stay.
Meals	Self-catering.
Closed	Never.

Biscuits, a chew, sometimes a piece of ham. Outside bath for dogs who love to roll in fox poo or muddy puddles (candles optional!). Deck to sit on – what better doggy heaven than sharing an evening BBQ with their owners!

Canopy & Stars
Up^,
Coldharbour Road,
Brockweir, NP16 7PH

Tel	+44 (0)117 204 7830
Email	enquiries@canopyandstars.co.uk
Web	www.canopyandstars.co.uk/up

Entry 81 Map 2

Legg Barn

Ted and Paddy's barn is a surprise. Tucked off the High Street, it has four acres of garden with space for pigs, chickens, veg, sunny seats, trees – and for collie Bill to chase squirrels. The long hall has a quirky line of antique high chairs, and there's a soaring living space beyond with a big wood-burner and comfy sofas; the white theme throughout contrasts with honey-coloured wood and the odd splash of colour. Bedrooms – one up spiral stairs on the sitting room mezzanine – have lovely linen and piles of pillows. Paddy is a good cook – her generous breakfasts often include their own sausages. Walk from the door into the Forest of Dean. *Forest walks nearby; meadow to romp in which is surrounded by a brook – perfect for muddy dogs to get clean in.*

Rooms	1 double; 2 doubles sharing bathroom: £80-£90. Max. 2 dogs.
Meals	Restaurant 2-minute walk; pub 10-minute walk.
Closed	Christmas & occasionally.
	Dog bowls and dog beds.

Paddy Curtis
Legg Barn,
Church Square,
Blakeney, GL15 4DP
Tel +44 (0)1594 510408
Email paddy@leggbarn.co.uk
Web www.leggbarn.co.uk

Entry 82 Map 2

The Grange

The largest green in England and this house is at a leafy corner. Rosanne has that happy knack of making you feel at home. Gibraltarian and a keen cook, her breakfasts come with a continental edge – eggs with chorizo, homemade baked beans; her Spanish soup suppers are hearty. The house has stories – ask about Miss Kickler… Family photos, art and quirky monkeys add warmth, the guest sitting room has original wood panelling with the Clifford Crest, inviting bedrooms are all different; there's an indoor pool, gym, playroom, places to read – dogs Spud and Otto keep you company. Walk to Slimbridge, have fun at Frampton's festivals. *Garden completely enclosed – Houdini the Labrador has tested it! Walks from front gate away from roads; sheep in some fields. Lakes for swimming; beautiful wooded areas.*

Rooms	1 twin/double; 2 doubles with separate bathroom: £95-£125. 1 single sharing bath with nearby double: £50. Dogs £10 per stay.
Meals	Soup with bread, £10. Restaurant/pubs 3 miles.
Closed	Rarely.
	Bowls, high-quality dog food, beds, hose for washing muddy paws and local ID dog tag.

Rosanne Gaggero-Brodermann
The Grange,
The Green, Frampton on Severn,
Gloucester, GL2 7DX
Tel +44 (0)1452 740654
Email rockape@mac.com
Web www.atthegrange.com

Entry 83 Map 2

The Guest House

Your own timber-framed house with masses of light and space, a sunny terrace, and spectacular valley and woodland views… A peaceful secluded place, it's full of books and mementoes of Sue's treks around the world; the large living room has wooden floors, lovely old oak furniture and French windows onto the rose-filled garden. Sue brims with enthusiasm and is a flexible host: breakfast can be in her kitchen with delicious farm shop sausages and bacon, or continental in yours at a time to suit you. There's a wet room downstairs, and you hop up the stairs to your charming up-in-the-eaves bedroom with oriental rugs and a big comfy bed. Wonderful! *Minimum stay: 2 nights at weekends Easter – October. Two and a half acres of fenced garden in glorious rural Cotswolds with walks straight from the door. Dogs must be completely sheep-proof as surrounded by breeding ewes.*

Rooms	1 double, with sitting room & kitchenette: £140-£160. 3-6 night breaks £133-£152 per night; £935 per week.
Meals	Dinner, 2 courses, from £17.50; 3 courses, from £22.50; 4 courses, from £28. Pub 1 mile.
Closed	Christmas.

Dog-sitting, towels for drying and advice on walks.

Sue Bathurst
The Guest House,
Manor Cottage, Bagendon,
Cirencester, GL7 7DU
Tel +44 (0)1285 831417
Email thecotswoldguesthouse@gmail.com
Web www.cotswoldguesthouse.co.uk

Entry 84 Map 3

The Close

Up a hill of pretty Cotswold-stone houses, this large Queen Anne house with handsome sash windows delivers what it promises. Step into a stone-flagged hall with grandfather clock and Georgian oak staircase; take welcoming tea with Karen in the drawing room – all gracious sofas and charming chandelier; then upstairs to three light and airy bedrooms softly furnished with antiques. Window seats, shutters and views over garden or pretty street add to the restful atmosphere. Karen, as gracious and relaxed as her house, serves excellent breakfasts in the polished dining room. An elegantly hospitable base for exploring the Cotswolds. *Minimum stay: 2 nights at weekends. Garden, lots of public footpaths and dog walks on beautiful Minchinhampton Common. Many dog-friendly pubs/cafés nearby.*

Rooms	2 doubles, 1 twin: £85-£95. Singles £65-£75. Dogs £10 per stay.
Meals	Pubs/restaurants 1-minute walk.
Closed	January.

Advice on walks and large dog-friendly garden.

Karen Champney
The Close,
Well Hill, Minchinhampton,
Stroud, GL6 9JE
Tel +44 (0)1453 883338
Email theclosebnb@gmail.com
Web www.theclosebnb.co.uk

Entry 85 Map 3

The Wellington Arms

Lost down a web of lanes, the 'Welly' draws foodies from miles around. Cosy, relaxed and decorated in style – old dining tables, crystal decanters, terracotta floor – the newly extended bar-dining room fills quickly, so make sure you book to sample Jason's inventive modern cooking. Boards are chalked up daily and the produce mainly home-grown or organic. Kick off with home-grown courgette flowers stuffed with ricotta, parmesan and lemon zest, follow with rack of home-reared lamb with root vegetable mash and crab apple jelly, finish with elderflower jelly, strawberry and raspberry sorbet. Migrate to the huge garden for summer meals and views of the pub's smallholding: pigs, woolly sheep, bees and almost 100 assorted hens; buy the eggs at the bar. Stay over and get cosy in any one of the four rooms, housed in the former wine store and pig shed. Expect exposed brick and beams, vast Benchmark beds topped with goose down duvets, fresh flowers, coffee machines, mini-fridges, and slate tiled bathrooms with underfloor heating and walk-in rain showers. Breakfast too is a treat. *Open fields and woodland walks; public footpath from the pub.*

Rooms	4 doubles: £110-£200. Dogs £10.
Meals	Lunch, 2-3 courses £17.50-£19. Dinner £11-£21.
Closed	Rarely.

Lily's Kitchen Bedtime Biscuits, bones, sheepskin rug, water bowl, towels for drying, maps and advice on walks.

Jason King & Simon Page
The Wellington Arms,
Baughurst Road,
Baughurst, RG26 5LP
Tel +44 (0)118 982 0110
Email hello@thewellingtonarms.com
Web www.thewellingtonarms.com

Entry 86 Map 3

Riverside Cottage

Lavender beds, wild flowers, yoga, treatments… Heaps to dip into, and it's a great place to share with family and friends: thatched Cottage and a separate Lodge. A lit wood-burner in the Cottage hall welcomes you, as well as bubbly, nibbles and soft drinks. It's a relaxed, lived-in house with three sets of stairs leading to simply done bedrooms (a quirky hatch joins two), family bathrooms (one tiny), places for children to play hide-and-seek. The two sitting rooms are stuffed with beams; art, family photos, books, colourful rugs, more fires make you feel at home. The dining sun room has a huge table – book a chef or there's a fully kitted Aga kitchen. The Lodge has its own drive and is tucked away behind hedging: a snug bolthole for two (plus two nimble children up on the mezzanine), with an airy sitting room warmed by a modern wood-burner, comfy bedroom looking over the lavender, swish shower. There's a large garden, a yurt in the field (becomes a café with set events in the summer) and a pool with the Lodge (this can be used by the Cottage if you let both houses). Head off for river walks from the door; nearby Winchester is a treat. *Minimum stay: 2 nights; 7 in high season. Wonderful enclosed garden; great walks from the door. Dog sitting; dog relaxation and meditation; dog training: please pre-book.*

Rooms	1 house for 4: £1,000 per week. 1 cottage for 8: £2,000-£2,200 per week. Short breaks available. Extra bed/sofabed available at no charge. Dogs £25 per stay. Max. 2.
Meals	Dinner available by arrangement. Restaurants 2 miles.
Closed	Rarely.
	Doggy treats for nicely tired out hounds.

Clare Scott Dryden
Riverside Cottage,
Bransbury, Barton Stacey,
Winchester, SO21 3QJ
Mobile +44 (0)7973 215407
Email riversidehampshire@gmail.com
Web www.riversidelifestyle.co.uk

Entry 87 Map 3

The Rother

The Rother yurt at Adhurst, in the ancient woodland of the South Downs National Park just an hour and a half from London, is a perfect place for getting back to nature. Owners Guy and Alison are passionate about sustainable living and invite you to set the fire, tramp through the woods and immerse yourself in a slower, more basic, way of life. The site is completely off-grid and the yurt, made from local wood, has been decked out with solar fairy lights, wood-burners, storm kettles and wind-up radios. It shares a camp kitchen with the three other yurts, a gas-powered shower and compost loo. A wood-burner keeps the yurt warm, and can be used to make tea, but there is also a storm kettle which can be lit with nothing more than twigs, leaves and a match. Once you've had a cup of tea, you'll be ready to explore the woods (look out for the zip wire), try a bit of horse riding or fly fishing, head over to Cowdray to watch the polo, or admire the beautiful scenery of the South Downs Way. *Yurts are spaced far enough away from each other to not confuse dogs about their territory. River & woods. Dog-friendly pubs in walking distance.*

Rooms	Yurt for 4 (2 camp beds for children): from £153 per night. Max. 2 dogs – please call before booking.
Meals	Self-catering.
Closed	November – April.
	Advice on walks, and river swims!

Canopy & Stars
The Rother,
Steep,
Adhurst, GU31 5AD

Tel	+44 (0)117 204 7830
Email	enquiries@canopyandstars.co.uk
Web	www.canopyandstars.co.uk/rother

Entry 88 Map 3

Wriggly Tin

Wriggly Tin shepherd's huts was born out of a family holiday where Alex Evans and his two daughters got out into the countryside and never looked back. Although that defining stay was actually in tipis, Alex's love of all things mechanical led him to hand build these lovely off-grid huts in a wooded corner of Hampshire. Butser, a two person hut named after the highest point in the area, sleeps 2 people and there are 4 other huts, varying in size up to Boundary who can accommodate up to 5 guests but all have enough space for a dog to sleep in comfort. Showers and loos are shared and housed in, unsurprisingly, an even more cunningly converted shepherd's hut. You're far enough apart to feel on your own, with a personal fire pit, tripod, cast iron griddle and plenty of wood and kindling for some daring experiments in campfire cooking. 100-year-old Old Winchester even has a private wood fired hot tub to soak in. Wriggly Tin gives you a chance to settle in to the slow lane. Keep a pan of water on the wood-burner for tea and stroll through the surrounding bluebell woods with your canine companion. *Dogs to be kept on lead while on site. Think twice before bringing a wolfhound, as space is limited! Butser, Barrow & Old Winchester have most space for a dog bed.*

Rooms	3 shepherd's huts for 2; 1 shepherd's hut for 3; 1 shepherd's hut for 5: from £93 per night. Dogs £6 per dog per stay. Max. 2.
Meals	Self-catering.
Closed	Never.

Map showing the best places for walks and advice on days out.

Canopy & Stars
Wriggly Tin,
15 Beckless Cottages, Brook Lane,
Hambledon, PO7 4TF

Tel	+44 (0)117 204 7830
Email	enquiries@canopyandstars.co.uk
Web	www.canopyandstars.co.uk/wrigglytin

Entry 89 Map 3

Brook House Woods

Brook House Woods is home to Penny & Will's woodland wonderland and the Green Wood Workshop. There are six woody spaces to choose from: Hobbit Hut, Yurt, three treehouses and a tree tent. The Hobbit Hut fits a surprising amount inside: king-size bed, fairy lights and wood-burner (there's something very satisfying about pulling the circular door closed behind you). Find a private fire pit and deckchairs outside; the kitchen is in the communal workshop: cook on an open fire or make pizzas in the cob barrel oven. The treehouses give elegance, simplicity and adventure in perfect balance: roll top tub on the deck, chaise longue, smoker and barbecue. Spot shooting stars while tucked up in bed in the colourful yurt under the trees. There are plenty of on-site activities: green wood-working with Will, yoga with qualified instructors and tasting sessions at the honesty bar, which features a host of locally produced tipples. For supper order something in from good local caterers and tuck into it around the huge banqueting table. Take a dip in the secret lake, wander along the river Frome, follow miles of trails. *Babies welcome. 350 acres of off-lead private paths through fields, forest & orchards; river paths. Map of walks – all ending up in a dog-friendly pub. Dog-friendly taxi service too.*

Rooms	Hobbit hut for 2 from £80. Yurt for 2: from £90. 3 tree cabins for 2: from £135. Tree tent for 2: from £100. Prices per night. Dogs £10 per dog per stay. Max. varies by space.
Meals	Self-catering.
Closed	Never.
	Pond & little stream for doggy paddling in summer; a dog-stop in the workshop where you can snuggle by the fire with them; a veranda where you can wash down muddy hounds.

Canopy & Stars
Brook House Woods,
Brook House Farm, Avenbury Lane,
Bromyard, HR7 4LB

Tel	+44 (0)117 204 7830
Email	enquiries@canopyandstars.co.uk
Web	www.canopyandstars.co.uk/brookhouse

Entry 90 Map 2

Drover's Rest

Through a tunnel of trees you'll find your meadow-dwelling safari tents – African in looks, but Welsh in spirit. The tents are far enough away from each other to be private but neighbourly enough that you can borrow a box of matches for the campfire. Your first tell-tale sign is the chimney of a log-burner popping out of the top of each tent and a rattan sofa with huge cushions on the porch. Beyond the farmhouse-worthy kitchen and living area padded out with sheepskins and cushions, there are two bedrooms, each with cast iron beds, Welsh blankets and sheepskin rugs. All tents have their own hot monsoon shower and flushing loo in a fully heated stable block, just a couple of minutes' walk from the tents and torches are provided for night time trips. The Hayloft barn is yours to share with other glampers and has WiFi, a café, a cocktail bar and its own farm shop. There's also a lounge with bean bags and movie screenings and a dining area for group suppers. Pizzas, curries and barbecues are served up on different days of the week but there's a barbecue area outside each tent and a heavy-duty pot for cooking chillies and stews. *Walks direct from the door. Dogs allowed in communal chill-out barn while you have dinner. Working farm so animals around.*

Rooms	5 safari tents for 4: from £75 per night. Dogs £20 per dog per stay. Max. 2; will come into contact with owners' dog.
Meals	Self-catering.
Closed	Never.
	Water bowls, doggy treats and advice on walks.

Canopy & Stars
Drover's Rest,
Llanycoed Farm, Nr Hay-on-Wye,
Dorstone, HR3 6AG

Tel	+44 (0)117 204 7830
Email	enquiries@canopyandstars.co.uk
Web	www.canopyandstars.co.uk/droversrest

Entry 91 Map 2

Brooks Country House

Led Zeppelin used to stay here when recording at studios on a nearby farm, and there's definitely a bit of a rock-star feel to the place. A big house in the country, a swimming pool in the kitchen garden and its own vineyard that produces wine for the restaurant…There's a rather good view, too, a clean sweep over ten miles of rolling country to rising mountains. The house once stood in 1,000 acres and now has a mere 15, but the land beyond is owned by the National Trust and you can walk straight out, skirt a copse and find yourself at a 14th-century church. As for the hotel, it's going to make a small splash – Andrew and Carla are far too down-to-earth for anything bigger. It's a total refurbishment – smart, but relaxed, a place to feel at home. Expect an open fire in the sitting room, wood floors in the restaurant, then cowhide rugs in a bar that opens onto a sun-trapping garden. Nicely priced rooms are scattered about, some grander, others smaller, all with good beds, warm colours and lovely bathrooms. As for the food, it's earthy stuff; homemade soups, a local rib-eye, a sinful chocolate tart. Hard to beat. *Minimum stay: 2 nights at weekends. Acres of garden and lovely walks; sheep in the field so dogs on lead. Four big courtyard rooms with plenty of space for dogs.*

Rooms	14 twin/doubles, 6 four-posters: £79-£169. 2 suites for 2: £99-£169. 3 trucks for 2: £99-£139. Singles £89-£119. Dinner, B&B £60-£80 per person. Extra bed/sofabed £10-£20 p.p.p.n.
Meals	Dinner £18-£24 (not Sundays). Sunday dinner from £19-£23.
Closed	Never.
	Dog biscuits, basket with a snug blanket and toys.

Carla & Andrew Brooks
Brooks Country House,
Pengethley Park,
Ross-on-Wye, HR9 6LL
Tel +44 (0)1989 730211
Email info@brookscountryhouse.com
Web www.brookscountryhouse.com

Entry 92 Map 2

The Stables

A joy for couples looking for solid, understated style inside and rolling country walks and cycling from the door – without heading for the wilds. On the fringe of pretty Berkhamsted – with its castle, art-house cinema, tempting shops and cafés – there are glimpses of a sheep-dotted landscape beyond as you take the No Through Road at the top of Castle Hill. Here, the Groves' handsome brick and timber Stables conversion stands near their magnificent Great Barn. They've designed and organised the space so well you could happily live here. Sturdy oak floorboards are heated from below; lighting is elegant and discreet. There's a good collection of DVDs and cookery books; a slick, well-equipped kitchen with retro country touches; a deep leather sofa and scrubbed dining table; a beautifully turned out bed beneath the beams, and a snug bathroom with plump towels. The odd French and rustic piece – like the water jug, brass candlesticks and Cézanne-style prints – add to the charm of the place. Bird-song peace, a 10-minute walk from good eateries, the train station (Euston 35 minutes), and Waitrose! *Short breaks available. AONB. Dogs need to be kept on lead initially due to sheep field nearby.*

Rooms	1 cottage for 2: £650 per week. Short breaks £125 per night. Dogs £10 per stay. Max. 2.
Meals	Self-catering.
Closed	Rarely.

Woodland walks from the doorstep.

Sarah Groves
The Stables,
Castle Hill,
Berkhamsted, HP4 1HH

Tel	+44 (0)1442 874767
Mobile	+44 (0)7885 676136
Email	timandsarahgroves@icloud.com

Entry 93 Map 3

Heron House

Welcome to Heron House – spruce and perfectly placed, between the high street and the sea. Its restoration, from 'sorry state' to much-loved home (neat-as-a-pin but not precious) is down to Julie, who has thought in much detail about your stay. Her passion for the place, and her love of Whitstable and all it offers, will rub off on you the moment you meet her. Downstairs are two sitting rooms, one smaller (with a wood-burner), one large, and a kitchen-diner in the extension, in beautiful, bright, Victorian-modern style. Find a table topped with candles and a basket of nice things, and doors to a pretty courtyard with a garden room for dreaming on a day bed. Bedrooms on the upper floors are a mix of vintage pine pieces and Farrow & Ball colours, new rugs on stripped floors, bathrooms with thick towels and shining sash windows – only the best. For a group of friends or two families it's perfect. Wander through trendy Whitstable which has it all: shops, galleries, restaurants, pubs, oysters, chips, beach huts, and a proper coffee shop in Tankerton called JoJo's. *Minimum stay: 3 nights; 7 in high season. See website for availability. Secure small garden, beach and woodland walks and dog-friendly restaurants and pubs. Further information and walking routes provided.*

Rooms	1 house for 8: £1,260-£1,990. 3-night stay £960-£1,245. Max. 3 dogs.
Meals	Pubs/restaurants 2-minute walk.
Closed	Never.
	Towels, blankets, biscuits and water bowls.

Julie FitzGerald Vitelli
Heron House,
Nelson Road,
Whitstable, CT5 1DP
Mobile +44 (0)7734 663589
Email info@heronhousewhitstable.co.uk
Web www.heronhousewhitstable.co.uk

Entry 94 Map 4

Albion House

This is quite some house, a Regency pile that dates to 1790, with huge rooms, high ceilings and grandeur at every turn. It stands at the top of a hill in the middle of town with fine views over the Royal Harbour. Incredibly, it was left to decay by its last inhabitants, Ramsgate Town Council, whose headquarters this was until 2008. Now, after a long renovation, interiors shine, mixing contemporary design with the feel of a colonial gentleman's club. There's a fire in reception, watery views through big windows in the restaurant, then a fabulous bar with grand piano, exotic pot plants, a roaring fire, and sofas everywhere. Classical prints are jammed on the wall, the bar itself came from the town hall. The whole place is a work of art, nothing is here by accident. A treatment room, a steam room and a vaulted cavern for wine tastings are coming for summer 2018. Big bedrooms get smaller as you climb the house, but the best views are at the top. Expect good beds, crisp linen, neutral colours, robes in white marble bathrooms. Beaches, gardens and cliff-top walks wait, but don't miss afternoon tea. *Minimum stay: 2 nights at weekends April-September. Great beach for dog walks just a stone's throw away. Local green to take your dog for a quick walk in the mornings and evenings.*

Rooms	13 twin/doubles: £89-£245. 1 suite for 2: £180-£345. Dinner, B&B from £80 per person. Dogs £30 per stay. Max. 2 small.
Meals	Lunch from £5. Afternoon tea £16. Dinner, 3 courses, £25-£35. Sunday lunch from £16.
Closed	Never.
	Dog bed, chews to gnaw on, toys to play with and water bowl.

Ben & Emma Irvine
Albion House,
Albion Place, Ramsgate, CT11 8HQ
Tel +44 (0)1843 606630
Email enquiries@albionhouseramsgate.co.uk
Web www.albionhouseramsgate.co.uk

Entry 95 Map 4

Stable West

Who would imagine, at the end of the humble track, fields of blackcurrants, a newly planted vineyard and a beautifully converted Edwardian stable block? The friendly owners live at one end of the stables, you're at the other, and all you hear are birds and sheep. There are free logs for the wood-burner, wine and flowers for the table, and heaps of country-house space. So: enter a hall with white paintwork and chequer tiles, a lofty sitting room in duck-egg blue, a big fresh kitchen/dining room with all you need, and an airy sun room, perfect for perusing the papers. The en suite bedroom is downstairs and the rest are up: a twin/double; a single; a bathroom under the eaves. Colours are muted, carpets soft, beds comfortable and everything shines. Outside? Rolling views of Kentish countryside from a well-tended pretty garden, a pool enclosed by a rose-tumbled wall, a wild meadow sprinkled with flowers. Tennis can be arranged, historic Canterbury is up the road, and if you fancy a well-pulled pint – or a top-notch Sunday roast – you simply stride across the fields. *Minimum stay: 3 nights; 7 nights in high season. Secure garden with beautiful dog walking countryside direct from the door.*

Rooms	1 house for 5: £800-£1,200 per week. 3-night stay from £525. Max. usually 2 dogs.
Meals	Pub 15-minute walk.
Closed	Rarely.
	Dog biscuit treats, rugs for the furniture and towels for drying.

Charlie Markes
Stable West,
Heppington, Street End,
Canterbury, CT4 7AN
Mobile +44 (0)7779 350305
Email stablewest@btinternet.com

Entry 96 Map 4

The Inn at Whitewell

It is almost impossible to imagine a day when a better inn will grace the English landscape. Everything here is perfect. The inn sits just above the river Hodder, and doors in the bar lead onto a terrace where guests can enjoy five-mile views across parkland to rising fells. Inside, fires roar, newspapers wait, there are beams, sofas, maps and copies of *Wisden*. Bedrooms, some in the Coach House, are exemplary and come with real luxury, perhaps a peat fire, a lavish four-poster, a fabulous Victorian power shower. All have beautiful fabrics, top linen and gadgets galore; many have the marvellous view – you can fall asleep at night to the sound of the river. There are bar meals for those who want to watch their weight (the Whitewell fish pie is rightly famous) or a restaurant for splendid food, so dig into seared scallops, Bowland lamb, a plate of local cheese (the Queen once popped in for lunch). Elsewhere, a wine shop in reception, seven miles of private fishing and countryside as good as any in the land. Dogs and children are very welcome. Magnificent. *The river Hodder that runs adjacent is a favourite for walkers, and their dogs of course! Dogs are welcome in all areas of inn except the main dining room.*

Rooms	17 doubles, 5 twin/doubles: £120-£215. 1 suite for 2: £210-£240. Singles £92-£204.
Meals	Bar meals from £8. Dinner £25-£35.
Closed	Never.
	Dog beds, bowls and towels upon request.

Charles Bowman
The Inn at Whitewell,
Dunsop Road, Whitewell,
Clitheroe, BB7 3AT
Tel +44 (0)1200 448222
Email reception@innatwhitewell.com
Web www.innatwhitewell.com

Entry 97 Map 6

Breedon Hall

Through high walls find a listed Georgian manor house in an acre of garden, and friendly Charlotte and Charles. Make yourselves at home in the fire-warmed drawing room full of fine furniture, art and furnishings in the richest reds and golds. Charlotte is a smashing cook: homemade granola and marmalade, local eggs, bacon and sausages for breakfast; you can book a three-course dinner too. Bedrooms are painted in soft colours, beds are covered in goose down; bathrooms are immaculate. The old stabling now houses three neat self-catering cottages too. Borrow a bike and discover the glorious countryside right on the cusp of two counties. *Minimum stay: 2 nights in high season. Secure garden. Both pubs in the village accept dogs, and there are plenty of places for dogs to run.*

Rooms	5 doubles: £80-£150. Dogs £5 a day.
Meals	Supper £25. Dinner, 3 courses, £35. Pub/restaurant 1-minute walk.
Closed	Rarely.
	Advice on walks.

Charlotte Meynell
Breedon Hall, Main Street,
Breedon-on-the-Hill, DE73 8AN
Tel +44 (0)1332 864935
Mobile +44 (0)7973 105467
Email charlottemeynell1963@gmail.com
Web www.breedonhall.co.uk

Entry 98 Map 6

Photo: Stanley Richardson

Washingborough Hall

In its day Lincoln was one of the most important cities in England. Its castle holds a copy of the Magna Carta and was built by William the Conqueror in 1068; its cathedral dates to 1090 and remains one of the finest in Europe. All of which makes it a great city to visit, and if you want to beat a peaceful retreat into the country at the end of the day, this is the place to stay. It sits two miles east of town in a small village on the river Witham – footpaths by the water lead back into town. As for this Georgian rectory, you'll find smart lawns to the front, then a big welcome within – Edward and Lucy go out of their way to make your stay special. There's a wood-burner in the hall, a breakfast room with garden views, a sitting-room bar for afternoon tea, then a light-filled orangery restaurant. Stylish bedrooms offer unstinting comforts. Rooms at the front are bigger and have the view, all have good beds, bold wallpapers, excellent bathrooms, a sofa if there's room. As for the food, there's posh fish and chips in the bar or sea bass with spring greens in the orangery. *Small woodland in grounds, open countryside within half a mile.*

Rooms	12 doubles, 3 twin/doubles, 2 four-posters: £85-£175. 1 suite for 2: £175-£195. 2 singles: £65-£85. Dogs £10. Max. 2.
Meals	Lunch from £5.50. Dinner, 3 courses, £25-£35. Sunday lunch from £18.50.
Closed	Never.
	Bowls, biscuits and advice on walks.

Lucy & Edward Herring
Washingborough Hall,
Church Hill,
Washingborough, LN4 1BE
Tel +44 (0)1522 790340
Email enquiries@washingboroughhall.com
Web www.washingboroughhall.com

Entry 99 Map 6

The Lifeboat Inn

You're in heaven here, under the big skies of Norfolk's north coast with its sweeping salt marshes, nature reserves and sandy beaches. The Lifeboat, newly captained by Agellus, sails a smooth and stylish path with glowing fires and scrumptious seafood. Tucked down a hidden lane in pretty Thornham, the inn's darkly-beamed bar conjures a smugglers retreat, while the conservatory and restaurant are light, bright and contemporary. Settle by a crackling fire with a pint of Woodforde's Wherry and plan a day's bird- or seal-spotting. In summer, the sun-trap courtyard beckons, or book one of two cedarwood pavilions for private dining. Wherever you settle, the menu will tempt you with seasonal specials, cream teas, hearty sandwiches and children's treats. Our Brancaster moules were the juiciest and tastiest we've eaten, and where else could you find roast beef in a Yorkshire pudding with horseradish sauce and a jug of gravy as a (bargain-priced) bar snack? *Minimum stay: 2 nights at weekends. Walks in marshes, on nearby beaches & on Thornham Harbour.*

Rooms	13 doubles: £145-£215. Dinner, B&B £145-£215 per person. Extra bed/sofabed available £25 per person per night. Dogs £10 per dog per night. Max. 2.
Meals	Starters from £6.25. Lunch from £6.50. Dinner from £9.95.
Closed	Never.
	Dog blanket and bowl with treats in room on arrival. Treats behind the bar and a sausage for breakfast.

James Green
The Lifeboat Inn,
Ship Lane,
Thornham, PE36 6LT
Tel +44 (0)1485 512236
Email info@lifeboatinnthornham.com
Web www.lifeboatinnthornham.com

Entry 100 Map 7

The Chequers Inn

Cheerful Chequers, beloved by locals and visitors alike, is thriving under the new care of Agellus. General Manager Martin takes the helm and all is smooth sailing – with some of the best seafood you'll find in this lovely part of the world. Thornham is a pretty little village nestled along the coast, close to spectacular scenery and nature reserves, where Chequers gleams with its whitewashed walls and red pantiles. Inside, the fireplace glows and crackles, fresh flowers sit on scrubbed tables and the menu beckons. Our tempura of Brancaster mussels with tartar espuma and chilli vinegar (part of their Norfolk tapas range) was bursting with delicate flavours, but you might try slow-cooked crispy belly of pork with cider potato fondant, black cabbage, black pudding bonbon and grain mustard velouté. Pizzas are a treat too (crispy duck caught our eye) and there's private dining in the all-weather Pavilions outside. Both Sandringham and Holkham Hall are close. *Minimum stay: 2 nights at weekends. Maps with local walks available.*

Rooms	11 doubles: £120-£195. Extra bed/sofabed available £25 per person per night. Dogs £10 per dog per night. Max. 2.
Meals	Breakfast from £15. Starters from £3.95. Tapas from £3.95. Lunch from £8.95. Mains from £13.95.
Closed	Never.
	A dog blanket in the room and a tasty sausage for breakfast. Four-legged guests' gallery on the website.

Ewen Thomson
The Chequers Inn,
High Street,
Thornham, PE36 6LY
Tel +44 (0)1485 512229
Email info@chequersinnthornham.com
Web www.chequersinnthornham.com

Entry 101 Map 7

The Globe Inn at Wells-next-the-Sea

It's as English as can be – a beautiful inn on a Georgian green, where Nelson used to catch the coach to London. Potter down to the water and find a sandy beach for family fun, then a small harbour, where day boats land their catch on the quay. As for the Globe, it's an inn for all seasons. Outside, there's a sun-trapping terrace at the front, a flower-filled courtyard where you can eat in summer, then a colourful roof terrace for guests. Inside, wood-burners sit at both ends of the bar, there are sofas and armchairs, games for rainy days, and local ales and excellent wines to wash down delicious food. You eat in an airy restaurant with local art of the walls, perhaps clam linguini with chilli and garlic, dressed Wells crab or a rib-eye steak, then chocolate mousse with pistachio ice cream. Rooms above have the comfiest beds in the land. Those at the front have views of the green, all have crisp linen, padded heads and vintage tiles in sparkling bathrooms. Rooms connect for families, boat trips can be arranged and Sandringham is up the road. *Minimum stay: 2 nights at weekends. Huge beautiful beach, dogs off lead. Pine woods & miles of N. Norfolk Coast Path to explore. Come home to The Globe on the coasthopper bus when you and the pooch have had enough!*

Rooms	4 doubles, 3 twin/doubles: £110-£170. Extra bed/sofabed available £30 per person per night. Dogs £15 per night. Max. 2 small or 1 large per room. 3 dog-friendly rooms.
Meals	Lunch from £6. Dinner, 3 courses, £25-£30.
Closed	Rarely.
	Homemade biscuits, blankets, towels and soft-cushioned bed, water and food bowls, feeding mat, poo bags. Drying room too.

Antonia & Stephen Bournes
The Globe Inn at Wells-next-the-Sea,
The Buttlands,
Wells-Next-The-Sea, NR23 1EU
Tel +44 (0)1328 710206
Email hello@theglobeatwells.co.uk
Web www.theglobeatwells.co.uk

Entry 102 Map 7

Dockings Cottage

In the grounds of Hindringham Hall is a long brick and flint barn with a red-tiled roof, pretty paintwork and a bridlepath running past. It was converted after the war for herdsman Mr Docking, who lived here with his bride. Now lovely new oak floorboards (great for dogs) add charm, there's a traditional sitting room with Freeview and WiFi, a neat airy kitchen opening onto the garden and, at either end, comfortable carpeted bedrooms (not for dogs) with sweet little windows and a bathroom apiece. What's great is that the garden is enclosed so young children are as safe as the pooches, and there's solid oak furniture on the lawn. Outside the door: Hindringham Hall's gorgeous borders, wild garden, water garden, kitchen garden, 12th-century moat and medieval pond; all this free to guests on Wednesdays and Sunday afternoons throughout the summer. The coast is close, and dogs will love the wide sands of Holkham and Wells-next-the-Sea, and the enticing aromas of Stiffley Marshes. Don't miss the six villages called the Burnhams, the best-known being Burnham Market – 'Chelsea on Sea.' *Short breaks only available in winter. Minimum stay: 3 nights Nov-Apr. Fenced rear garden. Beside bridle path. Space for dog baskets. Advice on walks and dog-friendly beaches.*

Rooms	1 cottage for 4: £475–£900 per week.
Meals	Self-catering.
Closed	Rarely.
	Towels for drying.

Lynda Tucker
Dockings Cottage,
Hindringham Hall, Blacksmiths Lane,
Hindringham, NR21 0QA
Tel +44 (0)1328 878226
Email info@hindringhamhall.org
Web www.hindringhamhall.org

Entry 103 Map 7

Saracens Head

Lost in the lanes of deepest Norfolk, an English inn that's hard to match. Outside, Georgian red-brick walls stand to attention at the front, but nip round the back and find them at ease in a beautiful courtyard where you can knock back a pint of Wherry in the evening sun before slipping inside to eat. Tim and Janie upped sticks from the Alps, unable to resist the allure of this lovely old inn. A sympathetic refurbishment has worked its magic, but the spirit remains the same: this is a country-house pub with lovely staff who go the extra mile. Downstairs the bar hums with happy locals who come for Norfolk ales and good French wines, while the food in the restaurant is as good as ever: Norfolk pheasant and rabbit terrine, wild duck or Cromer crab, treacle tart and caramel ice cream. Upstairs, there's a sitting room on the landing, then six pretty rooms. All have have smart carpets, wooden furniture, comfy beds and sparkling bathrooms. There's masses to do: ancient Norwich, the coast at Cromer, golf on the cliffs at Sheringham, Blickling Hall, a Jacobean pile. Don't miss Sunday lunch. *Many local walks for dogs and their owners; beaches nearby too. Dogs on leads please as there are sheep and cattle nearby.*

Rooms	5 twin/doubles: £110-£130. 1 family room for 4: £110-£160. Singles £75. Extra bed/sofabed available £25 per person per night. Dogs £5 per night. Max. 2.
Meals	Lunch from £6.50. Dinner, 3 courses, £25-£35.
Closed	Rarely.
	Dog bed, and towels for drying off wet, nicely tired out dogs.

Tim & Janie Elwes
Saracens Head,
Wolterton,
Norwich, NR11 7LZ
Tel +44 (0)1263 768909
Email info@saracenshead-norfolk.co.uk
Web www.saracenshead-norfolk.co.uk

Entry 104 Map 7

The Willows Cottage

Two cottages – two staircases – neatly woven into one, and a tiny sun room tucked onto the end. This is a sweet Norfolk brick and flint house, 180 years old, quintessentially English and idyllically positioned on a small village road close to the coast. Over the garden gate is a huge wildlife-rich nature reserve of reed beds and woodland bisected by pushchair-friendly boardwalks – a privileged spot. Step through the door and into the dining room to low ceilings, a wooden floor and a lovely feeling of homeliness. Then the kitchen: low-beamed, well-equipped – the bathroom too is off here – and the sitting room, cosy with books, sculptures, squishy sofas and a wood-burner with logs on the house. Then up the steep narrow stairs to inviting bedrooms with sloping ceilings, low windows and doors to duck; the twin is nautically themed, the double a dream, with a carved mahogany bed and a glass chandelier. Feather toppers, scented candles, gorgeous linen… you are shamelessly spoiled. Brilliant for families, walkers, romantic couples – and dogs, enticed with biscuit snacks, holiday tags and a list of all the best walkies. *Dogs free to roam in secure garden, walks from the front door, splashy river and dog-friendly beach nearby.*

Rooms	1 cottage for 4: £470-£695 per week. Short breaks £315-£455. Dogs £15 per stay.
Meals	Self-catering.
Closed	Rarely.

Tasty biscuits, bowls for feeding, blankets for snuggling, throws for furniture.

David Sewell
The Willows Cottage,
Lower Street,
Southrepps, NR11 8UL
Tel +44 (0)1608 686351
Email norfolkholidaycottage@gmail.com
Web www.norfolk-cottage-holiday.co.uk

Entry 105 Map 7

Mill Farm Eco Barns

In the grounds of Mill Farm where the owners live (he's an ecologist, she's an organic food specialist), is a big beautiful barn that will make your heart soar. Views reach over farmland, paddock and Shetland ponies, while brick and flint walls and willow screens create privacy from next door: the big patio is a safe place for children. Enter a great open-plan living room with vaulted ceilings and a bright airy feel, and a central oak staircase that winds you to mezzanine and bedrooms upstairs (two up, two down). Fossil-stone slabs line the floor, the end wall is of exposed brick, sleek leather sofas are deliciously comfy and children will love the hanging chair. Delightful Emma welcomes you in, gives you a fabulous hamper (veg from the allotment, home-baked cake and more), logs for the wood-burner, and has a wonderful eye for colour and design. Bedrooms are large and calming, one with a balcony for sundowners; bathrooms are the bee's knees. You can walk to pub, fish shop, small store and beach, there are books, games, TV with surround sound, bikes to borrow and seats for toddlers. *Check owners' website for availability. Short breaks outside peak season. Secure garden; all-year dog-friendly beach; country walks and walking guide. Chickens, so sadly no puppies.*

Rooms	1 cottage for 2: £345-£550 per week. 1 barn for 8: £845-£1,950 per week. Dogs £15 per dog per stay. Max. 2 in each barn.
Meals	Self-catering.
Closed	Never.
	Dog treats on arrival and dog bowls provided.

Emma Punchard
Mill Farm Eco Barns,
Mill Farm, Hemsby Road,
Winterton-on-Sea, NR29 4AE
Mobile +44 (0)7900 376462
Email millfarmecobarn@gmail.com
Web www.millfarm-ecobarn.co.uk

Entry 106 Map 7

The Old Rectory

Conservation farmland all around; acres of wild heathland busy with woodpeckers and owls; the coast two miles away. Relax in the spacious drawing room of this handsome 17th-century rectory and friendly family home, set in lovely mature gardens (NGS) full of trees and unusual planting. Fiona loves to cook and bakes her bread daily, food is delicious, seasonal and locally sourced, jams are homemade. Comfortable bedrooms have *objets* from diplomatic postings and the spacious suite comes with mahogany furniture and armchairs so you can settle in with a book or plan your rambles on the Broads or long sandy beaches nearby. Super views, friendly dogs, tennis in the garden and masses of space... *The garden is not enclosed. Occasional dog sitting if owners have to leave their dogs for the day. Dog-friendly beaches nearby.*

Rooms	1 double: £75-£85. 1 suite for 2: £75-£90. Singles £50.
Meals	Dinner from £25. Pubs 2 miles.
Closed	Rarely.

Locally made dog biscuits and wonderful walks.

Peter & Fiona Black
The Old Rectory,
Ridlington, NR28 9NZ
Tel +44 (0)1692 650247
Mobile +44 (0)7774 599911
Email ridlingtonoldrectory@gmail.com
Web www.oldrectorynorthnorfolk.co.uk

Entry 107 Map 7

Brinkburn Northumberland

This is heavenly countryside, and Brinkburn Priory (built in 1135) has an unrivalled position within it. Solitude and peace are yours in a dramatic wooded ravine along the meandering river Coquet – no wonder the monks who built it felt serene. Mark and Emma Fenwick have renovated (beautifully) three lovely old buildings: The Stables, perfect for a big family or friends' gathering with plenty of outdoor space, Priory Cottage – a cosy bolthole for two, and Bel House with its private south-facing garden. All have superb kitchens and bathrooms, comfortable sofas and chairs by wood-burning stoves, good fabrics and gentle colours. Nothing is other than generous and all has been thought of, even down to bathrobes and good lotions and potions. It's so romantic you may even be inspired to get married here, in a marquee on the terrace in summer or in the elegant White Room in winter. There are more than 30 acres for you to explore, with woodland walks along the river and lots of wildlife; beaches are peerless and yet you are close to good road and rail links, and the airport. Newbies to Northumberland will fall in love. *Short breaks available.Woodland walks, beach walks, rivers to jump in. Dogs over 1 welcome. Dogs downstairs only please.*

Rooms	1 cottage for 2: £425-£670. 1 cottage for 8: £700-£1,690. 1 house for 4: £350-£870. Prices per week. Both properties can be booked together. Extra bed/sofabed £9 per person per night. Logs £10 per crate. Dogs £20 per stay. Max. 2.
Meals	Self-catering.
Closed	Never.

Towels, bowls, and great dog walking from the door.

Mark Fenwick
Brinkburn Northumberland,
Longframlington,
Morpeth, NE65 8AR
Tel +44 (0)1665 570870
Email athome@brinkburnnorthumberland.com
Web www.brinkburnnorthumberland.com

Entry 108 Map 9

Sky Den

The Sky Den was built by William Hardie Designs with George Clarke during the second series of his *Amazing Spaces* programme. It's made up of three different shapes which blend together the best of outdoors and indoors, taking in everything from the red squirrels in the trees around you to the sweeping river below. The square is the central point of the Den and your main living space, with glass doors opening onto a wide balcony with captivating views over the river. Inside, George has created an impressively versatile space, with a functional kitchen in a clutter-phobe's paradise of fold-away furniture (including two single beds) and wet room. Then there's the circle, a simple viewpoint of corrugated iron, where you can have a picnic and brew up a cuppa over the wood-burning stove. Finally the triangle is the loft space of your already lofty suite, accessed by steps from the outside deck. In good weather open the whole roof for an unobstructed view of the Northumberland Dark Skies. You're in the Kielder Water & Forest Park so wildlife lovers and adventure-seeking families will be happy. Bring warm clothes! *Maps of the area provided. Please note that dogs are not allowed in the centre building unless they are assistance dogs.*

Rooms	Treehouse for 4: from £155 per night. Dogs £50 per dog per stay. Max. 1
Meals	Self-catering.
Closed	Never.

Food and water bowls, and advice on walks through the forest and along the Lakeside Way.

Canopy & Stars
Sky Den,
Calvert Trust, Kielder,
Hexham, NE48 1BS

Tel	+44 (0)117 204 7830
Email	enquiries@canopyandstars.co.uk
Web	www.canopyandstars.co.uk/skyden

Entry 109 Map 9

East Cottage

You'll fall in love with this rugged county, for its beauty and its space; no crowds, no traffic jams, no rush. Stay in a 19th-century byre and a granary (the original feeding troughs stand outside, spilling flowers in summer), immaculately converted, alongside two others, in an eco-friendly way. Solar panels heat the water, the logs are on the house, electricity comes from renewable sources. Step into East Cottage to find a light modern space with soaring ceilings, tiles warm underfoot, bright rugs and cushions and a wood-burning stove. The kitchen glows at the other end: hand-built Shaker-style units, granite tops, an old pine dresser with plenty of china, a table for lazy breakfasts; owner Dee delivers a sizzling full English if you want, all local and seasonal. Up the spiral stairs are super bedrooms with buttermilk walls, wooden floors, pastel-striped blankets and exquisite beds; bathrooms are dazzling white, the twin has a wet room, the towels are thick and white. You can walk to a superb pub; or take a sundowner to the patio, and choose a home-cooked supper from the honesty freezer. *Buy home-produced rare breed Dexter beef and pork sausages from the owners' farm shop. North Tyne river walks, a stream to splash in and a public footpath right by the gate.*

Rooms	1 cottage for 2: £360-£650 per week. 1 cottage for 4: £400-£800 per week. Dogs £30 per stay. Max. 2.
Meals	Self-catering.
Closed	Never.

Drying room, towels and Bonedrybed dog bed. Advice on walks, and hose pipe area for muddy paws. Birthday cakes on request and 37 acres to explore.

Charles & Dee McGowan
East Cottage, Southlands Farm, Gunnerton,
Hexham, NE48 4EA

Tel	+44 (0)1434 681464
Mobile	+44 (0)7876 455620 / +44 (0)7900 271455
Email	dee@southlandsfarmcottages.co.uk
Web	www.southlandsfarmcottages.co.uk

Entry 110 Map 9

The Waiting Room

Staward Station had trains puffing in and out for over 80 years. It closed in 1950 along with the traditional waiting room and is now owned by Deb and Steve, who live nearby. You'll be sleeping in the old ticket office; in fact the original ticket hatch is still in use, opening onto the reading room (although morning cups of tea might be more appreciated than tickets these days). It's also a bit cosier than it used to be, with new double glazing on the replica south-facing windows and with insulation material used by NASA lining the roof. There's still the main entrance from the platform, leading into the sitting room, and if you go through the fully-equipped kitchen you'll find another door leading out the back to your private courtyard garden. The old stone railway bridge is just at the end of the platform, and from the top you can see over the tree tops down into Staward gorge and across to Hadrian's Wall – perfect for planning your walking route through the surrounding countryside. A good one to start with is the John Martin trail, a ten mile off-road walk that you can join just at the bottom of the garden. *Secure area of garden; woodland, advice on dog-friendly walks away from farm stock. (No bitches in season.)*

Rooms	Cabin for 4: from £80 per night. Dogs £25 per dog per stay; multiple dogs may be brought by arrangement, please call to discuss.
Meals	Self-catering.
Closed	Never.
	Leads, bowls, furniture throws and poo bags.

Canopy & Stars
The Waiting Room, Staward Station,
Langley upon Tyne, Hexham, NE47 5NR

Tel	+44 (0)117 204 7830
Email	enquiries@canopyandstars.co.uk
Web	www.canopyandstars.co.uk/thewaitingroom

Entry 111 Map 6

Lord Crewe Arms at Blanchland

Originally the abbot's lodge and kitchens (and its garden the cloisters), the Lord Crewe Arms has become a Grade II*-listed inn. The village, in a sheep-clad valley on the moors' edge, was built with stone from the abbey's ruins. Inside: ancient flags, inglenook fireplaces, fortress walls and a classy country décor. Public areas range from lofty to intimate and the atmospheric bar is in the vaulted crypt. With a head chef from Mark Hix's 'stable', the robust modern British menu includes steaks, chops and spit-roasted meats, fresh crab salad and ruby beets. Puddings hark back to ancient times: sea buckthorn posset, rhubarb fumble. Wines include great burgundies and clarets; ales range from Allendale's Golden Plover to Nel's Best from High House Farm; there are water bowls for dogs in the garden. If you stay, you're in for a treat. Most rooms are divided between The Angel, a simple, beautiful, listed ex-inn across the way, and the former tied cottages. Some bedrooms have exposed stone walls and real fires, all have soft carpets, fine fabrics, divine beds and deep baths. *Rivers to jump in. Sheep in fields so dogs to be kept on leads.*

Rooms	19 doubles: £119-£192. 1 suite for 2: £144-£212. 1 family room for 4: £189-£252. Dogs £10. Max. 2.
Meals	Lunch & dinner from £12.75. Sunday lunch, 2-3 courses, £18-£24.
Closed	Rarely.
	Dog bed, towel, bowl and advice on walks.

Tommy Mark
Lord Crewe Arms at Blanchland,
The Square,
Blanchland, DH8 9SP

Tel	+44 (0)1434 677100
Email	enquiries@lordcrewearmsblanchland.co.uk
Web	www.lordcrewearmsblanchland.co.uk

Entry 112 Map 6

The Killingworth Castle

The family behind the Ebrington Arms has renovated this 17th-century inn, around the corner from Blenheim Palace, to its former glory with beautifully restored bedrooms too. Wood floors sweep from side bar to main bar to dining room, burners in brick fireplaces belt out heat and the set menu is a steal. Smiling staff ferry own-brewed Yubby Bitter, Goldie and Yawnie to locals, dog walkers and drinkers; the rest are here for the food: roast venison and faggot croquette with beetroot dauphinoise, kale and juniper; blackberry and frangipane tart. And the best chips in Oxfordshire! Famous for their real ales, the focus is on small brewers; wines showcase independent makers; there's a nifty selection of malt whiskies, or try a pint of their home-brewed in the big beer garden. Oh, and the bedrooms! Some upstairs, some down, all with handpicked art, handmade sturdy beds and the softest linen. Muted tartan blankets keep you warm on winter nights, roll top baths sit on patterned tiled floors and there's a complementary decanter of sherry to start you off. Glorious. *Seven-mile walk Wychwood forest; eight and a half mile Wootton Circular walk; short rambles too. 1 dog-friendly room.*

Rooms	10 doubles: £99-£180.
Meals	Starters £6-£8. Mains £13-£21. Midweek set menu, 2 courses, £11.95.
Closed	Rarely.
	A box of dog treats, water bowls and a beer garden to sit in.

Claire & Jim Alexander
The Killingworth Castle,
Glympton Road, Wootton,
Chipping Norton, OX20 1EJ
Tel +44 (0)1993 811401
Email reservations@thekillingworthcastle.com
Web www.thekillingworthcastle.com

Entry 113 Map 3

The Greyhound Inn

Close to the white chalk horse at Uffington – the walking is grand round here – is a beautiful red-brick pub on a quiet road that winds through Letcombe Regis. The new owners have kept the fine old windows and the irresistible fireplaces and have added a garden at the back, a bright, cheerful décor, and a diamond of a chef in Phil Currie. Whether you go for guinea fowl with truffle, choux gnocchi and consommé, or battered haddock and chips and salad, this is cooking of a high order. Our two-course 'Midweek Fix' was a steal: a cheddar and leek tart followed by new season lamb chunk steak, both delicious. If the pub is Georgian on the outside, it's country-trendy within; racing scenes adorn the walls, dog biscuits beautify the bar, and up the carpeted stairs are eight sympathetically, tastefully refurbished rooms. Our favourite is the family suite under the eaves (beams, sloping ceiling, simple country antiques, turquoise roll top tub). Beds are Hypnos, cushions are plush, bathrooms luxurious, breakfasts a treat. You can pop in for a latte, a well-kept pint, or a hedonistic meal: it's the sort of place we all love. *Secure garden; country walks; maps. Close to Ridgeway path; woods, streams & fields too (horses & sheep so some signs for dogs on leads). 2 dog-friendly rooms.*

Rooms	4 doubles, 2 twin/doubles: £90-£135. 1 suite for 4, 1 suite for 5: £135-£195. Singles £75-£120. Extra bed/sofabed available £20 per person per night. Dogs £15 per dog per night.
Meals	Starters from £ 5.50. Lunch from £7. Dinner from £11.
Closed	24-26 December, 7-18 January.
	Four-legged friends are offered a selection box of tasty treats, comfy bed, water bowl, a towel to dry muddy paws after country walks and poo bags.

Catriona Galbraith
The Greyhound Inn,
Main Street, Letcombe Regis,
Wantage, OX12 9JL
Tel +44 (0)1235 771969
Email info@thegreyhoundletcombe.co.uk
Web www.thegreyhoundletcombe.co.uk

Entry 114 Map 3

The Olive Branch

A lovely pub in a sleepy Rutland village, where bridlepaths lead out across peaceful fields. It dates to the 17th century and is built of Clipsham stone, as is York Minster. Inside, a warm, informal, rustic chic hits the spot perfectly with open fires, old beams, stone walls and choir stalls in the bar. But there's more here than cool design. This is a place to come and eat great food, the lovely, local seasonal stuff that's cooked with passion by Sean and his brigade, perhaps potted pork and stilton with apple jelly, haunch of venison with a juniper fondant, then a boozy rhubarb trifle. Bedrooms in Beech House across the lane are gorgeous. Three have terraces, one has a free-standing bath, all come with crisp linen, pretty beds, Roberts radios and real coffee. Super breakfasts – smoothies, boiled eggs and soldiers, the full cooked works – are served in a stone-walled barn with flames leaping in the wood-burner. The front garden fills in summer, the sloe gin comes from local berries, and Newark is close for the biggest antiques market in Europe. Picnic hampers can be arranged. A total gem. *Dogs welcome in ground floor rooms. Lots of countryside walks nearby.*

Rooms	5 doubles: £115-£205. 1 family room for 4: £115-£255. Singles from £97.50. Extra beds £30. Dogs £10.
Meals	Lunch from £8.50. Dinner, 3 courses, £28.50-£40. Sunday lunch from £24.50.
Closed	Rarely.
	Advice on walks.

Ben Jones & Sean Hope
The Olive Branch,
Main Street, Clipsham,
Oakham, LE15 7SH
Tel +44 (0)1780 410355
Email info@theolivebranchpub.com
Web www.theolivebranchpub.com

Entry 115 Map 6

Hambleton Hall Hotel & Restaurant

Hambleton is matchless, one of the seven wonders of English country-house hotels. It sits on a tiny peninsular that juts into Rutland Water. You can sail on it, cycle round it, or watch terns and osprey commute across it. Back at the house the undisputed wonders of Hambleton wait: sofas by the fire in the panelled hall, a pillared bar in red for cocktails, a Michelin star in the elegant dining room. French windows in the sitting room – beautiful art, fresh flowers, the daily papers – open onto fine gardens. Expect clipped lawns and gravel paths, a formal parterre garden that bursts with summer colour and a walled swimming pool with views over parkland to the water. Bedrooms are flawless: hand-stitched Italian linen, mirrored armoires, Roberts radios and marble bathrooms. Stefa's eye for fabrics, some of which coat the walls, is impeccable; the Pavilion, a two-bedroom suite, has its own terrace. Polish the day off with ambrosial food, perhaps beetroot terrine with horseradish sorbet, fallow venison with Asian pear, passion fruit soufflé with banana sorbet. Barnsdale Gardens are close. *Minimum stay: 2 nights at weekends. Great walks around Hambleton; maps provided. Livestock in many of the footpath fields – out of respect to our farmer friends please keep dogs on leads.*

Rooms	15 twin/doubles: £270-£725. 1 suite for 4: £290-£725. Singles £200. Dinner, B&B £210 per person. Dogs £10. Max. 2.
Meals	Lunch from £29. Dinner, 3 courses, £69. Tasting menu £92. Sunday lunch £58.
Closed	Never.
	Leads, bedding, poo bags, bowls, food and biscuits. Crates, cuddly toys, waterproof coats and towelling for muddy paws.

Tim & Stefa Hart
Hambleton Hall Hotel & Restaurant,
Ketton Road, Hambleton,
Oakham, LE15 8TH
Tel +44 (0)1572 756991
Email hotel@hambletonhall.com
Web www.hambletonhall.com

Entry 116 Map 6

Offa's Dyke Yurt

The two pod set up, spectacular views from the glass doors and complete privacy make Offa's Dyke Yurt a great place for any kind of escape. You can bring the family down and watch the kids play in your personal play park, or go it alone and lounge in the spacious yurt camp. The main living area is beautifully decorated with rich, glowing woods and soft fabrics and the big double bed is housed in a separate, but adjoined mini yurt, giving extra space and privacy. On the same soaring deck are your own gas-powered shower, flushing loo and the wood-store. There's also some outdoor furniture, the centrepiece of which, a big wooden chaise longue, is perfect for napping in front of the views of the rolling hills. As the name suggests, the yurt is rather well placed for the Offa's Dyke Path, with some hearty hiking to be done for about 180 miles in both directions and miles of world class mountain biking trails all around. You can also do courses in everything from fruit tree grafting to bench making and woodwork; Jo and Wilf are happy to take you badger spotting in an adjoining field after the chickens have settled. *Best to keep dogs under control as sheep may be in next field. River & plenty of walks. Own garden but dogs could get out – they can be secured with little trouble.*

Rooms	Yurt for 4: from £100 per night. Max. 2 dogs – please bring your own bedding and keep them off the furniture.
Meals	Self-catering.
Closed	Never.
	Advice on walks.

Canopy & Stars
Offa's Dyke Yurt,
The Barn, Fron Uchaf,
Weston Rhyn, SY10 7NQ

Tel	+44 (0)117 204 7830
Email	enquiries@canopyandstars.co.uk
Web	www.canopyandstars.co.uk/offasdyke

Entry 117 Map 5

Pen-y-Dyffryn Country Hotel

In a blissful valley lost to the world, a small country house that sparkles on the side of a peaceful hill. This is one of those lovely places where guests return again and again, mostly due to Audrey and Miles, who run a very happy ship. Outside, fields tumble down to a stream that marks the border with Wales. Daffodils erupt in spring, the lawns are scattered with deckchairs in summer, paths lead into the hills for fine walking. Lovely interiors are just the ticket: Laura Ashley wallpaper and an open fire in the quirky bar; colourful art and super food in the pretty restaurant; the daily papers and the odd chaise longue in the sitting room. Bedrooms hit the spot. Most have the view, one has a French sleigh bed, a couple have jacuzzi baths for two. Four lovely rooms outside are dog-friendly and have their own patios. You get warm colours, crisp linen, pretty fabrics and sparkling bathrooms. After a day in the hills come back for a good dinner, perhaps wild mushroom risotto, pan-fried wood pigeon, hot chocolate fondant with vanilla ice cream. Offa's Dyke and Powis Castle are close. *Minimum stay: 2 nights at weekends. Secure garden; 20 local walking leaflets; 100-acre wood next to the hotel open to walkers. Dogs welcome in bedrooms, and in the public areas until 6pm.*

Rooms	8 doubles, 4 twins: £120-£190. Singles £90-£99. Dinner, B&B £99-£136 per person. Extra bed/sofabed £35 p.p.pn. Max. 2 dogs.
Meals	Light lunch (for residents) by arrangement. Dinner £30-£37.
Closed	Rarely.

Doggy box in every pet owner's bedroom with towels and cloths, dog mat, lead, bowl, treats and poo bags.

Miles & Audrey Hunter
Pen-y-Dyffryn Country Hotel,
Rhydycroesau,
Oswestry, SY10 7JD
Tel +44 (0)1691 653700
Email stay@peny.co.uk
Web www.peny.co.uk

Entry 118 Map 5

The Shippen

An old stone shippen on a remote hillside in an AONB valley, with designer décor, delightful owners, and a glass-and-oak gable for heaven-sent views. No longer a cattle shed, this is one big living, sleeping and eating space with a south-facing decked veranda that gazes on Shropshire's sweet hills. Timbers have been re-used, the slate roof raised, and the stone floor replaced by pristine planks of oak. Not a building in sight, other than Jeannie and Paul's discreet farmhouse… just a sloping grass garden, a mini orchard and masses of wildlife. It's heaven for couples or families (there's a sofabed if you've little ones in tow), and perfect in every season; snuggle up by the the log-burner in winter and barbecue in summer. There's a filter for spring water, Freesat, Netflix, PlayStation, a wet room that takes a wheelchair, and a robot vacuum cleaner (a Sawday's first?!). Stroll the cobbled streets of Bishop's Castle and Shrewsbury, enjoy a local pint by the river, hike to the top of the Long Mynd. Then back to board games by the fire, bright starry skies, and owls that hoot you to sleep. *Minimum stay: 3 nights. Miles and miles of woodland and fields for walking. Use the Shropshire Way (right on the doorstep) or walk on the lanes.*

Rooms	1 cottage for 2: £495-£535 per week. Extra bed/sofabed available £10 per person per night. Max. 2 dogs.
Meals	Pubs/restaurants 2.5 miles.
Closed	Never.
	Dog biscuits, medium-sized dog bed, 2 bowls and towels for drying.

Jeannie McGillivray
The Shippen, Little Wood House,
Linley, Bishop's Castle, SY9 5HP

Tel	+44 (0)1743 387873
Mobile	+44 (0)7747 115935
Email	jeannie@remotenewmedia.com
Web	the-shippen.com

Entry 119 Map 5

The Castle Hotel

This thriving medieval market town sits amid some of the loveliest country in the land, a launch pad for walkers and cyclists alike, with Offa's Dyke, Long Mynd and the Kerry Ridgeway all close. After a day in the hills, roll back to this quirky hotel for a night of gentle carousing. You'll find heaps of country comforts: hearty food, impeccable ales, super rooms with honest prices. Downstairs, there's a coal fire in the pretty snug, oak panelling in the breakfast room, and Millie the short-haired dachshund who patrols the corridors with aplomb. Stylish bedrooms upstairs have all been refurbished. Expect good beds, warm colours, flat-screen TVs, an armchair if there's room. Some are up in the eaves, several have views of the Shropshire hills, two have baths in the room. Back downstairs you find the sort of food you'd want after a day in the hills, perhaps hot garlic prawns, beef and ale pie, sticky toffee pudding. Don't miss the hugely popular real ale festival in July, the beer drinker's equivalent of Glastonbury. The garden terrace, with long country views, is a fine spot for a sundowner. *Dogs are welcome with you at the table for all meals in bar areas. Let us know on booking, so we can give you a dog-friendly table throughout your stay.*

Rooms	9 doubles, 1 twin: £95-£150. 2 family rooms for 4: £130-£155. Singles from £75. Dinner, B&B from £82.50 p.p. Extra beds for children £20.
Meals	Lunch from £4.50. Dinner, 3 courses, about £25.
Closed	Christmas Day and 10 days in January.
	Dog Welcome Box in the room for your pet which includes a feeding mat, food bowl, towel, lead, treats and poo bags.

Henry & Rebecca Hunter
The Castle Hotel,
Bishops Castle, SY9 5BN
Tel +44 (0)1588 638403
Email stay@thecastlehotelbishopscastle.co.uk
Web www.thecastlehotelbishopscastle.co.uk

Entry 120 Map 5

Walcot Hall

Lose yourself in the grounds of Walcot Hall – play croquet, go fishing, boating, biking, hiking and discover all the quirky treasures…There's the Dipping Shed, with stunning views of the Long Mynd, a rough outer shell and a beautifully decorated interior with a high, beamed ceiling. On a grassy hill nearby is Buffalo Springfield Yurt with a great, fur-covered bed and Crazy Horse Yurt with a big brass bed and sheepskins, share a modern loo in the former hen house and a gas-powered shower in the AA caravan, as well as spectacular views. After The Gold Rush, for the more adventurous, is perched high above two secluded fishermen pools, shares the loo and has a wood-burner, double bed and sofa bed. Deep in the arboretum and a 500-yard walk from the nearest parking sits The Chapel: a delightful airy bolthole, with subtle modern comforts and an organ you can play; curtains shield two separate beds from the fray. Then there's Green Glory an authentic showman's caravan and The Wheelwright's Shop, a cavernous workshop cabin adorned with antiques and curiosities…If you like things idiosyncratic you must visit this place! *Plenty of walking, small pools to swim in, a large arboretum to explore; dog-friendly pubs nearby. Sometimes livestock around estate.*

Rooms	2 cabins for 4: from £100. 1 cabin for 4: from £95. 1 wagon for 2: from £45. 2 yurts for 2: from £65. 1 yurt for 4: from £73. Prices per night. Max. 2-3 dogs.
Meals	Self-catering.
Closed	Never.
	Walks, lots of space and many dog-loving staff!

Canopy & Stars
Walcot Hall,
Lydbury, SY7 8AZ

Tel	+44 (0)117 204 7830
Email	enquiries@canopyandstars.co.uk
Web	www.canopyandstars.co.uk/walcothall

Entry 121 Map 2

Lakeside Retreat

Off-piste drivers will delight in the approach – down a bumpy farm track, over an open field, across a ford and through grassy woodland. You land in a dreamy, bucolic setting with an arboretum and views over two deep water lakes (yes you may swim, yes you may use the little boat) with island, waterfalls, a small summerhouse that revolves, and a stream teeming with wildlife. A veranda and patio with table and chairs face south so you won't miss a thing; writers, artists and those clutching a large drink may take root here on less chilly days. Your wooden cabin is comfortable and very cosy: find one fresh and airy living/dining room with a fully formed kitchen area and plenty of good seating; glass doors open out to the terrace. The main bedroom has a giant bed with a pretty rose-strewn bedspread and a cream rug; the bunk room is fine for adults or children but it's all so romantic you may want to farm them out! Owner Victoria, who lives nearby, leaves you jam from her damsons and raspberries, local apple juice, something baked, and fresh flowers. A gorgeous little watery retreat. *Children over 5 welcome. Secure 15 acres of garden and woodland.*

Rooms	1 cabin for 4: £395-£795 per week. Weekly bookings (Fri-Fri) or 3-night weekends (Fri-Mon). Additional night's stay booked upon request. Dogs £30 per stay. Max. 2.
Meals	Self-catering.
Closed	Never.
	Dog treats, blankets and advice on walks.

Victoria Orchard
Lakeside Retreat,
Old Hall Farm, Milson, Cleobury Mortimer, DY14 0BH
Tel +44 (0)1299 270780
Email info@ludlowholidaylet.co.uk
Web www.ludlowholidaylet.co.uk

Entry 122 Map 2

Cleeton Court

Rare peace: a tiny lane leads to this part 14th-century farmhouse, immersed in the countryside with views over meadows and heathland. You have your own entrance, and the use of the pretty drawing room, elegantly comfortable with sofas and a log fire. Beamed bedrooms are delightfully furnished, one with a magnificent, chintzy four-poster and a vast bathroom; recline in the cast-iron bath with a glass of wine, gaze on views from the window as you soak. Bring your boots: the walking is superb, and charming Ros gives you a smashing, locally sourced breakfast to get you going. *Secure garden; wonderful walks over the hills from the house. There are sheep around sometimes so leads needed; avoid cattle fields.*

Rooms	1 twin/double, 1 four-poster: £80-£90. Singles £65. Max. 2 dogs.
Meals	Pubs/restaurants 1.5-4 miles.
Closed	Christmas & New Year.
	A Bonio at bedtime.

Rosamond Woodward
Cleeton Court,
Cleeton St Mary, Ludlow, DY14 0QZ
Tel +44 (0)1584 823379
Mobile +44 (0)7778 903136
Email roswoodward1@gmail.com
Web www.cleetoncourt.co.uk

Entry 123 Map 2

Hopton House

Karen looks after you very well – she's such an expert on B&B she runs courses on how to do it. And how to do it beautifully: unwind in this fresh converted granary with old beams, high ceilings and a sun-filled dining/sitting room overlooking the hills. You sleep over in the barn: choose between two bedrooms – one up, one down – each with its own entrance. Find beautifully dressed beds, silent fridges, good lighting, homemade cakes. Bathrooms have deep baths (and showers) – from one you can lie back and gaze at the stars. Karen's breakfasts promise Ludlow sausages, home-laid eggs, fine jams and homemade marmalade. *Minimum stay: 2 nights. Over 16s welcome. Secure garden; local woods to walk in. Free-range chickens in garden, and resident dogs.*

Rooms	2 doubles: £125-£135. Check owner's website for availability calendar & booking engine.
Meals	Restaurant 3 miles.
Closed	19-27 December.
	Throws, dog bowls, towels and advice on walks and places to eat. Downstairs room has direct access to enclosed garden.

Karen Thorne
Hopton House,
Hopton Heath,
Craven Arms, SY7 0QD
Tel +44 (0)1547 530885
Web www.shropshirebreakfast.co.uk

Entry 124 Map 2

The Yurt Sanctuary

This pretty yurt camp sits behind a wicker fence under the trees, through your own private meadow at Orchard House. It has stunning views of the Mendips and owners Michele and Dan have thought of everything: big, iron-framed double bed, chunky wooden furniture, quirky trinkets, colourful rugs. There are cosy locals for hearty pub food, but you might choose to rustle up something in the kitchen hut and crack open the welcoming supply of local cider. After dinner, lounge by the wood-burner, watch the sunset from the bench swing, fire up the hot tub for soaking and stargazing. There are camp beds for children but you can also bring tents – lots of space; they'll love to join the early morning feeding of chickens and pygmy goats. Michele offers grooming or training for your four-legged friends and you could take advantage of Dan's sports therapy work with the slightly larger beasts of Bath Rugby team by booking a massage. A peaceful place (occasional road sound at busier times) with warm, caring hosts who make you feel instantly at home. *Canine sensory enrichment garden for dogs to explore. Wonderful walks nearby including Cheddar Gorge; 3 dog-friendly local pubs.*

Rooms	Yurt for 2 (space for 2 children on camp beds): from £95 per night. Dogs £20 per dog per stay. Max. 6.
Meals	Self-catering.
Closed	October – March.

Doggy treat tin: anything from pig's ears/pizzle sticks & cow's hooves to dried banana & sweet potato; bowls aplenty. And ultimate treat: book your dog in for bath, brush & pamper, with a blueberry & vanilla facial!

Canopy & Stars
The Yurt Sanctuary, Orchard House,
Emborough, Radstock, BA3 4SA

Tel	+44 (0)117 204 7830
Email	enquiries@canopyandstars.co.uk
Web	www.canopyandstars.co.uk/yurtsanctuary

Entry 125 Map 2

The Queens Arms

Stride across rolling fields, feast on Corton Denham lamb, retire to a perfect room. Buried down several Dorset/Somerset borders lanes, Gordon and Jeanette Reid's 18th-century stone pub has an elegant exterior – more country gentleman's house than pub. The bar, with its rug-strewn flagstones and bare boards, pew benches, deep sofas and crackling fire, is most charming. In the light, bright dining room that doubles up as a cinema on week nights, and on the terrace in summer, robust British dishes are distinguished by fresh ingredients from local suppliers. Try pheasant, pigeon and black pudding terrine, follow with monkfish with chive velouté, make room for a comforting crumble. Bedrooms are beautifully designed in soothing colours, and all have lovely views over the village and surrounding hills. New coach house rooms are super, too: underfloor heating, down duvets, brass and sleigh beds, iPod docks and immaculate wet rooms. Expect Gyle59 on tap, homemade pork pies on the bar, Gloucester Old Spot bacon at breakfast (from 8am daily), and stunning walks from the door. *Guests can eat with their dogs in bar for all meals. Ground floor bedroom dog-friendly. Great dog-friendly printed walks in lanyards on back of door.*

Rooms	6 doubles, 2 twin/doubles: £125-£190. Singles £95-£120. Family room £200. Dogs £15 per dog per night. Max. 2.
Meals	Main meals from £10.50, starters from £6.25.
Closed	Never.
	Dog bed & bowl, towel to dry paws & small pack of doggy treats. Hose outside room for washing off, or wet room ideal for showering them. Dog biscuits on the bar.

Gordon & Jeanette Reid
The Queens Arms,
Corton Denham, Sherborne, DT9 4LR
Tel +44 (0)1963 220317
Email relax@thequeensarms.com
Web www.thequeensarms.com

Entry 126 Map 2

Farmers Arms

A lovely inn lost in peaceful hills on the Somerset Levels – a great base for a night or two of affordable luxury. Outside, free-range hens potter about, cows graze neighbouring fields and glorious views from the beer garden drift downhill for a couple of miles – a perfect spot for a pint in summer. Inside, you'll find friendly locals, sofas in front of an open fire and a timber-framed bar, where one airy room rolls into another giving a sense of space and light. There are beamed ceilings, boarded floors, tongue-and-groove panelling and logs piled high in alcoves. Bedrooms – of varying sizes – are just the ticket. They come with whitewashed walls, pretty beds, the odd chaise longue, then power showers or double-ended baths. One has a daybed, others have sofas, another has a private courtyard. Good food flies from the kitchen, perhaps ham hock terrine, crab and crayfish linguini, white chocolate and blackberry brûlée; in summer you can eat in the courtyard garden. There are local stables if you want to ride and great walking, so bring your boots. Taunton is close for cricket in summer. *Woodland walks, secure garden and open field; information on walks available.*

Rooms	4 doubles, 1 twin/double: £105-£125. Singles £75. Extra beds/sofabeds from £10. Dogs £10 per stay.
Meals	Lunch & dinner £5-£35.
Closed	Never.
	Dog biscuits, water bowls, hose for washing muddy dogs after after walks.

Alison Medley
Farmers Arms,
West Hatch, Taunton, TA3 5RS
Tel +44 (0)1823 480980
Email info@fawh.co.uk
Web www.farmersarmssomerset.co.uk

Entry 127 Map 2

Streamcombe Farm Shepherd's Hut

A peaceful spot in the woods just south of Exmoor: a break from city life. Karen and Ian have started a cookery school (where you can learn game or fish cookery during your stay). The area is a dark sky reserve completely unspoilt by light pollution and the woods near the hut shelter a herd of wild deer among other forest creatures. You can see them all on the two-mile hike over the hills to Dulverton, where you'll find some lovely pubs and shops. The Shepherd's Hut itself was built in the late 19th century and retains its original oak panelling and floors. It has been redecorated in the simple plain colours of Shaker style and positioned near the house but shielded by the barn, set up to catch the morning sun on the front door. The hut is off grid, lit with candles and heated by the big wood-burner. The shower, sink and organic chemical loo are all housed in the barn a few yards away. As the presence of an on-site cookery school suggests, the food available is superb. You can book BYO evening meals or have breakfast and lunch hampers delivered to the hut, so you can eat surrounded by the sounds of the country. *Free-range chickens and sheep everywhere: leads at all times please. Exmoor is a walker's paradise.*

Rooms	Shepherd's hut for 2: £75 per night. Max. 2 dogs.
Meals	Self-catering.
Closed	November – March.
	Maps and advice on local walks.

Canopy & Stars
Streamcombe Farm Shepherd's Hut,
Streamcombe Lane, Dulverton, TA22 9SA

Tel	+44 (0)117 204 7830
Email	enquiries@canopyandstars.co.uk
Web	www.canopyandstars.co.uk/streamcombe

Entry 128 Map 2

The Ship

Once a great port, Dunwich is now a tiny (but famous) village, gradually sinking into the sea. Its well-loved smugglers' inn, almost on the beach, overlooks the salt marsh and sea and pulls in wind-blown walkers and birdwatchers from the Minsmere Reserve. In the old-fashioned bar – nautical bric-a-brac, flagged floors, simple furnishings and a stove that belts out the heat – you can tuck into legendary fish and chips washed down with a pint of Adnams. There's also a more modern dining room where hearty food combines with traditional dishes: try Lowestoft crispy cod cheeks with Romesco sauce, smoked paprika and rocket, or tuck into their terrific Scotch eggs with black pudding and homemade piccalilli, or hot smoked salmon and horseradish. Up the fine Victorian staircase are spruced up bedrooms – simple, uncluttered – with period features, cord carpets, brass beds, old pine, little shower rooms. Rooms at the front have glorious salt marsh views, two new rooms overlook the garden, courtyard rooms are cosy with pine, and the family room under the eaves is fabulous: single beds, a big futon-style bean bag, and a flat-screen for the kids. *Special midweek rates off season. Huge garden. Great walks on heaths, in forests and on the all-year-round dog-friendly beach.*

Rooms	12 doubles, 1 twin: £120-£140.3 family rooms for 4: £140. Dogs £7.50.
Meals	Lunch from £6.95. Bar meals from £9.75. Dinner from £9.95. Sunday lunch £11.95.
Closed	Never.
	Dog biscuits, water bowls and maps with local walks.

Gareth Clarke
The Ship,
St James's Street, Dunwich,
Saxmundham, IP17 3DT
Tel +44 (0)1728 648219
Email info@shipatdunwich.co.uk
Web www.shipatdunwich.co.uk

Entry 129 Map 4

The Crown & Castle

A great place to wash up for a few lazy days. Orford is hard to beat, a sleepy Suffolk village blissfully marooned at the end of the road. River, beach and forest wait, as does the Crown & Castle, a welcoming English hostelry where the art of hospitality is practised with unstinting flair. The inn stands in the shadow of Orford's 12th-century castle. Uncluttered interiors have a warm, airy feel with stripped floorboards, open fires, wonderful art and flickering candles at night. Chic bedrooms have Vi-Spring beds, fancy bathrooms, lovely fabrics, the odd armchair. Four in the main house have watery views, the suite is huge, the garden rooms big and light, the courtyard rooms a real delight. All have crisp white linen, TVs, DVDs and digital radios. Wellington boots wait at the back door, so pull on a pair and explore Rendlesham Forest or hop on a boat and chug over to Orfordness. Ambrosial food awaits your return, perhaps potted brown shrimps, a faultless steak and kidney pie, crushed pistachio meringue with a chocolate ice-cream sundae. Sutton Hoo is close. *Minimum stay: 2 nights at weekends. Children over 8 welcome. Lots of walking both by the river and in the forest.*

Rooms	18 doubles, 2 twins: £130-£260. 1 suite for 2: £265-£335. Dinner, B&B from £95 p.p. Dogs £10 for up to 2 dogs per room per night. Max. 2.
Meals	Lunch from £8.50. À la carte dinner around £35.
Closed	Rarely.
	Homemade treats, towels, walks, and a bookable "doggie table" in the restaurant.

David & Ruth Watson
The Crown & Castle,
Orford, Woodbridge, IP12 2LJ
Tel +44 (0)1394 450205
Email info@crownandcastle.co.uk
Web www.crownandcastle.co.uk

Entry 130 Map 4

Kesgrave Hall

This Georgian mansion sits in 38 acres of woodland and gardens, sound-proofing it from the outside world. It was home to US airmen during WWII, but the locals have reclaimed it as their own now and they come for the easy style, the excellent service, the delicious food and the informal vibe. The emphasis here is firmly on the food, so it's almost a restaurant with rooms, albeit quite a grand one. Inside, you find wellington boots in the entrance hall, high ceilings in the big sitting room, stripped boards in the humming bistro and doors that open onto a terrace in summer. Colourful bedrooms have lots of style. One is huge and comes with a free-standing bath and a faux leopard-skin sofa. The others might not be quite as wild, but they're lovely nonetheless, some cosy in the eaves, others in beautifully refurbished outbuildings. Expect warm colours, crisp linen, good lighting and fancy bathrooms. Back downstairs, tasty food flies from the kitchen, perhaps smoked haddock fishcakes, a char-grilled steak, a delicious coffee cheesecake with Tia Maria ice cream. Suffolk's magical coast waits. *Woods to roam in, lawns to run on. Beach and rivers about 20 minutes away.*

Rooms	10 doubles, 7 twin/doubles: £130-£230. 6 suites for 2: £275-£300. Dogs £10.
Meals	Breakfast £10-£16. Lunch & dinner, 3 courses, £25-£30.
Closed	Never.
	Blankets, towels, walks, bowls and doggy dinners.

Oliver Richards
Kesgrave Hall,
Hall Road, Kesgrave, Ipswich, IP5 2PU
Tel +44 (0)1473 333741
Email reception@kesgravehall.com
Web www.milsomhotels.com

Entry 131 Map 4

The Sheepyard Barn

A wood-fired pizza oven, a 'resistance' indoor pool, a cosy home cinema and a hot tub with bucolic views: Sheepyard Barn is eco-chic, high spec, and spectacular. You pootle past four woody lakeside lodges and down the twisting track until, at last, a long low barn comes into view, in a commanding position on a gentle hill, with rolling fields all around. Enter to find streaming light, heaps of space, everything on one floor, and bedrooms divided from living areas by a heavy wooden sliding door. It's the perfect multi-generational place to stay. Every little thing has been considered, from hooks for children's coats and a trampoline sunk into the grass, to storage for outdoor cushions (note the patio sofas) and, on arrival, fresh flowers, homemade cake and eggs from the farm where the friendly owners live. Stock up with provisions in Hadleigh, return to a wow of a kitchen, a pleasure to work in and sociable too; no chef could be lonely here. Spot wildlife at Wolves Wood, book in a spa therapist, enjoy tea in Lavenham, or stroll to Flatford. Then retire to the 'Field Shelter' and catch the evening sun. *Minimum stay: 4 nights on weekdays; 3 at weekends; 7 in high season. Walks from the door. Large open garden for dogs to run free in. Safely 0.5 miles from the road.*

Rooms	1 house for 10: £2,200-£3,890 per week. Extra double bed £60. Dogs £20 per dog per stay.
Meals	Pubs/restaurants 2 miles.
Closed	Never.

Dog's own welcome letter, biscuits, water and food bowls, walking lead and spare poo bags. Underfloor heated boot room for dogs to sleep in.

Andrew Bryce
Northlands Farm, Hintlesham IP8 3NX

Tel	+44 (0)1473 652149
Mobile	+44 (0)7957 461011
Email	info@suffolkescape.co.uk
Web	www.suffolkescape.co.uk/barnescapes/sheepyard-barn/

Entry 132 Map 4

Hare Field Cabin

Hare Field Cabin is an effortless escape for the work-weary city dweller. Just a hop out of London takes you to a quiet spot in the heart of Suffolk countryside, but the cabin's modern elegance keeps the best of urban comfort close to hand. Laze in the king-size bed to the sound of birdsong, pad across the heated floor to the monsoon shower, then throw open the doors to the terrace while you cook breakfast in the fabulous kitchen. Owners Richard and Rachel have considered the environment in everything from the reclaimed wood of the veranda and the air-source heat pump, to the careful positioning that blends the cabin into its surroundings and hides it even from their house just over the drive. Follow the miles of footpaths and bike trails that criss-cross the sleepy landscape to medieval towns and villages, or make a day trip to the coast. Come home via the local farm shop to pick up something for the barbecue or marshmallows for the firepit, then lie back on the loungers and watch the stars. There's even a spa nearby, although with the cabin itself working its mellowing magic on you, you'll hardly need it. *Public footpath opposite cabin; large field that dogs can roam; advice on other nearby walks, including a riverside one for a quick dip. Lots of dog-friendly pubs in Long Melford.*

Rooms	Cabin for 2: £100 per night. Dogs £30 per dog per stay. Max. 1 small/medium dog.
Meals	Self-catering
Closed	Never.

Dog treats, water bowl and towel (any items owners might have forgotten can be supplied too: leads, spare bed, food).

Canopy & Stars
Hare Field Cabin,
Mill Road, Foxearth, Sudbury, CO10 7JF
Tel +44 (0)117 204 7830
Email enquiries@canopyandstars.co.uk
Web www.canopyandstars.co.uk/harefieldcabin

Entry 133 Map 4

Oak Tree Farm

A magnificent ancient oak tree stands guard over this 300-year old Georgian-fronted farmhouse. John and Julian love all things Art Nouveau/Art Deco and their home is filled with pieces from those periods, including china with masses of different patterns; fine books galore too, and peaceful bedrooms with smart white linen. Breakfast is a moveable feast: in the conservatory in summer, or by the fire in the dining room in winter; the bird feeders get moved too so you're kept amused while you tuck in! You can wander the five-acre garden and meadows, pretty Yoxford village has antique shops to browse, and Snape Maltings is a hop. *Minimum stay: 2 nights at weekends. Plenty of space to exercise dogs & throw balls. Dogs don't usually need to be on leads (check in case our chickens are free-ranging). Many lovely walks around the area.*

Rooms	3 twin/doubles: £90. Singles £70.
Meals	Pubs/restaurants 5-minute walk.
Closed	November – February.

Doggy towels and poo bags.

Julian Lock & John McMinn
Oak Tree Farm, Little Street,
Yoxford, Saxmundham, IP17 3JN

Tel	+44 (0)1728 668651
Mobile	+44 (0)7969 459261
Email	oaktreefarmyoxford@gmail.com
Web	www.oaktreefarmyoxford.co.uk

Entry 134 Map 4

Photo: istockphoto.com

8 Coastguard Cottages

Step through a white gate, down the garden path and into the porch of your cottage; one in a neat row of whitewashed 19th-century dwellings. Downstairs there's a fresh nautical feel with white, grey and blue tones and seascapes on the walls. The cosy living room, dining area and well-stocked kitchen are all open plan; and the spick and span family bathroom is downstairs too. Take your morning Nespresso outside to the terrace while you plan your day – perhaps a yomp through miles of rolling Sussex landscape, a jaunt to boaty Chichester or a wander down to wonderful West Wittering beach, a ten minute walk, for some twitching: swifts and swallows in spring, oyster catchers and geese in autumn. You're left a generous pile of logs for the open fire, a TV and plenty of books and board games – there's also a shed in the garden bursting with outdoorsy things: bikes, body boards, buckets, spades and crabbing nets. Upstairs to three restful bedrooms that continue the seafaring theme, the double has a distant view of the sea and one of the twin rooms is best suited to little ones. *Secure garden; coastal walks, dog-friendly sandy beach nearby. Don't leave dogs alone if they bark or cry, and do keep them off beds and furniture.*

Rooms	1 cottage for 6: £865-£1,350 per week. Short breaks occasionally available up to 6 weeks in advance. Dogs £10 per stay. Max. 3 (depending on size and age).
Meals	Pubs/restaurants 5-minute walk.
Closed	Never.
	Dog bowls and towels for drying.

Pilar Lafuente
8 Coastguard Cottages,
8 Coastguard Lane,
West Wittering, PO20 8AT
Tel +44 (0)20 7351 6009
Email admin@snowhillproperties.com
Web www.snowhillproperties.com

Entry 135 Map 3

Rubens Barn

Pheasant strut, shy deer bounce by – sure signs that you're immersed in the Goodwood Estate. This little flint barn is tucked into one of the most unspoilt woody corners of Sussex. Rush hour here, on a leafy lane, consists of the occasional tractor, car or combine. Renovated and decorated to the highest order – in duck-egg blue with hints of gold – this is one stylish retreat. Downstairs, a luxurious bedroom with a huge bed, silk throws, velvet cushions and a shower room with slate tiles, heated rails and fluffy bathrobes. In the living room, cream sofas, fresh flowers, a Shaker kitchen. Upstairs, a big twin bedroom, a roll top bath, soft lights and white towels. A welcome pack of fruit, ham, cheese, coffee and croissants is provided by the lovely owners who live in the main house – as are binoculars so you can spy on the wildlife! Sit out on the neat little patio through the French windows, enjoy a game of tennis, borrow the barbecue. Or set off for East Dean – it has two wonderful pubs. Sussex at its best, hidden well away yet never far from civilisation: historic Chichester is close by. *Minimum stay: 2 nights. Short breaks available. Secure garden, surrounded by walks through forests and farmland. Area of Outstanding Natural Beauty in the South Downs National Park.*

Rooms	1 barn for 4: £500-£1,200 per week. Dogs £30 per dog per stay. Max. 2.
Meals	Self-catering.
Closed	Rarely
	Advice on walks and dog-friendly pubs nearby.

Rob & Rachel Hill
Rubens Barn,
Droke Lane, East Dean, PO18 0JJ
Tel +44 (0)1243 818187
Email info@rubensbarn.co.uk
Web www.rubensbarn.co.uk

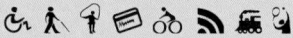

Entry 136 Map 3

The Welldiggers Arms

A true country classic where the views stretch for miles and the staff are warm, friendly and attentive. The kitchen turns out delicious modern British dishes; start with duck hash, hen's egg and crispy bacon crumb followed by pan-fried hake with spiced lentils and pot-roasted cauliflower and fennel. Finish up with a moreish pudding and coffee. Or just pop in for a drink and a bar snack: the large convivial space is full of happy diners making the most of the knock out views over the South Downs. The bar and dining area of this 300-year-old stone, slate-roofed inn has a fresh yet traditional feel: roaring fire, bespoke oak furniture, local art. Drink in the picture-perfect vistas or spill onto the terrace. And they've got 14 en suite bedrooms, some in the pub and some in a separate courtyard. The calm contemporary rooms have top quality Hypnos beds with attractive upholstered headboards; and all of them make the most of the scenery, while some windows frame spectacular views. Excellent walking all around; Chichester, sailing and National Trust properties are close. *Five and a half mile walk from the pub created for us by iFootpath. Fields to roam with lots of wildlife. Dogs allowed in bar area; same menu & service runs throughout whole establishment.*

Rooms	14 doubles: £90-£155. Extra bed available. Dogs £15 per stay.
Meals	Bar snacks from £3.95. Starters from £7. Mains from £11.95.
Closed	Rarely.
	Dog beds and bowls in rooms. Free dog biscuits at the bar; 'dog beer' for sale!

The Manager
The Welldiggers Arms,
Low Heath, Petworth, GU28 0HG
Tel +44 (0)1798 344288
Email enquiries@thewelldiggersarms.co.uk
Web www.thewelldiggersarms.co.uk

Entry 137 Map 3

Merrion Farm

Local and sustainable are the two principles at the heart of Merrion Farm. Withyfield Cottage is half rustic log cabin, half comfortable cottage, this incredible straw bale structure was designed by Ben Law, builder and permaculture expert whose project was voted the most popular ever to feature on Channel 4's *Grand Designs*. Throughout, modern comfort blends seamlessly with rustic design. It's a graceful work of art: exposed timber beams sweep down from the high, arched ceiling and sink into the worktops and floor, framing the open plan kitchen and living room. One of the bedrooms has its own bathroom, two are on the ground floor; all are simply decorated, letting the breathtaking quality of the workmanship shine through. From the veranda, you can see the very woodlands where the timber to clad the exterior was cut and then replenished. A ten-minute walk away and sharing the woods with badgers, woodpeckers and barn owls, you'll find Withywood Shepherd's Hut, a private hideaway for up to 4. Further afield is the Sussex landscape, criss-crossed with walking trails taking in places of history and beauty. *Heaps of lovely walks, private garden – and lots of good smells for dogs!*

Rooms	Cottage for 6: from £127 per night. Shepherd's hut for 4: £100 per night. Dogs £15 per dog per stay in hut (max. 1). £20 per dog per stay in cottage (max. 2, extras by arrangement only).
Meals	Self-catering.
Closed	Never.
	Towels, advice on walking and walks from the door. Dog sitting if you want to go out without your dog.

Canopy & Stars
Merrion Farm,
Partridge Green, Horsham, RH13 8EH

Tel	+44 (0)117 204 7830
Email	enquiries@canopyandstars.co.uk
Web	www.canopyandstars.co.uk/merrionfarm

Entry 138 Map 3

The Cat

Owner Andrew swapped grand Gravetye Manor for the buzzy, pubby atmosphere of The Cat in 2009; he hasn't looked back. The 16th-century building, a fine medieval hall house with a Victorian extension, has been comfortably modernised without losing its character. Inside are beamed ceilings and panelling, planked floors, splendid inglenooks, and an airy room that leads to a garden at the back, furnished with teak and posh parasols. Harvey's Ale and some top-notch pub food, passionately put together from fresh local ingredients by chef Alex Jacquemin, attract a solid, old-fashioned crowd: retired locals, foodies and walkers. Tuck into rare roast beef and horseradish sandwiches, Rye Bay sea bass with brown shrimp and caper butter, South Downs lamb chops with dauphinoise (and leave room for treacle tart!). The setting is idyllic, in a pretty village opposite a 12th-century church – best viewed from two of four bright and comfortable bedrooms. Crisp linen on big beds, rich fabrics, fawn carpets, fresh bathrooms and antique touches illustrate the style. A sweet retreat in a charming village backwater. *Lots of walks in the area.*

Rooms	4 doubles: £125-£165. Singles £95-£110. Dogs £10 per stay. Max. 2.
Meals	Lunch & dinner from £12. Bar meals from £6. Sunday lunch, 3 courses, £26.
Closed	Rarely.
	Poo bags, dog biscuits and towels.

Andrew Russell
The Cat,
Queen's Square, West Hoathly,
East Grinstead, RH19 4PP
Tel +44 (0)1342 810369
Email thecatinn@googlemail.com
Web www.catinn.co.uk

Entry 139 Map 3

Boxwood

In a bright clearing in the forest, surrounded by leafy Wildlife Trust reserve, is a simple, contemporary, architect-designed home, a place to unwind and recharge. Spanning two floors, the living area is above, the bedrooms are below and the palest of pale flooring (solid oak) runs throughout. All is white, light and serene: walls, ceilings and modernist kitchen. Upstairs is open plan with a pitched roof and velux windows, and there are two lovely decks for summery meals, one at each end. Airy by day, cosy by night – the wood-stove glows, the floors are toasty – this charming cabin-house is a comfortable retreat, with more heated floors in super-mod bathrooms, and bedrooms uncluttered and pristine. Wild boar and deer roam, rabbits scamper, birds sing, yet the nearest shop is under a mile so if you run out of basics there's no need to panic. Bexhill is along the coast, and quirky, literary Rye is 15 minutes: stroll along the cobbled streets, check out the tea shops, and puff your way up the tower of St Mary's Church for a brilliant coastal view. *Minimum stay: 3 nights on weekdays; 2 nights at weekends; 7 nights in high season. Children over 2 welcome.Woodland setting with no fences. Site shared with another holiday let so dogs need to be kept from straying.*

Rooms	1 house for 6: £700-£1,900 per week. Max. 2 dogs.
Meals	Restaurant 1.5 miles.
Closed	Never.
	Woodland walks straight from the door and dog bowls.

Tim Bushe
Boxwood,
Bixley Lane,
Beckley, TN31 6TH
Mobile +44 (0)7973 149521
Email tim@walkerbushe.co.uk
Web www.boxwood-retreat.co.uk

Entry 140 Map 4

Strand House

As you follow the Royal Military Canal down to miles of sandy beach, bear in mind that 600 years ago, you'd have been swimming in the sea. This is reclaimed land and Strand House, built in 1425, originally stood on Winchelsea Harbour. Outside, you find wandering wisteria, colourful flowerbeds and a woodland walk that leads up to the village. Inside, medieval interiors have low ceilings, timber frames and mind-your-head beams. There are reds and yellows, sofas galore, a wood-burner in the sitting room, an honesty bar from which to help yourself. It's a home-spun affair: Hugh cooks breakfast, Mary looks after guests in style. Quirky bedrooms sweep you back in time. One has an ancient four-poster, some have wonky floors, three open onto a terrace, all have good beds and robes for tiny shower rooms. As for the cottage, airy rooms have more space, and the suite, with its balcony and views across fields, is a treat. The house, once a work house, was painted by Turner and Millais. Local restaurants wait: Webbe's at The Fish Café, The Kings Head in Rye, top notch food at the Curlew in Bodiem. *Minimum stay: 2 nights at weekends & in high season. 3 dog-friendly rooms. Canal towpath to walk along just in front of the hotel. Lots of local walks and places to eat too.*

Rooms	5 doubles, 1 twin/double; 1 double with separate bath: £80-£150. 1 suite for 4: £180. 5 triples: £80-£150. Singles from £60. Extra beds £25 per person. Dogs £7.50.
Meals	Dinner for groups by arrangements (minimum 8 people)
Closed	Rarely.
	Homemade dogs biscuits, towels and drying room.

Mary Sullivan & Hugh Davie
Strand House,
Tanyards Lane, Winchelsea,
Rye, TN36 4JT
Tel +44 (0)1797 226276
Email info@thestrandhouse.co.uk
Web www.thestrandhouse.co.uk

Entry 141 Map 4

The Big Green Bus

A mixture of upcycled furniture, bright retro splashes of colour and original bus features (tickets, please!) the Big Green Bus narrowly escaped destruction before it was rescued by owner Adam. Now enjoying a leisurely retirement in an East Sussex field – apart from a recent starring role in George Clarke's *Amazing Spaces* on Channel 4 – it has oak flooring, painted walls, and a beautifully custom-made kitchen and shower room. All thoroughly modern, it sports chrome LED lights, Farrow & Ball paint, even charging sockets for your iPhone. The log-burner downstairs keeps the whole bus toasty and a boiler ensures you have hot water – a shower on the side of the bus means you can enjoy it outside too! Everyone knows the best views are from the top deck – up here, thick carpet, and two bunks and two comfy doubles in individual sleeping pods are cosy at night. Lounge around on lime green sofas or just enjoy the rural setting within an hour of London – you have plenty of space around the bus itself, and your hosts' house is close by if you need anything. Bring the gang – it's great for groups. *Woodland walks. Dogs not allowed on the top deck.*

Rooms	Bus for 6: from £175 per night. Dogs £25 per dog per stay. Max. 2.
Meals	Self-catering.
Closed	Never.
	Advice on walks.

Canopy & Stars
The Big Green Bus,
Broomham Lane, Wealden, BN8 6JL

Tel	+44 (0)117 204 7830
Email	enquiries@canopyandstars.co.uk
Web	www.canopyandstars.co.uk/biggreenbus

Entry 142 Map 4

The Flint Barns

An extraordinarily beautiful setting in the South Downs with views all the way to the sea… this pioneering English vineyard (take a tour and discover the story) is an unusual place to stay. Find huge style with a homely feel thanks to cheery Ade. More poshtel than hostel, there are chunky doors, reclaimed oak, bedrooms with luxurious mattresses and small sparkling shower rooms. A fabulous communal sitting room has a roaring wood-burner and books; breakfast (and dinner if you want) is at long tables in the lofty dining room: lovingly cooked and local. Spill onto the courtyard for barbecues, walk straight onto the South Downs Way. *Direct access to South Downs Way, Friston Forest close by; beach walks.*

Rooms	3 doubles, 1 twin/double, 1 twin: £95-£150. 1 family room for 3, 3 family rooms for 4, 1 family room for 5: £200-£250. Dogs £5 per night. Max. 2 per booking.
Meals	Dinner, 2 courses, £20. Pubs 2-3 miles.
Closed	Mid-January to mid-February; end of September to end of October.
	Treats, poo bags and advice on walks.

Adrian Lamb
The Flint Barns,
Rathfinny Wine Estate, Alfriston,
Polegate, BN26 5TU
Tel +44 (0)1323 874030
Email flintbarns@rathfinnyestate.com
Web rathfinnyestate.com/flint-barns/

Entry 143 Map 4

The George Townhouse

Celebrate the refurbishment of this gloriously handsome inn with a pint of Brakspear Oxford Gold at the long bar that gleams with speciality gins and wonderful wines. Slap-bang in the centre of pretty Shipston, the George is a treat of a place to eat, drink and be merry. Full of snug corners and private spaces (free to book) for family gatherings, you'll struggle to find a more cheering spot so close to Stratford. Deep blue velvet banquettes, mustard yellow chairs, your choice of log burners to sit beside as you tuck into local menus (pork and beef from award-winning Todenham Manor Farm; artisan bread). Our Welsh rarebit with roasted tomato was excellent, with a hearty mug of potato and leek soup, but you might fancy wild mushroom and tarragon risotto with spring onions and truffled crispy egg, or the locals' favourite fishcakes. Bedrooms are above – some cosy, others spacious – all with kingsize beds, Feather & Black mattresses and blackout blinds to ensure a good night's sleep. The Cotswolds Distillery is nearby, as is the Wychwood Brewery. Smashing. *Dogs free to be anywhere in bar area. 2 dog-friendly rooms. Scenic walk through Tysoe; track and fields.*

Rooms	14 doubles: £100-£180. 1 suite for 2: £200-£240. Extra bed available £20 per person per night. Dogs £20 per night.
Meals	Starters from £5. Lunch from £9. Dinner from £9.
Closed	Rarely.
	Dog biscuits in the bar area and dog bowls available.

Dan Turner
The George Townhouse,
8 High Street,
Shipston-on-Stour, CV36 4AJ
Tel +44 (0)1608 661453
Email book@thegeorgeshipston.co.uk
Web www.thegeorgeshipston.co.uk

Entry 144 Map 3

The Fuzzy Duck

Nestled in the rolling folds of the Cotswold countryside, close to Stratford-upon-Avon, is this 18th-century coaching inn, polished to perfection by Tania, Adrian and their team. Beautiful fireplaces and gleaming tables, fine china and big sprays of wild flowers tell a tale of comfort and luxury, while the smiling staff are rightly proud of this gem of a pub. You dine like kings and queens in the sparkling bar, or in the clever conversion at the back, overlooking grounds that are part-orchard, part-walled-garden. Try Cotswold chicken breast with slow-cooked chorizo and white bean stew, or a splendid ploughman's with warm Scotch quail's egg. For pudding, try the zingy lemon posset, or treacle tart with orange scented milk ice. If you over-indulge, borrow wellies in your size for a bracing walk then back to your beautiful bed above the bar; rooms are sound-proofed and two have double loft beds (up very vertical ladders) for families. Best of all, the generous team has provided indulgent treats: lovely slippers; a nightcap tipple – come prepared to be spoiled. Bliss. *Secure outside garden; lots of walks on the doorstep. Some livestock nearby.*

Rooms	2 doubles: £110-£140. 2 family rooms for 4: £180-£200.
Meals	Starters from £4.50. Mains from £9.95.
Closed	Never.

Dog biscuits, pig's ears, water, dog beds, blankets and advice on walks.

The Manager
The Fuzzy Duck,
Ilmington Road, Armscote,
Stratford-upon-Avon, CV37 8DD
Tel +44 (0)1608 682 635
Email info@fuzzyduckarmscote.com
Web www.fuzzyduckarmscote.com

Entry 145 Map 3

Marston House

A generous feel pervades this lovely family home; Kim's big friendly kitchen is the hub of the house. She and John are easy-going and kind and there's no standing on ceremony. Feel welcomed with tea on arrival, delicious breakfasts, oodles of interesting facts about what to do in the area. The house, with solar electricity, is big and sunny; old rugs cover parquet floors, soft sofas tumble with cushions, sash windows look onto the smart garden packed with birds and borders. Bedrooms are roomy, traditional and supremely comfortable. A special, peaceful place with a big heart, great walks from the door and Silverstone a short hop. *Electric bikes available to rent. Good walks all around but sheep and cattle in the field in summer. Dog-sitting offered.*

Rooms	1 twin/double with separate bath, 1 twin/double with separate shower: £95-£110. Singles £80. Max. 2 dogs.
Meals	Supper, 3 courses, from £30. Dinner £35 (min. 4). Pub 5-minute walk.
Closed	Rarely.
	Dog bed, water bowls, a hose for washing off muddy paws – and a sausage for breakfast.

Kim & John Mahon
Marston House, Byfield Road,
Priors Marston, Southam, CV47 7RP

Tel	+44 (0)1327 260297
Mobile	+44 (0)7813 831028
Email	kim@mahonand.co.uk
Web	www.ivabestbandb.co.uk

Entry 146 Map 3

The Wagon

The unusual craftsmanship and design that have gone into The Wagon reflect, perhaps, the county's history and mysticism. Using the natural forms of Sussex Oak, forester and furniture maker James Noble conjures wonders out of wood. The Wagon is one of them. A carefully crafted living space, it has a comfy bedroom, a mini kitchen with all you need and a seating area, cleverly contrived using a few well placed hinges. Perfect seclusion means that you can swing in the hammock, laze by the lake and shower with only the trees for company – naturists will swoon! During the day, explore some of Britain's most famous archaeological sites, take tea in attractive market towns and walk in miles of rolling countryside. At night, light the barbecue or fire up the clay pizza oven, open the wine and let yourself sink into the comfort of a slower life. There's a lovely walk from Marlborough to Avebury that crosses the Ridgeway – only a few hours each way so you can arrive back in Marlborough for dinner or linger in Avebury for lunch. The Kennet & Avon canal has gentler walks, or cycles, along the tow path. *Lake and river to jump in.*

Rooms	Wagon for 4: £110 per night. Max. 2 dogs.
Meals	Self-catering.
Closed	December – March.

Maps and advice on walks – and towels if required.

Canopy & Stars
The Wagon,
Pewsey, Puckshipton, SN9 6HG
Tel +44 (0)117 204 7830
Email enquiries@canopyandstars.co.uk
Web www.canopyandstars.co.uk/thewagon

Entry 147 Map 3

Bridges Court

You're in the heart of the village with its small shop, friendly pub and the Melvilles' lovely 18th-century farmhouse. It's a comfortable, relaxed home; dogs wander, horses whinny, and there's a beautiful garden to wander with a Kiftsgate rose and a swimming pool for sunny days. On the second floor, off a corridor filled with paintings, are three florally inspired bedrooms: comfortable, bright and spacious with views to the village green. Breakfast leisurely on all things local at the long table in a dining room filled with silver and china. There's a pleasant guests' sitting room to relax in too. *Enclosed walled garden and lots of walks in beautiful countryside. Close to the Badminton estate & Westonbirt Arboretum where dogs are welcome.*

Rooms	1 double; 1 double with separate bath, 1 twin: £90. Singles £65. Discount for 3 nights or more, excluding Badminton w/e.
Meals	Pub in village.
Closed	Rarely.

Dog treats, water bowls, towels for drying, advice on walks – and dog bed if required.

Fiona Melville
Bridges Court,
Luckington, SN14 6NT
Tel +44 (0)1666 840215
Mobile +44 (0)7711 816839
Email fionamelville2003@yahoo.co.uk
Web www.bridgescourt.co.uk

Entry 148 Map 3

Hop Pickers' House

Down winding country lanes in the depths of the Welsh Marches, an Elizabethan farmhouse sitting in nine acres and surrounded by attractive barns. The Hop Pickers' House was used by hop workers, and it sits at right angles to an open barn. Step in to find an airy feel, open-plan upstairs and down, with white walls, old beams, wooden floors and a charming mix of pretty china, comfy chairs, throws and jugs of flowers. The kitchen area is cosy and rustic with a painted dresser, pine table for four and wood-burner (plenty of logs); a welcome hamper includes some local fare and, of course, apple juice. Hop up painted stairs to a big four-poster with diaphanous drapes – be lulled to sleep by the hoot of an owl, the bleat of a lamb. Stroll through woodlands, wild flowers, fern gulley and orchards; rest by a babbling brook. In a distant corner with a view of the setting sun is a makeshift barbecue. The owners are in the farm next door through a rose-strewn pergola but you'll feel very private. Guests will purr with happiness here, and can stock up with food from famous Ludlow only 15 minutes away. A mouth-watering snug of a nest. *Minimum stay: 2 nights. Woodland walks and pretty brooks to explore. 'Doggie' version of guest pack sharing dog-friendly places to eat, drink and walk.*

Rooms	1 cottage for 2: £450-£510 per week.
Meals	Pubs/restaurants 2 miles.
Closed	Never.

Cosy blankets to snuggle up in, towels, dog bowls and poo bags provided.

Steven Hickling & Stephen Snead
Hop Pickers' House,
Berrington, Tenbury Wells, WR15 8TJ
Mobile +44 (0)7736 341906
Email stephensnead@yahoo.co.uk
Web www.brookfarmberrington.org

Entry 149 Map 2

The Coach House

Head for the hills…and the dancing daffodils. In the grounds of a 16th-century timber-framed house, the perfect retreat à deux. Way up a simple track, your stone-walled, stone-tiled hideaway was built almost entirely from reclaimed materials. Inside is open plan and easy. Recline on your leather chesterfield, toes directed at a wood-burner stacked with logs from the woods. The kitchen, of hand-crafted oak, has a double Belfast sink and a sweep of wood floor, the well-dressed bed is to the side, and the shower room is a step away. Follow the brook through this ancient orchid-dotted woodland, rest awhile at the owner's little treehouse (with hammocks), then come home to your own little patch and magnificent views across open pastures to the Teme and Kyre valleys. Venture further to foodie Ludlow, book-lined Hay-on-Wye and the grand industrial heritage that is Ironbridge. Take to the slow life on the steam railway, stride out on the Mortimer Trail, meander through Herefordshire villages. Buzzards soar overhead, rabbits scamper in the fields that surround you. *Seven acres of specially fenced land for carefree scampers and no roads for miles.*

Rooms 1 house for 2: £700 per week.
Meals Self-catering.
Closed Never.

Towels, water bowls and dog treats.

Ellie Van Straaten
The Coach House, Vine Lane, Kyre,
Tenbury Wells, WR15 8RL
Tel +44 (0)1885 410208
Mobile +44 (0)7725 972486
Email ellie_vanstraaten@yahoo.co.uk
Web www.a-country-break.co.uk/coach-house/

Entry 150 Map 2

Long Cover Cottage

Stealing its name from the backdrop of ancient undisturbed woodland, the cottage and its surrounds make a natural family home – for both frazzled humans and local badgers. Winding your way up the long peaceful track to this converted stable, you catch glorious glimpses of the Teme and Kyre valleys; the setting is spectacular. On arrival, you're greeted by the delightful Ellie, whose grounds and beautifully tended English country garden you share. Generous windows flood rooms with light that bounces off polished elm floorboards; a wood-burner and Aga keep things cosy, the kitchen is handcrafted, the views are long and bucolic. Upstairs, bedrooms are brass-bedded and floral, tucked under the eaves in that cottagey way. You get a handy loo and basin up here, and a sparkling bathroom with a roll top tub downstairs. Lucky children have seven acres to romp in, and a secret treehouse with hammocks and a barbecue for midnight feasts. Resting on the borders of three counties, this is prime walking country. Bustling Ledbury and Ludlow, England's Slow Food capital, are just a drive away. *Seven acres of specially fenced land for carefree scampers and no roads for miles.*

Rooms	1 cottage for 6: £900 per week.
Meals	Self-catering.
Closed	Never.
	Towels, dog bowl and dog treats.

Ellie Van Straaten
Long Cover Cottage, Vine Lane, Kyre,
Tenbury Wells, WR15 8RL
Tel +44 (0)1885 410208
Mobile +44 (0)7725 972486
Email ellie_vanstraaten@yahoo.co.uk
Web www.a-country-break.co.uk/long-cover/

Entry 151 Map 2

Cider Mill Cottage

If you want to get off the beaten track, this is the bucolic bolthole for you. A rustic road with beautiful Malvern views ends at a cluster of Victorian farm buildings in a sea of fields. Pleasant, organised owner Catherine – dogs in tow – welcomes you to a neat stone cottage opposite the main house. On the open plan ground floor, sofas cluster around a wood-burner, a small dining table tucked in beside them. The brick and terracotta floor is swathed in Persian rugs, but otherwise the house is decorated with a pared-back elegance, letting the venerable beams and walls sing. At the far end of the room, a Victorian mill wheel is cleverly incorporated into a stylish modern kitchen complete with Aga and welcoming goodies like wine, homemade jam, bread and milk. Up the spiral staircase and you're in the eaves, with space for an armchair on the landing, a cosy double room warmed by the wood-burner flue, a sunny single room and a pristine modern bathroom beneath the beams. Outside, breakfast al fresco on your little patch of lawn, or roam Catherine's beautifully tended garden. *Short breaks available. Fantastic footpaths leading to fields and woods with streams nearby for doggie swimming and splashing. Large private paddock for safe, free runs.*

Rooms	1 cottage for 3: £410-£650 per week. Dogs £15 for 1 large dog or 2 small.
Meals	Pubs serving food nearby.
Closed	Rarely.
	Cosy basket and box of dog treat biscuits.

Catherine Prindezis
Cider Mill Cottage, Ayngstree,
Clifton Upon Teme, WR6 6DS

Tel	+44 (0)1886 812156
Mobile	+44 (0)7590 073084
Email	info@cidermill-cottage.co.uk
Web	www.cidermill-cottage.co.uk

Entry 152 Map 2

Lilla Stugan

Lilla Stugan, or 'little cottage', was inspired by the long summers Martin and Annika spent in their Swedish summer house. And what's not to love about a country that designates whole days to celebrating sugary cakes and buns? To top off these sweet credentials, the hut lives at the bottom of its very own apple orchard and you can try beekeeping or cider making, depending on the season. A private gate leads straight out onto the beautiful Knapp and Papermill Nature Reserve. In warmer months, the orchard is awash with daffodils, blossoming trees, long meadow grasses and rare orchids. Come autumn, the trees are heavy with bright red apples, pears and plums, ripe for picking and juicing. Wander into the trees and you'll stumble across a huge fire pit, complete with a cooking pot to winch your bubbling stews up and down; you can order a dinner hamper – and breakfast one too. Strum the guitar or let the nearby weir and the crackle of the fire be your soundtrack. *Dogs free to roam in orchard; horses & chickens elsewhere on farm. Public footpaths. Mill Race & Leigh Brook for dog swims. Nature reserve with signed woodland walks.*

Rooms	Cabin for 2 (space for extra 2 children on a futon & fold out bed): from £100 per night. £10 per child per night. Dogs £20 per dog per stay. Max. usually 1 dog.
Meals	Self-catering.
Closed	January – March.
	Doggy bed/basket, bowls, hose pipe & towels. 2 butchers within 10 minutes' drive for meaty dog treats (pig's ears & bones can be ordered, by prior arrangement).

Canopy & Stars
Lilla Stugan,
Millham Farm, Millham Lane,
Alfrick, WR6 5HS
Tel +44 (0)117 204 7830
Email enquiries@canopyandstars.co.uk
Web www.canopyandstars.co.uk/lillastugan

Entry 153 Map 2

The Burgoyne Hotel

Reeth is one of those English throwbacks, a beautiful village in the Dales that's hardly changed in 200 years. It was mentioned in the Domesday Book, has the finest grouse moors in the land and its sweeping views over Swaledale stretch for miles. The Burgoyne looks out over it all – afternoon tea in the garden on a sunny day is hard to beat. Inside, an elegant past lives on: a smart drawing room with a crackling fire where you gather for drinks before dinner; a restaurant in racing green where you feast on delicious Yorkshire food; country-house bedrooms full of comfort, with warm colours, good beds, white linen, a sofa if there's room. You'll find pine shutters, cushioned window seats, a four-poster in the old snooker room; all but one has the view. The food is old-school, but utterly delicious, perhaps pheasant and venison terrine, Dover sole with brown shrimps, lemon tart with raspberry sorbet. Best of all are Julia and Mo, who run the place with unstinting kindness. There are maps for walkers, fishing can be arranged, a market passes on Fridays. Richmond is close, too. A delight. *The hotel has 2 black Labs and can give details of walks and pubs that are dog-friendly in the Dales. Dogs are allowed in the sitting rooms.*

Rooms	4 doubles, 1 four-poster, 1 twin; 2 doubles, 1 twin with separate bathrooms: £130-£190. 1 suite for 2: £210. Singles from £112.50. Extra beds for children under 13: £25. Dogs £10 per night. Max. 2 (arrange with hotel if you'd like to bring more).
Meals	Dinner: 2 courses, £27; 4 courses, £40.
Closed	Midweek in January (Mon-Thurs).
	Towels for drying and advice on great walks.

Julia & Mo Usman
The Burgoyne Hotel,
Reeth,
Richmond, DL11 6SN

Tel	+44 (0)1748 884292
Email	enquiries@theburgoyne.co.uk
Web	www.theburgoyne.co.uk

Entry 154 Map 6

The Mollycroft

The Mollycroft is a 1940s showman's living van, restored to gleaming glory and as eccentric as the people who once toured in it. Inside, a combination of dark wood and bright yellow and green décor creates a lively but homely feel. There are sofas in both the living room and the bunk room, which doubles as the kitchen, so you have plenty of space for lazy loafing in this tumbling, spacious wagon. You're far from the '40s in comforts: gas hobs and fridge in the kitchen, mains power and WiFi bring things up-to-date. Next to the Mollycroft is a fire pit complete with cooking gear, and the compost loo and outdoor shower are both a walk away (you're still camping, after all). With no other guests around, it's ideal for families or groups looking for peace, though the three-foot high deck makes it unsuitable for toddlers. The grounds hold rare bamboo gardens, a lake, and your host Greville has converted a chapel to display his modern art collection. Head off into the stunning Yorkshire Dales; don't miss the enormous Sunday market at Catterick racecourse – or the races, or course. *Secure garden, woodland and lakes. Dogs must be kept on lead.*

Rooms	Wagon for 4: from £95 per night. Max. 2 dogs.
Meals	Self-catering.
Closed	Never.

A lake for dog swimming, lovely walks on site, and a contained two-acre bamboo garden for comfort and safety.

Canopy & Stars
The Mollycroft,
Saint Paulinus, Brough Park,
Tunstall, DL10 7PJ

Tel	+44 (0)117 204 7830
Email	enquiries@canopyandstars.co.uk
Web	www.canopyandstars.co.uk/themollycroft

Entry 155 Map 6

A Place in the Pines

Matt is the brains behind these forest hideaways. He scoured the mountains of Switzerland in search of canvas-topped inspiration. He found that nothing quite beats waking up in the forest to the smell of stovetop coffee and bacon, with a day of trudging unknown lands ahead. And, lucky for you, he also scribbled down hot baths and homemade sloe gin on his list of must-haves. Easy to get to, not far off the main road, the four safari tents – all about 60 metres apart – each have their own personality. The super-stoves inside don't stop at keeping the whole family warm all night, they can slow cook a joint at the same time! It doesn't have to be Easter for an egg hunt here: you can collect your breakfast from the hens most mornings or pick up duck eggs from the honesty box by the pond. The sheep, pigs and ponies in the next field appreciate the odd carrot or apple on your way past too. Hop over the fence to explore the glorious Yorkshire Moors. If you go in August, you can glimpse local farmers battling it out for the title of longest pod of sugar peas or heaviest courgette at the famous Osmotherley show. *Site fenced off & away from roads. North Yorkshire Moors, streams for dogs to paddle in; advice on walks; local pubs all dog-friendly. Dogs on leads in some areas.*

Rooms	4 safari tents for 5: £120 per night. Dogs £10 per dog per stay. Max. 2.
Meals	Self-catering.
Closed	January – March.

Advice on walks and suggestions of local dog-friendly pubs.

Canopy & Stars
A Place in the Pines,
Keepers Cottage, Thimbleby, DL6 3PY

Tel	+44 (0)117 204 7830
Email	enquiries@canopyandstars.co.uk
Web	www.canopyandstars.co.uk/aplaceinthepines

Entry 156 Map 6

The Hayloft at Flamborough Rigg

On and on the road goes, deeper into the woods until the single track stops at an 1820s farmhouse surrounded by open fields. The gravelled drive crunches nicely under the tyres and the kitchen sports a hamper of local goodies (and, on occasion, home-brewed elderflower champagne!). Philip and Caroline love making guests feel at home and you may freely roam their super big garden with orchard, vegetable patch, loungers and barbecue. You can head off for a long walk over the rolling North Yorkshire Moors and come back to deep comfort. Snuggle up with a book in front of the wood-burner, watch a DVD, play a round of cards at the chunky table. There are quirky touches like old Singer sewing machines as table bases, a shelf of vintage china in the well-thought out kitchen/diner, and modern art on the walls. The bedrooms feel light and fresh with local oak furniture and cheerful cushions. Jump in the car for a trip to the coast or wander round the charming market town of Helmsley. The Hayloft feels as though it's in the middle of nowhere and yet moors, dales and the sea are wonderfully close. *Short breaks available. Large fully enclosed garden.*

Rooms	1 barn for 4: £595-£695 per week. Dogs no charge.
Meals	Pub within 3 miles.
Closed	Rarely.

A guide to local dog-friendly pubs and beaches.

Philip & Caroline Jackson
The Hayloft at Flamborough Rigg,
Middlehead Road, Stape,
Pickering, YO18 8HR
Tel +44 (0)1751 475263
Email enquiries@flamboroughriggcottage.co.uk
Web www.thehayloftatflamboroughrigg.co.uk

Entry 157 Map 6

Little Garth

In the gentle foothills of the North York Moors, four miles from the market town of Kirkbymoorside, lies Normanby, an ancient settlement blessed with a Norman church and a trout stream. And, tucked behind the village street, through the picket gate, this immaculate little cottage. Having swapped a farmhouse in the Lakes for Little Garth, Pippa has poured love into its revival. Now all is light, warm and cosy inside, with plenty of pretty things to catch the eye: old paintings, quirky pots, cheerful rugs on polished flagged floors. Fresh flowers glow on old pine tops, cotton-covered armchairs are deep and comfortable, and a super, bright, light kitchen with all the kit opens to a very private rose and honeysuckle garden. After a day's roaming the sheep-speckled moors, bliss to snuggle down here. Light the candles, throw another log on the fire, pop the cork, or stroll to the pub for a drink. For eating out, Pippa recommends The Sun Inn at Normanby, a short walk. Return to sweetly floral bedrooms with gleaming white woodwork and generously clad beds. A lovely, very comfy hideaway. *Minimum stay: 3 nights. Secure garden.*

Rooms	1 house for 5: £320-£700 per week. Max. 2 dogs.
Meals	Self-catering.
Closed	Never.
	Dog bowl.

Pippa Galloway
Little Garth,
Normanby, Sinnington,
York, YO62 6RH
Tel +44 (0)1904 431876
Email p.galloway@talk21.com
Web www.holidaycottage-normanby.co.uk

Entry 158 Map 6

Lodge Cottages

Two sweet escapes for two. One is tucked next to Rick and Sue's house in a quiet village, its charming roses-and-hollyhocks exterior does not disappoint and inside it's romantic with low beams and sheepskin rugs. Step straight into the low-beamed sitting room (tall folk beware) with its soft colours, bright gingham armchair and cream wood-burner. There's a smart kitchen, a table-for-two and upstairs a dove-grey bedroom with soft rugs on painted floorboards. The other is a little loft conversion at the bottom of the garden. A secret path lined with espaliered apple trees and tubs of flowers takes you to a dinky private courtyard. Walk through a glass door into a contemporary space: an open plan dining area and kitchen with upcycled furniture, pretty porcelain plates and a soft grey colour scheme enlivened with zingy limes and pinks. Vases burst with fresh flowers and skylights let in the light. Upstairs to your cosy double and funky en suite. Rick is a chef and it shows: for lazy suppers he can prepare meals to re-heat or you can slip next door to the pub. Ripon Cathedral and Harrogate's spa town are nearby or take bracing walks on the NorthYork Moors. *Short breaks available. Plenty of wonderful walks locally, and pub right next door which is very dog-friendly!*

Rooms 2 cottages for 2: £450-£600 per week.
Meals Dinner, 3 courses, £25.
Closed Never.

Advice on walks, and a lovely nature reserve just 2 minutes from the cottages.

Sue & Rick Hodgson
Lodge Cottages,
1 Lodge Cottage,
Main Street, Staveley
Tel +44 (0)1423 340700
Email info@lodgecottages.co.uk
Web www.lodgecottages.co.uk

Entry 159 Map 6

Bewerley Hall Cottage

Pretty pretty pretty! Once the home of Bewerley Hall's head gardener, this couple's hideaway is comfy, cute and at the tail of a terrace of stone cottages. Step in to a sitting room that envelops you in cheering warmth: a wood-burner in the inglenook; two squishy red sofas dotted with cushions; a bookcase brimming with books, an iPod dock, guides and maps. For muddy wellies there's a boot room, and next to this, a cottagey kitchen. Upstairs is a double with excellent linen and lovely views over cherry trees and the village green, and a bathroom with slipper bath and local lotions. On sunny days, follow the sun front or back, dine out and soak up the views over Bewerley Park, the river and town beyond. Walk from the door, along the river Nidd or to How Stean limestone gorge; you're in beautiful Nidderdale and the Yorkshire Dales are a few miles away. Explore by foot, bike or horse – a mountain bike centre and stables are nearby – and well-behaved dogs are welcome (downstairs). For a more sedate ramble, stroll to charming Pateley Bridge (5 minutes) and pick up your dinner – there's a deli, butchers and a good pub. Perfect. *Minimum stay: 3 nights. Great walks from the door, dog-friendly pubs along the way!*

Rooms	1 cottage for 2: £475-£650 per week. Dogs £20 per stay. Max. 2.
Meals	Pub within walking distance.
Closed	Never.
	Dog treats upon arrival.

Denise & Nigel McConnell
Bewerley Hall Cottage, 9 The Green,
Bewerley, Pateley Bridge, HG3 5HU

Tel	+44 (0)1765 658565
Mobile	+44 (0)7966 560716
Email	denisemcconnell11@gmail.com
Web	www.cottageinbewerley.com

Entry 160 Map 6

Gamekeepers Cottage & Cross Cottage

Gorgeous countryside in this neck of the woods, rolling and lush, with sheep round every corner. The house, cottages and six acres of orchard and paddock stand on their own, with heart-stopping views. Warm smiling Louise lives in the main house, keeps hens, ducks and geese and is passionate about North Yorkshire. Two stunning cottages – one new, though you'd never know it – with rug-cosy, stone-flagged sitting rooms and kitchens to love. The style is an enticing mix of modern and vintage: smartly upholstered wing chairs, a squishy old chesterfield, a fine pine cupboard. Gamekeepers Cottage has two bedrooms downstairs and a master up top. We loved the ground-floor double bedroom, calming and cosy, but the top suite is a wow, with a French-style bed. Cross Cottage has two charming ground-floor bedrooms. Snuggle up by the wood-burner for a cosy night in with a basket of logs; in summer, drift onto the patio (each cottage has its own garden) with furniture, barbecue and views. As for pubs, you're spoilt: the Coach & Horses at Bolton by Bowland, the Inn at Whitewell, the Spread Eagle at Sawley. Lovely. *See owner's website for availability. Minimum stay: 3 nights on weekdays; 7 in high season. Secure garden and dog-specific walks; livestock at property so dogs on leads.*

Rooms	1 cottage for 4: £399-£949 per week. 1 cottage for 6: £499-£1,199 per week. Short breaks available October-March. Dogs £30 per stay. Max. 2.
Meals	Self-catering.
Closed	Rarely.
	Blankets, throws, treats and bowls. Dog tags with our phone number; hose for cleaning muddy paws and towels for drying off.

Louise & Stephen McAneny
Wigglesworth House, Becks Brow,
Wigglesworth, BD23 4SA
Tel +44 (0)1729 840168
Mobile +44 (0)7715 459330
Email info@wigglesworthhouseandcottages.co.uk
Web www.wigglesworthhouseandcottages.co.uk

Entry 161 Map 6

The Traddock

A northern outpost of country-house charm, beautiful inside and out. It's a family affair and those looking for a friendly base from which to explore the Dales will find it here. You enter through the drawing room – crackling fire, pretty art, the daily papers, cavernous sofas. Potter about and find polished wood in the dining room, panelled walls in the breakfast room, then William Morris wallpaper in the sitting room bar, where you can sip a pint of Skipton ale while playing Scrabble. Bedrooms are gorgeous, some coolly contemporary, others warmly traditional. The star of the show is the new suite – sand-blasted timbers, a lovely big sofa, a stunning free-standing bath – but all are charming, with chic fabrics, warm colours, comfy beds and the odd claw-foot bath. Downstairs, a white-washed sitting room opens onto the garden for afternoon tea, while delicious food waits in the restaurant, perhaps seafood chowder, braised lamb shank, apple and calvados mousse. Walks start at the front door, there are cycle tracks, even caves to explore (one is bigger than St Paul's). Unbeatable. *Minimum stay: 2 nights on weekends March-November. Walks from the door in the Yorkshire Dales National Park.*

Rooms	8 doubles, 1 twin/double: £95-£165. 2 suites for 2: £180-£235. 2 family rooms for 4: £95-£175. Dinner, B&B £85-£160 per person. Extra bed/sofabed £25 p.p.p.n. Dogs £5. Max. 2 per room (some only 1).
Meals	Lunch from £9.50. Dinner, 3 courses, around £30. Picnics from £7.50. Afternoon tea from £15.95.
Closed	Never.
	Towels for drying and advice on walks.

Paul Reynolds
The Traddock,
Austwick, Settle, LA2 8BY
Tel +44 (0)15242 51224
Email info@thetraddock.co.uk
Web www.thetraddock.co.uk

Entry 162 Map 6

Stow House

Past ancient stone walls and fields of lambs you reach sleepy Aysgarth and this dignified rectory. Step inside to find – Shoreditch pizzazz! Sarah and Phil have swapped the world of London advertising for a dream house in the Dales; she does cocktails, he does breakfasts and their take on Victoriana is inspiring. Floors, banisters and sash windows have been restored, stairs carpeted in plush red, sofas covered in zinging velvet. Bathrooms are wow, bedrooms are soothing and the papier mâché hare's head above the bar says it all. A stroll down the hill are the Aysgarth Falls, beloved of Ruskin, Wordsworth and Turner. *Minimum stay: 2 nights at weekends. Magnificent walks and big garden. Owners to keep dogs on a lead when walking through livestock.*

Rooms	6 doubles: £110-£175. 1 family room for 3: £110-£175. Extra bed/sofabed £10-£20 per person per night. Max. 1 dog per room.
Meals	Pubs/restaurants 5-minute walk.
Closed	January & occasionally.
	Raw beef bones from the butcher, great dog walks, and towels.

Sarah & Phil Bucknall
Stow House,
Aysgarth, Leyburn, DL8 3SR
Tel +44 (0)1969 663635
Email info@stowhouse.co.uk
Web www.stowhouse.co.uk

Entry 163 Map 6

Pubs-for-a-pint

When you're away on a break with your dog it's handy to have a list of dog-friendly pubs to visit for a pint or a snack. Here is a small selection of pubs in England that welcome dogs in at least one area of the pub – most likely to be by the fire, at the bar or in the garden. Most pubs, though – even the dog-friendly ones – draw the line at allowing dogs in dining rooms, but if you want to check the details beforehand just give them a call.

We've visited each of these pubs and written about them ourselves. They're here because we like them. (We've not inspected any bedrooms they may have.) They are all taken from our hugely popular *Pubs & Inns of England & Wales* guide. Now in its fourteenth edition, this guide brings you a huge variety of pubs from the charming to the rustic and the real-aled to the Michelin-starred. Visit www.sawdays.co.uk/bookshop to buy the guide.

Here is an explanation of the symbols you'll find at the foot of each Pub's entry. They apply to bar areas.

- Wheelchair access to both bar and wcs.
- Children of all ages welcome in parts of pub (highchairs not necessarily available).
- Credit cards accepted, most commonly Visa and MasterCard.
- Pub serves four or more hand pumped ales.
- Pub serves eight or more wines by the glass.
- Wireless internet access available in the bar.

Photo: Elsie Esq

Bedfordshire

Pub

The George Inn

A well-heeled pub in a large, leafy Bedfordshire village: this 16th-century building, all newly spruced up, is encircled by ancient Maulden Wood and you're perfectly placed for yomping part (or all 40 miles!) of the Greensand Ridge Walk. Julian and Emma have always lived locally, they noticed that The George needed rescuing, snapped it up and have worked hard to transform it into a smart, funky pub. Lewis and his young, energetic team run the place with good humour. The kitchen turns out hearty, wholesome lunches and evening meals, Sunday roasts, and pizza night is always busy. There's a gin bar, ales on tap, wines by the glass and you can choose to cosy up by a roaring wood-burner or dine in the conservatory. *The pub is slap bang in the middle of The Greensand Ridge Walk – longest in the UK and great for walkers! Dogs welcome in all areas except restaurant at the back.*

Meals Starters from £5.
Lunch & dinner from £9.50.
Closed Open all day.

Dog biscuits on the bar, beef bone and pig's ears, water bowls and hose for washing off muddy paws.

Lewis Johnson
The George Inn,
6 George Street,
Maulden MK45 2DF
Tel +44 (0)1525 841559
Email info@thegeorgemaulden.com
Web www.thegeorgemaulden.com

Entry 163.1 Map 3

Brighton & Hove

Pub

The Ginger Dog

This gem of a pub is tucked away in Brighton's trendy Kemptown just a short stroll from the promenade. The Gingerman group have nailed it again with another trendy, chilled out, friendly sort of place. Expect hearty, traditional-with-a-modern-twist fare: beef jerky popcorn, mushroom soup with cep powder and parmesan, braised ox cheek with bone marrow polenta, and some very moreish liquid desserts! Outside it's an attractive townhouse – inside find classic stripped floorboards, a wood panelled bar and a wood-burner juxtaposed with interesting art (for sale) and bright red leather banquet seating. There's a mix of locals and out-of-towners who come to sample the menu or just for a drink, there's an exciting selection of local ales, wines and spirits. And the best of Brighton is right here: hit the arcades and the pier or shop till you drop. *Nice and blowy seafront walks.*

Meals Starters from £7.
Mains from £13.50.
Desserts from £7.50.
Closed 2.30pm-3pm.

Water bowls and treats, and a warm open fire in the winter months which dogs love.

Ben McKeller
The Ginger Dog,
12 College Place,
Brighton, BN2 1HN
Tel +44 (0)1273 620990
Email gingerdog@gingermanrestaurants.com
Web www.thegingerdog.com

Entry 164 Map 2

Bristol

Pub

The Pump House

Meander through the boatyards and find this grand ex-Victorian pumping station, with chef Toby Gritten at the helm. Inside: cool stone floors, high ceilings and big arched windows frame gorgeous views. Local guest beers and ales abound, but it's the gins that really pack a punch: there are over 400! Just ask the cool, young bar staff to guide your choosing. Upstairs it's both formal and fun; foodies travel far and wide to sample the tasting menu. Try seared Brixham scallops with sweetcorn and chicken wings, belly of suckling pig pork with apples, leeks and coco beans, then finish with a Tahitian vanilla brûlée. In summer, catch some rays out on the lavender-framed courtyard, tuck into a hearty ploughman's, watch the boats sail past, and see how many famous landmarks you can spot. The SS Great Britain and M Shed are close. *On the Bristol cycle network which is a great walk. Two pub dogs, Minnie and Scooby.*

Meals Starters from £5. Mains from £15.
Closed Open all day.

Dog bowls available at all times.

Toby Gritten
The Pump House,
Merchants Road, Hotwells,
Bristol, BS8 4PZ
Tel +44 (0)117 927 2229
Email info@the-pumphouse.com
Web www.the-pumphouse.com

Entry 165 Map 2

Buckinghamshire

Pub

The Royal Oak

The old whitewashed cottage stands in a hamlet on the edge of the common – hard to believe that Marlow is just a mile away. It's a thriving dining pub (and sister pub to the Alford Arms, Herts). Beyond the terrace is a stylish open-plan bar, cheerful with cream-coloured walls, fresh flowers, rug-strewn boards, cushioned pews and crackling log fires. Order a pint of local Rebellion and check out the daily chalkboard or printed menu. You might start with breaded Cornish fishcake slider, mashed peas and tartar sauce before tucking into slow-cooked breaded lamb croquettes with sticky braised red cabbage, creamy mash and mint, saving room for lemon posset with hedgerow fruits and brandy snap cream. The sprawling gardens are perfect for a summer game of table tennis on the lawn. *Just down the road from beautiful Marlow Common. Dogs welcome in the bar.*

Meals Lunch & dinner £11.75-£19.75.
Closed Open all day.

A huge garden to run around in. Dog biscuits on the bar, fresh water bowls outside and a large OS map by the front door. Lovely circular walk on iFootpath.

David & Becky Salisbury
The Royal Oak,
Frieth Road, Bovingdon Green,
Marlow, SL7 2JF
Tel +44 (0)1628 488611
Email info@royaloakmarlow.co.uk
Web www.royaloakmarlow.co.uk

Entry 166 Map 3

Buckinghamshire

Pub

The White Horse

In tiny Hedgerley village is a perfectly preserved slice of unspoiled pubbery. Whitewashed brick, horseshoes and cartwheels peer from shrubbery and window baskets, illuminated by ancient gas lamps on both street and façade. Inside, exposed wood is overlaid by carpet, while endless beams and supports for low ceilings are festooned with artefacts. As a serious ale house, seven ever-changing beers are drawn direct from cask and served via a hatch, the selection rotating on a seasonal basis. Food is from a pre deep-fryer age with ploughman's, quiches, cold meats and baps displayed at a chilled counter alongside the odd hot option of chunky lamb broth or maybe pheasant Wellington. A busy garden and marquee are a treat in summer – and house an aviary of finches. *Large garden and plenty of fields and woods for walking; bird sanctuary nearby.*

Meals Lunch £6-£10.
No food in evenings.

Closed Mon-Fri 2.30pm-5pm.
Open all day Sat & Sun.

Dog biscuits, bowls of water and open fires to snooze by.

Doris Hobbs & Kevin Brooker
The White Horse,
Village Lane,
Hedgerley,
Slough, SL2 3UY
Tel +44 (0)1753 643225
Email janet_brooker@yahoo.co.uk

Entry 167 Map 3

Cambridgeshire

Pub

The Blue Ball Inn

The Blue Ball takes its name from one of the first hot air balloons, which landed nearby in the 1750s. Ideally placed, with Granchester Meadows for a front garden and views across the river to the spires of Cambridge's colleges, this pretty country pub is thriving under the care of Toby and Angela. Taking pride of place in a row of cottages, the Blue Ball's bright whitewashed walls, bay window and flowing flower baskets is postcard-perfect. Inside all is spotless, scrubbed and poised to welcome hungry locals, walkers, twitchers and tourists. Tuck into shepherd's pie topped with cheese crusted leeks, or a bowl of hearty soup with a sandwich. At the back, a heated pavilion, shrine to the local cricket team, where you can while away a happy afternoon with a pint of Aspall's Harry Sparrow cider. Stroll across the Meadows to spend the day in Cambridge. *Fenced dog-proof back garden; river 200 yards.*

Meals Starters from £4. Lunch from £9.
Mains from £9.

Closed Open all day.

A dogs welcome sign at the front of the pub, dog biscuits behind the bar and bowls at the front door and in the back garden.

Toby Joseph
The Blue Ball Inn,
Broadway, Grantchester,
Cambridge, CB3 9NQ
Tel +44 (0)1223 846004
Email info@blueballgrantchester.co.uk
Web www.blueballgrantchester.co.uk

Entry 168 Map 4

Cheshire

Pub

The Three Greyhounds Inn

The bright, many-bottled bar winks and glows as you enter, while host Michael has a welcome for all. Fat purple cushions soften wooden benches around a huge dual-facing fireplace; reach for the 'Brandy Bible' and settle in. The clever layout makes the space cosy and intimate, with snugs around every corner – four with firesides – and nooks and crannies aplenty. Michael is proud of the atmosphere, and rightly so. Families nibble and natter with relish, while walkers and couples take their time over delicious smoked haddock and leek tart or pan-fried lamb's kidneys. During annual Cheshire Game Week you can tuck into dishes such as pheasant breast with sautéed white pudding and red leg partridge croquette.... Deep in the Cheshire countryside, this well-restored pub is conveniently close to the M6. *A secure garden and great walk around Shakerley Mere next to the pub.*

Meals	Lunch & dinner from £10.50. Bar meals from £5.95.
Closed	Open all day.
	Dog biscuits, dogs' dinner menu, Doggie Beer and water bowls. Shakerley Mere bird nature reserve walks, and a play in enclosed extensive gardens.

Michael Kettle
The Three Greyhounds Inn,
Holmes Chapel Road, Allostock,
Knutsford, WA16 9JY
Tel +44 (0)1565 723455
Email info@thethreegreyhoundsinn.co.uk
Web www.thethreegreyhoundsinn.co.uk

Entry 169 Map 6

Cheshire

Pub

The Bull's Head

You feel the warmth as soon as you walk through the door. Candles glow on the tables of this pretty village pub, fires crackle, and the staff couldn't be nicer. Under a low-beamed ceiling, seven hand pumps dispense the finest local ales from Storm, Wincle and Redwillow as well as the inimitable Mobberley Wobbly – ale is king! Add in a Highland extravaganza of over 100 whiskies and other tempting brews and you have the makings of a celebration. Chef Andy cooks 'pub classics from the heart' with full English flavours; the steak and ale pie is a fully encased masterpiece in itself, and the Irish whisky sticky toffee pudding too indulgent for words. With outside tables for sunny days, this is as good as it gets for a village pub. *A garden for dogs and the Whisky Snug. Beautiful Mobberley walk. Dog show every August: Saturday of the Bank holiday weekend or National Dog Day.*

Meals	Bar meals £2.85-£12. Lunch £3.95-£19.95. Sunday lunch £13.95.
Closed	Open all day.
	Biscuits on the bar, water bowls and Doggie Beer. A good pub walk between The Bull's Head and The Church Inn.

Barry Lawlor
The Bull's Head,
Mill Lane,
Mobberley, WA16 7HX
Tel +44 (0)1565 873395
Email info@thebullsheadpub.co.uk
Web www.thebullsheadpub.co.uk

Entry 170 Map 6

Cheshire

Pub

The Church Inn

Tim Bird and Mary McLaughlin's mini-pub empire continues to thrive and grow with the addition of the 18th-century Church Inn. Sister pub to the Bull's Head, also in Mobberley, it has been fully restored and refurbished, retaining the small intimate dining rooms with their wood and tiled floors, exposed brick and beams, soft lamplight, and glowing candles. On a wild winter's day it's hard to leave, with four craft ales on tap and decent wines to quaff and some great food: sautéed lamb's kidneys followed by grilled hake with tarragon and white wine sauce, then a sticky date bread and butter pud. Or try lighter lunch and afternoon dishes like smoked haddock tart or a sirloin steak sandwich with roast tomatoes and chips. Summer terraces give views of the church or across rolling fields. A village gem. *A secure terrace and garden. Own pub walk, lots more nearby and you can walk to sister pub in the village, the Bull's Head.*

Meals Lunch & dinner £15-£24.95.
Closed Open all day.

Dog bowls, dog biscuits and Doggie Beer too. A great pub walk, and extensive gardens and terrace to play in.

Simon Umpleby
The Church Inn,
Church Lane, Mobberley,
Knutsford, WA16 7RD
Tel +44 (0)1565 873178
Email info@churchinnmobberley.co.uk
Web www.churchinnmobberley.co.uk

Entry 171 Map 6

Cornwall

Pub

The Halsetown Inn

Built by a Victorian philanthropist in 1831 this inn has impeccable eco credentials and has won awards for its efforts. Inside, comfort and character abound with a choice of cosy corners, two open fires, an old Cornish range, and deep red walls. Tuck into the likes of pan-fried scallops with caramelised cauliflower and apple, followed by slow roasted pork belly with black pudding and cheddar hash brown, spring greens, cider gravy and onion rings. Leave room for puddings, especially rosewater panna cotta with pistachio biscotti. Vegetarians are well-served, children have their own menu, and monthly Wine and Dine evenings draw a happy crowd. You can walk from St Ives if the spirit moves you, then sit at the bar with a pint of Doom Bar or Skinner's ale or even a Cornish gin or a pastis! A pub with huge soul and great character. *We have a large field where dogs can round around and let off steam.*

Meals Starters from £3.
Lunch & dinner from £11.
Closed Rarely.

Dog treats and water bowls.

Julia & Stuart Knight
The Halsetown Inn,
Halestown,
St Ives, TR26 3NA
Tel +44 (0)1736 795583
Email info@halsetowninn.co.uk
Web www.halsetowninn.co.uk

Entry 172 Map 1

Gloucestershire

Pub

The Amberley Inn

Wend your way up Culver Hill to this impressive 1820 stone inn. The Amberley, encircled by National Trust AONB, has an enviable setting in the heart of the Cotswolds. Walkers and cyclists will be happy here; waggy friends are welcome too. Enter through the reception into an enticing bar area: oak panelled walls, parquet floors, open fireplaces, light pouring through lead windows. Hang out in the snug; eat in the bar or the more formal dining room, perhaps decent pub grub – burgers, pies, sandwiches; or opt for bistro-style dishes like whitebait with homemade tartar sauce, salt and pepper squid, rump of lamb with dauphinoise, steaks – much of the menu is gluten-free. There's a good selection of draught ales and ciders and heaps of books and games. Jane and Trevor gave up busy London lives, sailed the Med, and then chose this pub as their next project – and what a success it is! *Surrounded by NT Minchinhampton Common: 450 acres of lovely walks. Pub garden well-enclosed.*

Meals Starters from £4.95.
Lunch from £10.95.
Mains from £10.95.

Closed 2pm-6pm on weekdays.

Homemade biscuit in room. Water bowls, advice on walks, poo bags. Hose for mucky paws, towels after a good shake. Lounge bar & snug area for doggy dining – gluten-free breakfast sausages sometimes!

Jane & Trevor Bandey
The Amberley Inn,
Culver Hill, Amberley,
Stroud, GL5 5AF
Tel +44 (0)1453 872565
Email jane@theamberleyinn.co.uk
Web www.theamberleyinn.co.uk

Entry 173 Map 3

Gloucestershire

Pub

The Holford Arms

At the side of the long road that takes you into Tetbury sits this unassuming country inn with its shabby whitewashed exterior hiding more secrets than you can shake a stick at. Owners Pete and Tor have worked a special magic here. Whether it's building more stylish 'shacks' in the big field at the back, or pressing their own apples, they have a way with food, drink and atmosphere which would be the envy of many a new pub entrepreneur. Their hands-on approach means the little inn buzzes with happy locals and nature lovers who've popped in for a pint or a Sunday roast after exploring nearby Westonbirt Arboretum. Inside, all is snug and homely. The bar winks with bottles, or try one of the local ales. Young chefs serve up tasty classics and treats; on Wednesdays you can tuck into a three-course Thai feast for a bargain price. *Seven-acre garden and minutes away from wonderful walks in Westonbirt Arboretum.*

Meals Starters from £5. Lunch from £10.
Mains from £15.

Closed Christmas.

Dog treats and a water bowl.

Pete Heathcock
The Holford Arms,
Knockdown,
Tetbury, GL8 8QY
Tel +44 (0)1454 238669
Email info@theholfordarms.co.uk
Web www.theholfordarms.co.uk

Entry 174 Map 3

Hertfordshire

Pub

The Alford Arms

It isn't easy to find, so come armed with precise directions before you set out! In a hamlet enfolded by acres of National Trust common land, David and Becky Salisbury's gastropub is worth any number of missed turns. Inside are two interlinked rooms, bright and airy, with soft colours, scrubbed pine tables, wooden and tile floors. Food is taken seriously and ingredients are as organic, free-range and delicious as can be. You might start with grilled Cornish mackerel, Bucksum Farm beetroot and horseradish salsa then move onto rabbit leg bourguignon with smoked pancetta and creamy mash, saving room for coconut panna cotta and crispy malt loaf. Wine drinkers have the choice of 22 by the glass; service is informed and friendly. Arrive early on a warm day to take your pick of the tables on the sun-trapping front terrace. *Path into Ashridge Forest opposite, with thousands of acres of beautiful ancient beech woods. Dogs welcome in bar.*

Meals Lunch, bar meals & dinner £11.75-£19.75.

Closed Open all day.

Dog biscuits on the bar, fresh water bowls outside and a large OS map by the front door. Lovely circular walk on iFootpath.

David & Becky Salisbury
The Alford Arms,
Frithsden,
Hemel Hempstead, HP1 3DD
Tel +44 (0)1442 864480
Email info@alfordarmsfrithsden.co.uk
Web www.alfordarmsfrithsden.co.uk

Entry 175 Map 3

Northamptonshire

Pub

The Plough

It's a family affair here at The Plough; farmer owners Kim and Stephen keep sheep nearby and sell vintage furniture in the barn next door, leaving the bar in the capable hands of Uncle Barry. A seasoned, old-fashioned landlord and CAMRA-award winner, he welcomes both locals and strangers like old friends. Inside, character oozes: find a cosy log burner and open fire, exposed stone walls, quarry tiles and high wooden chairs at the bar. Ales change often but Doom Bar and Proper Job are regulars. The menus are short and locally-sourced: lunch on tart Provençal, dine on Everdon beef Bourguignon with dauphinoise potatoes, indulge in a treacle tart if you've room. The garden is a delight, with views for miles across the countryside, and there's a play area for little ones; all are warmly welcomed here. *Beautiful walks, short and long; when the bluebells are out in Everdon Stubbs people come from far and wide to walk through the woods.*

Meals Starters from £5.50.
Lunch from £4.95.
Dinner from £11.95.

Closed Open all day.

Water bowls inside and out. Solid floors throughout the pub so we are never fazed by muddy paws.

Kim Hopewell
The Plough,
High Street,
Everdon, NN11 3BL
Tel +44 (0)1327 361606
Email theploughinn.everdon@icloud.com
Web theploughinneverdon.com

Entry 176 Map 3

Somerset

Pub

The Bird in Hand

The Bird in Hand is an unassuming little pub on Long Ashton's high street. Enter the bar, sparkling and new, for a pint of Gem or the guest ale of the week; turn right for plain tables and deep blue-grey walls. Owner Toby Gritten is as excited about foraged ingredients as he is about 'heritage vegetables, forgotten cuts and wild fish', and his sentiments are echoed by those of head chef Sylvester and manager Dominic. Elegant dishes are served on white plates by friendly staff – chargrilled tenderstem broccoli, soft boiled duck egg, Berkswell cheese; haunch of wild venison, juniper, carrots, fondant potato; figgy pudding, stout and toffee sauce, cinnamon ice cream. Come on Sunday for champagne rhubarb fizz and a choice of two roasts, or gnocchi with artichokes and salsify. The food is satisfying, unshowy and steeped in flavour. *On the Bristol cycle network which provides a great walk with a dog. Two pub dogs, Minnie and Scooby.*

Meals Lunch & dinner from £9.
Sunday lunch from £12.50.
Closed Open all day (from 12pm).

Dog bowls available at all times.

Liz Pursey
The Bird in the Hand,
17 Weston Road,
Long Ashton, BS41 9LA
Tel +44 (0)1275 395 222
Email info@bird-in-hand.co.uk
Web www.bird-in-hand.co.uk

Entry 177 Map 2

Staffordshire

Pub

The Fitzherbert Arms

In the old village of Swynnerton on Lord Stafford's estate is the once-forlorn Fitzherbert, all spruced up. If you've visited before you're in for a surprise: bar, lounge and snug entwine with an open-plan feel, warmed by three delicious fires. A friendly vivacious team makes the place tick as they ferry platefuls of flavoursome food to elegant tables: seafood platters, steak and stout pies, crumbles, brownies and port-poached pears. They do a great line in comfort food, have a good list of local suppliers, and Staffordshire ales star at the pumps. There are 30 ports (more than any other pub in the country!), 16 wines by the glass and a real cider, too: something to be proud of. The 1818 building once held a forge and the Anvil Room is enticing: leather wingback chairs, a forge-like fire, hops above a soft-lit wall. *Autumn and winter pub walk available, enclosed garden, dogs welcome in the main bar area and snug.*

Meals Bar snacks from £3.
Starters from £5.75.
Mains from £12.95.
Closed Open all day.

Dog biscuit, water bowls and Doggie Beer.

Leanne Wallis
The Fitzherbert Arms,
Swynnerton,
Stone, ST15 0RA
Tel +44 (0)1782 796782
Email info@fitzherbertarms.co.uk
Web fitzherbertarms.co.uk

Entry 178 Map 6

Suffolk

Pub

The Westleton Crown

This is one of England's oldest coaching inns, with 800 years of continuous service under its belt. It stands in a village two miles inland from the sea at Dunwich, with Westleton Heath running east towards Minsmere RSPB Nature Reserve. Inside, stripped floors, smouldering fires, exposed brickwork and ancient beams sweep you back in time. Weave about and find nooks and crannies in which to hide, flames flickering in open fires, a huge map on the wall for walkers. You can eat in the conservatory amid big photos of local landscapes; in summer doors open onto a terraced garden for barbecues in the sun. Fish comes straight off the boats at Lowestoft, local butchers provide local meat, so try ham hock and pigeon terrine, filet of sea bass with a cockle chowder, dark chocolate fondant with pistachio ice cream. Aldeburgh and Southwold are close. *All year round dog-friendly beach just 3 miles away.*

Meals Lunch from £5.50.
Dinner, 3 courses, £30-£35.
Sunday lunch £19.95-£24.95

Closed Never.

Dog treats, water bowls, dog breakfast, blanket, map with local walks, dog wash and towels.

Gareth Clarke
The Westleton Crown,
The Street, Westleton,
Saxmundham, IP17 3AD
Tel +44 (0)1728 648777
Email info@westletoncrown.co.uk
Web www.westletoncrown.co.uk

Entry 179 Map 4

Sussex

Pub

Noah's Ark

In an idyllic setting – beside village pond and churchyard, overlooking a cricket green – the Ark restores faith in the future of the English country pub. In Henry and Amy's hands, this old village boozer has become a place of charm; no more darts, but a surprise at every turn. From bar to cosy dining areas – and one barn-like room – are beams, parquet flooring, open fires, traditional country furniture and a sprinkling of modern leather. The kitchen's insistence on good-quality (local, seasonal) produce results in a roll-call of British dishes; come evening, the simple bar menu is bolstered by such dishes as pan-fried wood pigeon breast with sautéed savoy cabbage and crispy pancetta. A cottagey garden to the side and picnic tables out front complete the very pleasing package. *Dogs are always very welcome in the bar. We have miles of wonderful walks from the door, as well as on nearby Blackdown.*

Meals Bar meals from £6.
Mains from £12.50.
Sunday lunch, 3 courses, £30.

Closed Open all day.

Dog treats on the bar; water bowls throughout the pub. Book a table with dogs and there will be a plate of dog biscuits waiting when you arrive. Great walks around the village too.

Henry Coghlan & Amy Whitmore
Noah's Ark,
Lurgashall,
Petworth, GU28 9ET
Tel +44 (0)1428 707346
Email amy@noahsarkinn.co.uk
Web www.noahsarkinn.co.uk

Entry 180 Map 3

Sussex

Pub

The Three Crowns

Landlord Tim Skinner's bonhomie helps to keep the customers coming at this convenient and convivial roadside pub. Exposed brick walls, parquet flooring and wooden beams give an old-time feel but it's bright and welcoming in the summer, cosy by the fire on cooler days. Relax in a comfy chair for afternoon tea, dine from wooden tables, or settle down beneath a heater on the large terrace to the rear. Local ingredients are used in innovative ways for the international and seasonal menu: chicken satay and Thai spiced crab; Sussex smoked haddock, seafood platter or Portobello mushroom burger. Sunday roasts come with their own mini versions for children. For grown-up tipples, try the Crown Inn Glory or guest ales. The gin menu – with nutmeg, with hibiscus, with grains of paradise – rather hits the spot. *In the quintessential village of Wisborough Green & set in the South Downs National park with many beautiful walks.*

Meals Starters from £7. Dinner from £10.
Closed Open all day.

Water bowl and dog bed in the bar, and doggy menu featuring biscuits and treats.

Tim Skinner
The Three Crowns,
Billingshurst Road,
Wisborough Green, TH14 0DX
Tel +44 (0)1403 700239
Email info@thethreecrownsinn.com
Web www.thethreecrownsinn.com

Entry 181 Map 3

Sussex

Pub

The Crown

Just a short stroll up from the beach, this old corner boozer oozes artful charm and hipster-cool. Décor is shabby-chic, the mood is laid-back, and the craft beer list is curated by an expert palate. With Tess and Andrew at the helm, the Crown celebrates fantastic local produce and menus bristle with local artisan producers: cured delights from Moon's Green in Northiam, meat from Winchelsea and homemade bread by Emmanuel Hadjiandreou. Enjoy a pint of Three Legs Pale with local herring fillet, beetroot and sour cream and horseradish croquette, or go the whole hog and tuck into Romney Marsh lamb suet pie with roast carrots, greens and mash. Community spirit rings throughout and everyone is welcome, including the dog. Anything goes, from live music, monthly quizzes and board games to regular events such as storytelling and craft groups. *Near to East Hill country park, and close to the beach. Dogs are welcome inside and outside.*

Meals Starters £4-£9. Mains £10-£16. Puddings £3-£7.
Closed Open all day.

Dog biscuits, water bowls – and a friendly welcome!

Tess Eaton & Andrew Swan
The Crown,
64-66 All Saints Street,
Hastings, TN34 3BN
Tel +44 (0)1424 465100
Email hello@thecrownhastings.co.uk
Web www.thecrownhastings.co.uk

Entry 182 Map 4

The Boot

In the pretty village of Berwick St James in the Till valley, sits this 'real British inn' where Giles and Cathy are working a quiet magic with food, ales and happy locals. The striking building – 17th-century Grade II listed, with flint and limestone bands – was once owned by Lord Malmesbury and later home to a boot and shoemaker who gave it its name. Inside, it's richly atmospheric, and very welcoming. You can sit snugly at the fireside with a ploughman's and a pint, or bring the family for Sunday lunch. Lush gardens, great Wadworth beers and proper pub food cooked with passion draws visitors and walkers. Tuck into lavender and cider roast ham with eggs and home-cut wedges, or Barnsley chop with bubble and squeak; for the more adventurous, try crab, whisky and sweetcorn risotto. Dogs and children welcome.

Meals	Light lunches from £6. Mains from £13.
Closed	Mondays all day (except Bank Holidays).
	Dog biscuits for our four-legged guests and a bowl outside. Their owners get mints with their bills

Giles & Cathy Dickinson
The Boot,
High Street, Berwick St James,
Salisbury, SP3 4TN
Tel +44 (0)1722 790243
Email cathy@theboot.pub
Web www.theboot.pub

Entry 182.1 Map 3

Wales

Photo: Troedyrhiw Holiday Cottages, entry 187

Wonderfully Wild

The safari tent lodges at Wonderfully Wild are a classic safari style with plenty of added Welshness, including slate hearths from local quarries and warm woollen rugs in the spacious living areas, not to mention the mountain views of Snowdonia from the outside decks. Derw, at one end of the field (and closest to the car park), is Welsh for Oak, and then there's Castan (Conker), Onnen (Ash) and Jacmor (Sycamore) at the far end. As well as the private showers, toilets and fully-equipped kitchens in each one, owners Victoria and Robin have toured the auctions to fill the lodges with quality upcycled furniture. You're surrounded by 200 acres of fields, woodland and streams – the nearest borders the field where you'll be staying. The Telor Cycle Route borders another side of the field and is a great way to explore this beautiful corner of Anglesey. It's a short drive to a choice of beaches, and just 40 minutes' walk to take you to the seaside town of Beaumaris – perfect for a day out. A big chest of board games and then comfy beds to come back to in the evening. *Fields and woodland to walk in, streams to play in; safe environment.*

Rooms	4 safari tents for 6: from £108 per night. Dogs £20 per dog per per stay. Max. 1.
Meals	Self-catering.
Closed	November – March.

Advice on dog-friendly pubs, beaches and days out.

Canopy & Stars
Wonderfully Wild,
Cichle Farm, Beaumaris, LL58 8PS

Tel	+44 (0)117 204 7830
Email	enquiries@canopyandstars.co.uk
Web	www.canopyandstars.co.uk/wonderfullywild

Entry 183 Map 5

Tŷ Cerrig Woodland Retreats

Come for silent nights and stargazing at these woodland retreats. Bwncath cabin is packed with sheep's wool insulation and has big French windows for flinging open onto the private deck when the sun comes up. It's built for spending time together with little pockets of places to gather around: the farmhouse table for lazy breakfasts, leather sofa and chairs by the wood-burner for playing board games, fire pit and picnic table outside for barbecues and drinks. Gwdihŵ the shepherd's hut has a goose feather duvet on a clever fold-down bed, wood-burning stove and bunks for little ones: talk about shepherd's delight! Both have a kitchen with all you need, hot shower and flushing loo. Make sure you keep an eye on the battery monitor to check your power usage or you might be reading your bedtime stories by torchlight. The spaces are about 100 metres apart, but the meadow is the only thing you'll be sharing. Pick up a map or guide and pack a picnic before you set off on adventures: beautiful long walks around the Vale of Glamorgan, kite-flying on the beach, visiting Cardiff, just half hour away. *Over 25 acres of woodland on site to run around in. Close to dog-friendly beaches and pubs.*

Rooms	Cabin for 4: from £95 per night. Shepherd's hut for 4: from £85 per night. Travel cot & Moses basket available. Max. 1 dog in shepherd's hut, 2 in cabin.
Meals	Self-catering
Closed	November – February
	Towels, and advice on walks and local dog-friendly pubs.

Canopy & Stars
Tŷ Cerrig Woodland Retreats,
Maerdy Newydd,
Bonvilston, CF5 6TR

Tel	+44 (0)117 204 7830
Email	enquiries@canopyandstars.co.uk
Web	www.canopyandstars.co.uk/tycerrig

Entry 184 Map 2

The Log House Studio

You may well be greeted by the ever-exuberant Charlie Brown, terrier and proprietor of Cwm Farm. Well, technically that's Tim, who lives with Charlie in the cottage across the field, and whose paintings festoon the walls of this raised, Swedish-style log cabin built from local timber. Step inside and you'll find an open-plan space, complete with artists' easel and desk, a comfortable double bed and a wood-burner to keep things cosy whatever the weather throws at you. Everything you might need for coffee brewing or sausage frying is also on hand and Charlie will be delighted to assist. The mezzanine level, reached by wooden ladder, provides space for extra guests or just to read a book. The private compost loo and wonderfully hot, gas-powered shower are reachable down a few steps. Although secluded, you'll never feel too alone here; there are cows and sheep in the fields, and from time to time you'll hear the odd barking from the kennels next door too. The surrounding countryside offers plenty of walks, some of Wales's best mountain bike trails, and a whole selection of ruined castles to explore. *Babies welcome. The fields are mostly fenced from livestock next door.*

Rooms	Cabin for 4: from £100 per night. Dogs £10 per dog per stay. Max. 2.
Meals	Self-catering.
Closed	Never.
	Advice on walks.

Canopy & Stars
The Log House Studio,
Cwm Farm, Capel Isaac,
Llandeilo, SA19 7UE

Tel	+44 (0)117 204 7830
Email	enquiries@canopyandstars.co.uk
Web	www.canopyandstars.co.uk/loghouse

Entry 185 Map 2

Ty Mawr Country Hotel

Pretty rooms, attractive prices and delicious food make this welcoming country house hard to resist. It sits in a very peaceful spot. You drive over hills, drop into the village, then wash up at this 16th-century stone house that comes in soft yellow. Outside, a sun-trapping terrace laps against a trim lawn, which in turn drops into a passing river. Gentle eccentricities abound: croquet hoops take odd diversions, logs are piled high like giant beehives, a seat has been chiselled into a tree trunk. Inside, original stone walls and low beamed ceilings give a warm country feel. There are fires everywhere – one in the attractive sitting room that overlooks the garden, another in the dining room that burns on both sides. Excellent bedrooms are all large. You get big beds, warm colours, crisp linen, good bathrooms. Some have sofas, all are dog-friendly, three overlook the garden. Back downstairs, the bar doubles as reception, while Welsh art on the walls is for sale. Steve's cooking is the final treat, perhaps Cardigan Bay scallops, organic Welsh beef, calvados and cinnamon rice pudding. Top stuff. *Children over 10 welcome. Dogs welcome in sitting room, bar and bedrooms (just not in the breakfast room or restaurant).*

Rooms	3 doubles, 3 twin/doubles: £115-£130. Singles £80.
Meals	Dinner £25-£30.
Closed	Rarely.
	Dog biscuits, beds, bowls, towels, leads and advice on walks.

Annabel & Steve Thomas
Ty Mawr Country Hotel,
Brechfa, SA32 7RA

Tel	+44 (0)1267 202332
Email	info@wales-country-hotel.co.uk
Web	www.wales-country-hotel.co.uk

Entry 186 Map 2

Troedyrhiw Holiday Cottages

Come for the wide wooded valley, the Preseli hills on show in the distance, and plenty of animals for children to befriend. You're down a rural track with other holiday makers; pygmy goats, Shetland ponies, kunekune pigs and chickens dot the fields around you and the owners (who will greet you) live on site should you need them. All the sitting rooms have wood-burners (logs are on the house), local art on the walls and comfy sofas and chairs; kitchens and bathrooms are modern (if slightly small) but fine for holiday needs. Bedrooms are spotless and bright – you'll sleep well, away from traffic noise. Each cottage has its own small garden or tranche of decking, plus barbecue and furniture so you can spill out for summertime meals and games. Fields lead down to the wide stream, perfect for welly (or barefoot in summer) splashing, and woodland walks. You're just a mile away from the nearest pub and shops and there are wide safe beaches for picnics and swimming; also walking, birdwatching, rugged mountain biking. Shopaholics will enjoy Cardigan, an appealing Welsh estuary town. *Short breaks available. Woodland walks, streams to jump in, hills to walk up and coast path to explore.*

Rooms	1 cottage for 2: £420-£550. 1 cottage for 3: £595-£875. 1 cottage for 4: £700-£955. 1 cottage for 6: £895-£1,225. 1 cottage for 8: £1,050-£1,750. Prices per week. Dogs £20. Max. 2.
Meals	Pub within 1 mile.
Closed	Never.

Advice on walks and dog-friendly beaches.

Rob & Michelle Silcox
Troedyrhiw Holiday Cottages,
Penparc, Cardigan, SA43 2AE

Tel	+44 (0)1239 811564
Email	info@troedyrhiw.com
Web	www.troedyrhiw.com

Penbontbren

You're lost in lovely hills, yet only three miles from the sea. Not that you're going to stray far. These gorgeous suites don't just have wonderful prices, they're heaped with comforts, too – this is a great spot to come and do nothing at all. Richard and Huw have thought it all through. You get crockery and cutlery, kettles and fridges, then you're encouraged to bring your own wine or to buy provisions from the farm shop for lunch. As for the suites, expect big beds, super bathrooms, sofas and armchairs in pretty sitting areas, then doors onto semi-private terraces – perfect for lunch in summer. You get iPod docks, flat-screen TVs, robes and White Company lotions, too. The new garden room is a little smaller than the others, but has a big terrace to compensate. Breakfast is served in the main house – the full Welsh works. Beautiful hills, sandy beaches, Cardigan and magical St Davids all wait. Good local restaurants are on hand: lobster from the sea, lamb from the hills. Don't miss The Shed in Porthgain for excellent fish and chips. A great place to unwind with discounts for longer stays. *Minimum stay: 2 nights in high season. Large gardens and country walks. No dogs on croquet lawns because that's where the bees are kept.*

Rooms	6 suites for 2: £99-£125. Singles £85-£99. 1 self-catering cottage for 7: £700-£1,150. Dogs free for guests via Sawday's. Max. 2 small or 1 large.
Meals	Restaurants within 3 miles.
Closed	Christmas.

Dogs truly welcome! Lovely gardens and lots of advice on beaches, local pubs and days out.

Richard Morgan-Price & Huw Thomas
Penbontbren,
Glynarthen,
Llandysul, SA44 6PE
Tel +44 (0)1239 810248
Email contact@penbontbren.com
Web www.penbontbren.com

Entry 188 Map 2

Locke's Cottage

It's difficult to know what to call the charming building sitting on the side of the Hoffnant valley – downstairs, thick stone walls give away this former barn's agricultural past, while the timber upper level with oak tree 'growing' through the centre has a distinctly cabin-like feel. In wonderfully thrifty style, many of the materials used in this unusual creation are recycled; floors and window sills have been cleverly fashioned from scaffold boards used during the renovation, the double-ended bath sits on a cradle handmade from reclaimed wood and the pan rack in the large downstairs kitchen was once an old meat spit found in the grounds. Big windows along the front look down over the valley, and double doors lead from the upstairs living area onto a balcony. You're so close to the sea that you can hear waves breaking when the wind is right. You have easy access onto the coastal path: follow the headland round to beautifully sandy West Wales beaches. Owners Kathryn and Geoff recommend the beach at Llangrannog for a great pub and unbeatable homemade ice cream from the beachside café. *Huge network of tracks, paths and hills to explore; 2 beaches within 1.5 miles, both dog-friendly all year round. Nearly all the surrounding pubs welcome dogs too.*

Rooms	Cottage for 5: from £99 per night. Dogs £10 per dog per stay. Max. 2.
Meals	Self-catering.
Closed	Never.

Towels for drying, feeding and water bowls, poo bags, nice dog biscuits and guided walks.

Canopy & Stars
Locke's Cottage, Troed Rhiw Fawr,
Brynhoffnant, SA44 6EF
Tel +44 (0)117 204 7830
Email enquiries@canopyandstars.co.uk
Web www.canopyandstars.co.uk/lockescottage

Entry 189 Map 2

One Cat Farm

In the wild meadows of a quiet valley live one cat, two owners, Jessie and Lyndon, and four grass-roofed dens, lovingly crafted by Lyndon. Helyg Den is pitched right by the pond so wildlife lovers, this one's for you. Next along is Celyg Den followed by Derwen Den, both overlooking the pond and a great spot for sunsets – and Onnen Den, pitched at the top. The grassy exteriors aren't the only thing Nordic here – the dens are simple and cosy inside and the flexible layout make them a perfect fit for families and couples. There is a double bed and two single beds, which stow away as a sofa. Once a home for saddlebacks, The Pig Shed is now a warm communal barn, a two-minute walk away from the dens, with a kitchen and a big dining table where you can get to know your fellow glampers. The hot showers and flushing loo are next door. Seek out the twin wood-fired outdoor baths for an evening of stargazing or dunking the muddy littlies after a day of adventures. With both beaches and mountains nearby, it's a perfect base for fishing, walking, horse riding and surfing. *Surrounded by working farmland so dogs must be kept on leads on site. Numerous walks from doorstep.*

Rooms	4 cabins for 4: from £80 per night. Dogs £20 per dog per stay. Max. 2 small or 1 large.
Meals	Self-catering.
Closed	Never.
	Water bowl and advice on walks.

Canopy & Stars
One Cat Farm,
Bronfre Fach,
Ciliau Aeron, SA48 7PT

Tel	+44 (0)117 204 7830
Email	enquiries@canopyandstars.co.uk
Web	www.canopyandstars.co.uk/onecatfarm

Entry 190 Map 2

Banceithin

Eco heaven doesn't have to come bereft of style: here are two neat cottages, formerly a pig sty and cowshed, now modernised with just the right amount of history in the mix: exposed stone walls, original archways, antique pieces, textiles from Jane Beck Welsh Blankets. David and Philippa who live in the farmhouse opposite have ten bountiful acres with an orchard, vegetable beds, humming bees, happy pigs and owl boxes. Each cottage has a private garden and shares a games room (table tennis, dart board, giant outdoor chess). Double height living/dining areas feel airy, the smaller cottage has a spiral staircase; both have wood-burning stoves, TV/DVDs and comfy seating. Kitchens and bathrooms have glossy red units, cheery tiles and eco-friendly products. The couple find time to make pies and preserves (buy yours from the honesty box), greet guests, and get involved in local life. Children will love collecting eggs, feeding animals, pond dipping, and building dens under the treehouse. Shops are three miles away, the coast seven and there's plenty of rolling countryside to tramp, including miles of coastal path. *Minimum stay: 2 nights; 7 in high season. Enclosed garden. Keep dogs on lead outside garden due to pets, chickens & sheep in fields. Evening dog-sitting available.*

Rooms	1 cottage for 2: £275-£440 per week. 1 cottage for 6: £400-£880 per week. Short break discounts: up to 3 nights 50%; 15% of weekly rate per additional night up to 6 nights Max. 2 medium/large or 3 small dogs.
Meals	Pub within 3 miles.
Closed	Never.
	Homemade biscuits, doggy guide with vet details, walks, dog-friendly pubs. Towels, blankets for the sofa, poo bags and scoop.

David & Philippa Pickworth
Banceithin,
Bethania, Llanon, SY23 5NP
Tel +44 (0)1974 272559
Mobile +44 (0)7794 738403
Email escape@banceithin.com
Web www.banceithin.com

Entry 191 Map 2

Pwll y Garth

The road twists and turns until you arrive at a small 19th-century slate house in a wild, magical setting. Step inside to oak floors, thick lime-plaster walls and beamed ceilings. This is not a place for luxury seekers, it's a modest, simple retreat without TV or dishwasher but with complete and utter tranquillity. There's a dining room with a wooden table and chairs, a dresser with glasses and crockery. The basic kitchen is off here; find local goodies, a Rayburn to cook on and deep slate windowsills. The cosy living room has a bookcase, Moroccan rugs, armchairs, a sofa and a wood-burner to belt out the heat – and enough wood to last a couple of days. Upstairs is a tiled bathroom, with Ecover smellies, and two simple bedrooms (one twin, one double) both with sloped ceilings and incredible views. Beds are draped with Welsh woollen throws. The delightful owners, who live close by, are the custodians of Ty Mawr, a 16th-century traditional Welsh house; Wil is passionate and can tell you its history. You're minutes from the A5 that takes you straight through Snowdonia but bring a torch, it's dark here at night. *River to jump in and endless amazing walks – many away from livestock (though sheep/ponies often in fields immediately next to cottage).*

Rooms	1 cottage for 4: £450-£550 per week. Max. 2 dogs.
Meals	Restaurant 6 miles.
Closed	During freezing weather.
	Advice on walks, a dog bowl, treats and a warm welcome.

Liz Green
Pwll y Garth,
Penmachno, Betws-y-Coed, LL25 0HJ
Tel +44 (0)1690 760296
Email info@pwllygarth.co.uk
Web www.pwllygarth.co.uk

Entry 192 Map 5

Plas Dinas Country House

The family home of Lord Snowdon dates to the 1600s and stands in 15 rural acres with an avenue of oak sweeping you up to the house. Princess Margaret often stayed and much of what fills the house belongs to the family: striking chandeliers, oils by the score, gilt-framed mirrors – an Aladdin's cave of beautiful things. There's a baby grand piano in the drawing room, where you find a roaring fire and an honesty bar, but potter about and find masses of memorabilia framed on the walls (make sure you visit the private dining room). Bedrooms – some with views across fields to the sea – mix a graceful past with modern design. You get four-posters, period colours, bold wallpapers, a sofa if there's room. A cute room in the eaves has mountain views, all have hot-water bottles, Apple TVs and excellent bathrooms, some with showers, others with free-standing baths. Good food waits in the restaurant, perhaps fishcakes with lime and ginger, lamb shank with a rosemary jus, chocolate tart with white chocolate ice-cream. Snowdon is close, as you'd expect, so bring walking boots and mountain bikes. *Minimum stay: 2 nights at bank holiday weekends. Fifteen acres of grounds. Three dog-friendly rooms: Buckley, Mount and South.*

Rooms	3 doubles, 5 twin/doubles: £109-£169. 2 suites for 2: £159-£249. Extra beds £50. Dogs £10 per night. Max. 2.
Meals	Dinner, 3 courses, £25-£35.
Closed	23-27 December.

Advice on dog-friendly dining, dog biscuits, dog towel, poo bags and suggestions for walks.

Neil Baines & Marco Soares
Plas Dinas Country House,
Bontnewydd, Caernarfon, LL54 7YF
Tel +44 (0)1286 830214
Email info@plasdinas.co.uk
Web www.plasdinas.co.uk

Entry 193 Map 5

Nantcol

If you want tarmac to the door, matching Ikea furniture and an absence of wildlife then eschew this place! Nature lovers and peace seekers however will be in heaven – it's a wildly romantic spot down a long winding road and completely remote. Walk in to find deep window sills for gazing at the Rhinog mountains and swirling ravens, wind-blasted buzzards, sometimes a mountain goat. Antique Welsh furniture is dotted about – a lovely old dresser, a grandfather clock – and the sitting room has a fireplace at each end (electric heaters too), plus interesting paintings, local maps, hefty beams and large rugs over ancient tiled floors – not for minimalist lovers. The kitchen, once home to the carthorse, has original slate tops and an old farmhouse table. Sleep soundly in bedrooms with heavenly views. The bathroom has a roll top, and children will adore the hayloft, with its own extra outside stair; there's also a playhouse outside. Llanbedr village is five miles down the winding road; the beautiful beaches of Shell Island offer safe swimming. *Please see owner's website for availability. Perfect walking from the door for dogs of all ages and sizes. Sheep country so be aware!*

Rooms	1 cottage for 7: £500-£950 per week. Low season short breaks available, 3-night stay from £300. Dogs £10 per dog per week. Max. usually 2.
Meals	Pub within 2 miles.
Closed	January/February.

Bonios and tap in downstairs loo for washing off muddy dogs.

Stephanie & John Grant
Nantcol,
Llanbedr, LL45 2PL
Tel +44 (0)1874 754786
Email johngrant6464@gmail.com
Web www.nantcol.com

Entry 194 Map 5

Bryn Adda

High up on private land, down the driveway, through the natural garden, and there it is, Bryn Adda – a rambling L-shaped stone building that dates from the 16th century. It's a fine house in anyone's book. Landscaped gardens drop away in all directions and you can walk to Dolgellau. Find a warren of little stairways and landings in the old part, larger rooms in the new and a low-ceilinged farmhouse kitchen right in the middle, with Belfast sinks and a big old Aga. You get a dining room for 18, two sitting rooms opening to terraces – one big and sunny, with a dog-dozy fire and an old-fashioned charm, the other with nut-brown sofas and gleaming parquet floor. There's a bedroom on the ground floor and seven more above, all comfy, all delightful, with various modern takes on traditional design. Bathrooms are new with a retro feel; antiques, pictures and books abound. Play hide-and-seek in the rhododendrons, table tennis in the barns, surf at Barmouth, hike in the forest, fish on their own stretch of river. Return to a blissful sauna – and toast your good fortune! *Short breaks available. Secure garden including woodland, within even bigger wild space. Dogs must be kept on leads near sheep.*

Rooms	1 house for 16: £1,260–£3,360 per week.
Meals	Pubs & restaurants within walking distance.
Closed	Rarely.
	Advice on walks and seven acres of garden to play in.

Sarah Watkins
Bryn Adda,
Dolgellau, LL40 1YA
Mobile +44 (0)7952 712104
Email distinctlywales@btinternet.com
Web www.brynaddasnowdonia.com

Entry 195 Map 5

Y Felin

Such a stunning drive through the Snowdonia National Park, down a long track to this remote water mill with the Dysynni river babbling past the front door. Inside is a symphony of local oak, slate and stone in a modern hi-tech interior with white walls and plenty of games and books; heat comes from an air-source pump and wood for the burner from the farm: you'll be cosy on the chilliest days. Cooks will be thrilled with the river view from the kitchen window – and the breadmaker. All has been beautifully considered. The three bedrooms are on the ground floor, the master has its own wood-burner and windows on three sides, the smaller double is bright and sweet. The bunk room is suitable for children and teenagers; the big bathrooms are fabulous. An honesty freezer is filled with local produce if you can't be bothered to shop, and there's a fire pit outside with wooden seats for flame-gazers. The owners can point you towards rugged mountain walking and bike rides, farm tours, fell running and sheep dog trials. Long sandy beaches are near, and the air is superb. *Secure garden and 2,000 acres beyond to roam. Dogs must be kept on leads near sheep.*

Rooms	1 cottage for 8: £610-£1,480 per week. Short breaks 3-4 nights, £280-£590.
Meals	Restaurant within 3 miles.
Closed	Rarely.
	Advice on walks, lots of private space and a river on the doorstep.

Sarah Watkins
Y Felin,
Maes y Pandy Farm,
Abergynolwyn, Tywyn, LL36 9AQ
Mobile +44 (0)7952 712104
Email distinctlywales@btinternet.com
Web www.distinctlywales.com

Entry 196 Map 5

The Slate Shed at Graig Wen

Sarah and conservationist John spent months travelling in a camper looking for their own special place and found this lovely old Welsh slate cutting mill… captivated by acres of wild woods and stunning views. You'll feel at ease as soon as you step into their eclectic modern home with its reclaimed slate and wood, cosy wood-burners, books, games, snug bedrooms (one downstairs) and superb bathrooms. Breakfast communally on local eggs and sausages, honey from the mountainside, homemade bread and granola. Hike or bike the Mawddach Trail, climb Cadair Idris, wonder at the views… and John's chocolate brownies. *Minimum stay: 2 nights at weekends & in high season. Children over 10 welcome. Dogs welcome in rooms & at breakfast. Advice on dog-friendly walks, beaches, places to eat & visit; doggie day care while guests take the train up Snowdon or visit Portmeirion.*

Rooms	4 doubles, 1 twin/double: £80-£130. Singles £65. Dogs £10 per dog per stay. Max. 2.
Meals	Packed lunch £6.50. Pub 5 miles.
Closed	5 November – 14 February.

Treats, towels and throws for muddy paws, and wonderful walks from the doorstep.

Sarah Heyworth
The Slate Shed at Graig Wen,
Arthog, LL39 1YP
Tel +44 (0)1341 250482
Email hello@graigwen.co.uk
Web www.slateshed.co.uk

Entry 197 Map 5

Coes Faen Lodge

Effortless simplicity is the key to this new spa B&B. A glass and rock entrance, a hallway suffused with light: this Victorian lodge on the edge of Mawddach Estuary has been stunningly, meticulously revived. Bedrooms are cocoons of sleek opulence, bathrooms are rich in slate and stone, and detailing is sublime: mood lighting, hands-free technology, pearlescent tiles that reflect the light. Choose a sauna smelling of cedar or a rooftop hot tub and terrace… Richard and Sara have Welsh roots and love both place and landscape. Acres of woodland garden await behind; breakfasts and dinners are original and exquisite. *Rooms have terraces with direct access to 20 acres of walled woodland gardens.*

Rooms	6 doubles: £135-£240. Dinner, B&B £100-£180 per person. Dogs £15 per stay. Max. 2.
Meals	Dinner from £35. Pubs/restaurants 0.5 miles.
Closed	Rarely.

Dog bed, dog blankets, biscuits, outside hot water shower, dog shampoo and towels.

Richard & Sara Parry-Jones
Coes Faen Lodge,
Coes Faen, Abermaw, LL42 1TE
Tel +44 (0)1341 281632
Email richard@coesfaen.com
Web www.coesfaen.co.uk

Entry 198 Map 5

Little Idyll

You'll be greeted by wildlife and livestock galore here. Birds, muntjac deer, alpacas, potbellied and kunekune pigs, ducks, chickens, turkeys… and a lively, curious pony in the sloping field next door, which you'll climb up to reach Little Idyll. Sharon's dogs are likely to pad up and say hello too – they're always excited to meet new people. Then hop into a wonderfully crafted shepherd's hut, decorated in subtle colours that complement the larch and oak panelling and worktops. Every comfort has been considered, from the bed occupying one whole end of the hut, to the nifty kitchen and the en suite compost loo; you can order a breakfast hamper too. Having retired from the police force, Sharon settled here to pursue her other dream of creating the perfect holiday spot and it's easy to see why she chose it: the view is breathtaking. The decking area with fire bowl is like a front row seat at a fabulous show, with countryside stretching across the Wye Valley and as far as the Cotswolds on a clear day. Head out for scenic walks and historic castles, canoeing, hiking and biking through the hills. *Enclosed garden; adjacent fields. Dogs on leads until they reach hut & when walking through livestock fields. Footpaths from hut; woodland walks a short drive; advice on walks. Dog-friendly pubs nearby.*

Rooms	Shepherd's hut for 2: from £95 per night. Up to 2 horses £15 per night, staying in the paddock (hay & water provided). Max. 1 small/medium dog.
Meals	Self-catering.
Closed	Never.
	Dog welcome pack with biscuits or gravy bones. Dog blanket and throws for protecting furniture so you can cuddle up.

Canopy & Stars
Little Idyll, Maybee Glamping, Maybee Cottage, Usk Road, Shirenewton, Chepstow, NP16 6TZ

Tel	+44 (0)117 204 7830
Email	enquiries@canopyandstars.co.uk
Web	www.canopyandstars.co.uk/littleidyll

Entry 199 Map 2

The Chickenshed

The Chickenshed completely belies its name, which makes for extra wonderment when you approach the stunning red cedar, glass and stainless steel structure. Put your shoes in the boot room and pad barefoot across the heated polished concrete floor. Owner Sue will show you round and explain how some of the space-age kitchen gadgets work. This is *the* place to truly enjoy cooking a feast. The floor-to-ceiling glass across the expansive open-plan living area creates a dramatic connection to the beautiful Wye Valley. The cabin's agricultural roots, like the corrugated roof and chunky wooden cladding, are kept soft and modern with striking greens, asymmetrical windows, and lights which appear to float around the glulam beams. Outside there are two private acres where the kids, big or small, can play safely, and a wood to wander through and gaze up at canopies of ancient trees. When you're sitting around the crackling flames of the fire pit on the paved terrace with the bats swooping above, and some sizzling steaks cooking... you'll see you don't have to do much to make days and evenings here perfect. *Surrounding area paradise for dogs. Large secure garden, field & woods beyond; safe for dogs to be off-lead for miles. Local guide, OS maps and walking books available.*

Rooms	Cabin for 8: from £210 per night. Reduced rates of 20% off may be available for groups of 2-4. Max 2.
Meals	Self-catering.
Closed	Never.
	Outside tap for cleaning muddy paws & blankets for drying off. Dog bed & crate available if needed. Sue & Nick have 2 active collies and are always happy to advise.

Canopy & Stars
The Chickenshed,
Parkhouse, Trellech, NP25 4PU

Tel	+44 (0)117 204 7830
Email	enquiries@canopyandstars.co.uk
Web	www.canopyandstars.co.uk/thechickenshed

Entry 200 Map 2

Old-Lands

This is a kindly place, in the family for 200 years; Clare and Sam introduce you, brilliantly, to the delights of rural life – or leave you to do your own thing. Two of the holiday cottages are in the old stable-yard, simple and attractive, divided by a flower-filled courtyard and next to the farm shop. Interiors are warm: curtains are made of Welsh blankets – family antiques, fresh flowers and pictures will make you feel at home. The third space is more contemporary, private and will suit romantic couples – although there's an outside bell tent or indoor loft den for smaller adventurers. You can roam the gardens and the 80-acre estate (perfect for dogs), send your children to Forest School (check the website for dates), row on the lake (little life jackets provided) and order home cooked food to be waiting for you. There is a gentle emphasis on sustainability, with sausages from their own pigs, honey from their bees, juice from their apples and seasonal produce from the bountiful kitchen garden. If gardening is your thing you can volunteer here too. Utterly special. *Minimum stay: 2 nights at weekends; 4 on weekdays; 7 in high season. Dogs welcome in Wood Barn & Stable Court. Lovely lake and masses of land to roam in – watch out for stock. Secure garden in one cottage.*

Rooms	1 apartment for 5: £465-£790. 1 barn for 4: £400-£690. 1 cottage for 5: £470-£790. Prices per week. Dogs £20 per dog per stay.
Meals	Pub/restaurant within 3 miles.
Closed	Never.
	Towels for drying off after lake swimming.

Clare Bosanquet
Old-Lands,
Dingestow Court,
Dingestow, NP25 4DY

Tel	+44 (0)1600 740141
Email	clarebosanquet@gmail.com
Web	old-lands.co.uk

Entry 201 Map 2

The Bell at Skenfrith

The position here is magical: an ancient stone bridge, a river snaking through the valley, glorious hills rising beyond, cows grazing in lush fields. It's a perfect spot, not least because providence blessed it with this chic little inn. Inside, you find a locals' bar for the odd game of rugby, sofas in front of a wood-burner in the sitting room, then an airy restaurant for some very good food. In summer, doors fly open and life spills onto a stone terrace with views of hill and wood – a fine spot for lunch in the sun. Elegant country-house bedrooms brim with light. Some are beamed, most are big, you'll find padded bedheads, Farrow & Ball colours, perhaps a walnut bed or a claw-foot bath in your room. Those at the front have river views, those at the back look onto the hills, some have sofas, all have robes in excellent bathrooms. Seven circular walks start at the front door with maps to show you the way. Delicious food awaits your return, perhaps Welsh rarebit with a poached egg, braised beef brisket with dauphinoise potatoes, apple doughnuts with toffee sauce and mulled cider. *Minimum stay: 2 nights at weekends. Secure garden; circular walks from the door. Beware of sheep and cows.*

Rooms	5 doubles, 3 twin/doubles, 3 four-posters: £150-£230. Singles £90. Dinner, B&B from £95 per person. Extra bed/sofabed available £10-£20 per person per night. Dogs £20 per dog per night. Max. 2.
Meals	Lunch from £5.95. Dinner, 3 courses, around £35. Sunday lunch from £12.95.
Closed	Rarely.
	Dog parlour and towels. Dog treats for well-behaved dogs.

Richard Ireton & Sarah Hudson
The Bell at Skenfrith,
Skenfrith,
Abergavenny, NP7 8UH
Tel +44 (0)1600 750235
Email enquiries@skenfrith.co.uk
Web www.skenfrith.co.uk

Entry 202 Map 2

Llys Meddyg

This beautiful small hotel has a little bit of everything: chic bedrooms that pack a punch, a cellar bar for cocktails before dinner, a stylish restaurant for delicious local food. In summer you decant into the garden, where a café/bistro opens up for coffee and cake or pizza from a wood-fired oven. There's a smokehouse out here, too, then a yurt tucked away around the corner that comes with a wood-burner and a hot tub. It's an intimate place, where staff stop to chat, locals pop in for a coffee and you can take home a jar of quince jelly made by Ed's mum. Food lies at the heart of the affair and you eat in a stylish restaurant with Welsh art on the walls, perhaps home-smoked salmon, slow-cook lamb, caramelized pear with blue-cheese ice-cream. Beautiful bedrooms are scattered about. Those in the main house have cool colours, vast beds and fancy bathrooms. Those in the mews have a rustic feel and garden views; all have fluffy bath robes. Pembrokeshire's coastal path waits for windswept cliffs and sandy beaches. Don't miss St Davids or the Preseli Hills. Dogs are very welcome. *Minimum stay: 2 nights at weekends. Estuary path, long sandy beach with dunes, mountain walks – all from the doorstep; OS explorer maps to borrow. Lovely garden. Three dog-friendly rooms.*

Rooms	8 doubles: £100-£180. 1 yurt for 2: £100-£120. Singles from £85. Dogs £15 per stay.
Meals	Lunch from £7. Dinner from £14.
Closed	Rarely.

Dog bowls and outside hose for washing off muddy paws. There is always a sausage at breakfast too.

Louise & Edward Sykes
Llys Meddyg,
East Street,
Newport, SA42 0SY
Tel +44 (0)1239 820008
Email info@llysmeddyg.com
Web www.llysmeddyg.com

Entry 203 Map 1

Cwtch Camping

The Welsh camping experience has been given a thoroughly contemporary spin by Beth, creator of the Cwtch (meaning a hug, or a snug place, in Welsh). The three handcrafted timber pods are a short walk through the trees from where you park your car, or a scenic cycle from local stations. Light pours through French windows, chunky brocante finds distinguish the interiors and a real double bed is bliss after a day in the fresh air. The cabins share a kitchen, shower and WC, but are privately sited with their own deck and picnic table. Local eggs, fresh bread and organic milk are among the goodies in your welcome hamper and Beth can supply extras for your private barbecue if you ask in advance. The Cwtch stands firm in all seasons in the midst of Pembrokeshire's natural beauty: follow the riverbank walk to a nature reserve teeming with bird life – and a family of otters – or take a boat trip to the Skomer Island. Camping has never been cosier! *Many dog-friendly pubs, restaurants and cafés nearby. Advice on the beaches without dog restrictions given.*

Rooms	2 pods for 2: from £68 per night. 1 pod for 4: from £80 per night. Max. 2 dogs.
Meals	Self-catering.
Closed	November – March.

Dog biscuits, towels, walking advice and 3 acres of woodland where dogs can run around off the lead.

Canopy & Stars
Cwtch Camping,
12 Vale Court, Houghton, SA73 1NQ
Tel +44 (0)117 204 7830
Email enquiries@canopyandstars.co.uk
Web www.canopyandstars.co.uk/cwtchcamping

Entry 204 Map 1

Beudy Banc

Five handmade and upcycled cabins surrounded by some of the best biking trails and beaches, wooded bridleways and ancient drovers' roads. Caban Coch, artfully crafted by its owner from an old hay trailer, has a wood-burning stove together with a kitchen/dining area with full-sized cooker, sink and storage, next to a sleeping area and the wet room with a shower. Cylindrical Caban Crwn has a ladder which leads up to the mezzanine bed and a lounge area (with a day bed single) off to the left. The compact compost loo and shower unit are through the hidden door in front of you. Caban Copa is framed by a domed ceiling, glass doors and porthole windows – a sofa sits by the wood-burner, opposite the kitchen and hidden behind is an ensuite compost loo. Up the ladder is your cosy bedroom. Caban Cader and Caban Cadno sit at the top of the hill – their walls festooned with collected treasures. Each has a living area with a double sofabed, a dining area, kitchen and a sleeping loft above with double bed. Perfect for all mud-seekers, adventurers and off-roaders, Beudy Banc has the quirky cabin just for you. *Nearby stream; marked walking routes on the farm.*

Rooms	1 cabin for 2: from £80. 2 cabins for 3: from £60. 2 cabins for 4: from £80. Prices per night. Dogs £10 per dog per stay. Max. 1.
Meals	Self-catering.
Closed	Never.

Water bowl and tether. Maps and routes for walks around the farm and local footpaths and bridleways.

Canopy & Stars
Beudy Banc,
Cwm Llywi Uchaf Farm, Abercegir,
Machynlleth, SY20 8NP
Tel +44 (0)117 204 7830
Email enquiries@canopyandstars.co.uk
Web www.canopyandstars.co.uk/beudybanc

Entry 205 Map 5

The Felin Fach Griffin

So what are the ingredients of one of the loveliest inns in the land? Well, it's quirky, homespun, and thrives on a mix of relaxed informality and colourful style. The bar resembles the sitting room of a hip country house, with timber frames, cool tunes and comfy sofas in front of the fire. Painted stone walls come in blocks of colour and you dine informally in the white-walled restaurant, with stock pots simmering on an Aga. The food is excellent, perhaps Portland crab, boeuf Bourguignon, chocolate mousse with mascarpone; much of what you eat comes from the half-acre kitchen garden, with meat and game from the hills around you. Pretty bedrooms have colour and style. Expect comfy beds and crisp linen, good bathrooms with fluffy towels, Roberts radios and a smattering of books (but no TV unless you ask). Breakfast is a leisurely treat: read the morning papers, make your own toast, scoff the full Welsh works. A road passes outside, but quietly at night, while lanes lead into the hills, so come to walk, ride, bike, canoe. Hay is close for books galore. Don't miss excellent off-season deals. *Large garden with plenty of space to run around and local rivers for swimming. Stunning walks in The Brecon Beacons.*

Rooms	7 doubles, 3 twin/doubles, 1 four-poster: £135-£175. 1 family room for 3: £175. Dinner, B&B £190-£230 (based on double occupancy).
Meals	Lunch from £7. Dinner, 3 courses, about £30. Sunday lunch from £20.
Closed	Christmas Eve & Day (evening). 4 days in Jan.
	Dog biscuits, blanket, towels, advice on walks, poo bags, dog bowls – and very friendly staff.

Charles & Edmund Inkin
The Felin Fach Griffin,
Felin Fach,
Brecon, LD3 0UB
Tel +44 (0)1874 620111
Email enquiries@felinfachgriffin.co.uk
Web www.felinfachgriffin.co.uk

Entry 206 Map 2

Danyfan Carriage

Danyfan Carriage is the latest project of Emma & Stevie, who fled London for the country life a few years ago. They found a perfect spot to make their home, and also the perfect place for a little glamping. The railway wagon, as far as they know, was built in the early 20th-century. In converting it they have kept as much of the original as possible, adding only what will complement the period feel, with a grand wicker-headboarded bed and a burnished walnut wardrobe. The whole site is completely off-grid, with a cleverly designed (piping hot!) gas shower and washing-up area, plus a separate compost loo, just steps from the carriage. Being off-grid doesn't have to mean hardship: the wood-burner keeps you beautifully warm, the bed is a wonder of mountainous soft pillows. Lanterns and torches give a soft light, and the gas hobs make cooking easy. Your corner of the garden is sheltered, with mountain views and a rushing stream. Walks through the Brecon Beacons National Park stretch out from the door and wildlife and nature surround you. *Large garden, owners' dog (lives next door) to play with, and wonderful walks up in the mountains. Livestock in neighbouring fields.*

Rooms	Train carriage for 2: from £80 per night. Max. 1 dog.
Meals	Self-catering.
Closed	Never.
	Biscuits, dog leads, bowls and advice on walks.

Canopy & Stars
Danyfan Carriage,
Danyfan, Cwmgwdi,
Brecon, LD3 8LG
Tel +44 (0)117 204 7830
Email enquiries@canopyandstars.co.uk
Web www.canopyandstars.co.uk/danyfan

Entry 207 Map 2

Hafod Y Garreg

A unique opportunity to stay in the oldest house in Wales – a fascinating, 1402 cruck-framed hall house, built for Henry IV as a hunting lodge. Informal Annie and John have filled it with a charming mix of Venetian mirrors, Indian rugs, pewter plates, rich fabrics and oak pieces. Dine by candlelight in the romantic dining room – all sorts of delicious dishes; tuck into a big breakfast in the sweet conservatory. Bedrooms are luxuriously comfortable with embroidered linen, quirky lamps, nifty bathrooms. Reach this relaxed retreat by a bumpy track up across gated fields crowded with chickens, cats… a peaceful, special place. *Hens here – so dogs to be on a lead in yard.*

Rooms	2 doubles: £92. Singles £90. Max. 2 dogs.
Meals	Dinner, 3 courses, £27. BYO. Pubs/restaurants 2.5 miles.
Closed	Christmas.
	Great walks from the house.

Annie & John McKay
Hafod Y Garreg,
Erwood,
Builth Wells, LD2 3TQ
Tel +44 (0)1982 560400
Email johnanniehafod@gmail.com
Web www.hafodygarreg.co.uk

Entry 208 Map 2

Ty'r Chanter

Warmth, colour, children and activity: this house is huge fun. Tiggy welcomes you like family; help collect eggs, feed the lambs, drop your shoes by the fire. The farmhouse and barn are stylishly relaxed; deep sofas, tartan throws, heaps of books, long convivial table; views to the Brecon Beacons and Black Mountains are inspiring. Bedrooms are soft, simple sanctuaries with Jo Malone bathroom treats. The children's room zings with murals; toys, kids' sitting room, sandpit – it's child heaven. Walk, fish, canoe, book-browse in Hay or stroll the estate. Homemade cakes and whisky to help yourself to: fine hospitality and Tiggy is wonderful. *River to swim and large field to run around in. But lots of livestock around – and mind the chickens!*

Rooms	3 doubles: £100. 1 twin (children's room with separate bath/shower, price per child): £20. Singles £55.
Meals	Packed lunch £8. Pub 1 mile.
Closed	Christmas.
	Sausages for breakfast, towels, dog bowls and walks.

Tiggy Pettifer
Ty'r Chanter,
Gliffaes, Crickhowell, NP8 1RL
Tel +44 (0)1874 731144
Mobile +44 (0)7802 387004
Email tiggy@tyrchanter.com
Web www.tyrchanter.com

Entry 209 Map 2

Scotland

Photo: The Old House
entry 213

Boutique Farm Bothies

Two upcycled bothies hidden away on a working farm in stunning rural Aberdeenshire, where Jane and James grow malting barley. They also breed sheep and grow strawberries, which you'll find tucked into your welcome hamper alongside homemade jam and Scottish treats. Barley Bothy's exterior is traditional, corrugated tin, and a veranda down its full length has an outside bike wash and storage for wet boots after those long countryside walks, perhaps up Bennachie or on the famous Malt Whisky Trail. Wool insulation, a log-burning range cooker and a vintage wood-burner will keep you warm even in Aberdeenshire winters. The two king-size cupboard beds have stargazing windows, as does the bathroom, which comes with a luxurious roll-top as well as a vintage loo. The Sheep Shed is easily recognised by its tin shell and huge windows framed in red. Inside, there are more pops of colour in the kitchen, a comfy sofa, wood-burner and a ladder leading up to the mezzanine bedroom. There's a flushing loo and a tin trough bath too! Step outside and take a long soak in the private wood-fired hot tub under clear starry skies. *Stream by Bothy & walks from the door. Fabulous dog-friendly beaches: Sandend and Cullen. Hill walks on Bennachie. Dogs to be kept on leads on farm.*

Rooms	Bothy for 4: from £95 per night. Bothy for 2: from £110 per night. Dogs £5 per dog per stay. Max. 3.
Meals	Self-catering.
Closed	Never.

Dog sleepover pack! Includes gravy bones, towel, blanket to put on the sofa, dog bed, bowls and lead. (Must keep off the beds!)

Canopy & Stars
Boutique Farm Bothies, Newton of Begshill, Drumblade, Huntly, AB54 6BJ
Tel +44 (0)117 204 7830
Email enquiries@canopyandstars.co.uk
Web www.canopyandstars.co.uk/boutiquefarmbothies

Entry 210 Map 9

Tiroran House

The setting is magnificent – 17 acres of gardens rolling down to Loch Scridian. Otters and dolphins pass through, buzzards and eagles glide above, red deer visit the garden. As for this 1850 shooting lodge, you'll be hard pressed to find a more comfortable island base, so it's no surprise to discover it was recently voted 'Best Country House Hotel in Scotland' for the second year in a row. There are fires in the drawing rooms, fresh flowers everywhere, games to be played, books to be read. Airy bedrooms hit the spot: crisp linen, beautiful fabrics, the odd chaise longue; some have watery views, all have silence guaranteed. You eat in a smart dining room with much of the delicious food from the island or waters around it, perhaps mussel and oyster broth, saddle of lamb with carrot purée, chocolate torte with vanilla ice cream. You're bang in the middle of Mull with lots to do: Tobermory, the prettiest town in the Hebrides; Calgary and its magical beach; day trips to Iona and its famous monastery; cruises to Staffa and Fingal's Cave. Come back for afternoon tea – it's as good as the Ritz. *Private beach, woodland walks: dog paradise!*

Rooms	5 doubles, 5 twin/doubles: £175-£220.
Meals	Dinner, 4 courses, £48.
Closed	Rarely.
	Dog biscuit.

Laurence & Katie Mackay
Tiroran House,
Tiroran,
Isle of Mull, PA69 6ES
Tel +44 (0)1681 705232
Email info@tiroran.com
Web www.tiroran.com

Entry 211 Map 8 + 10

Blue Cottage

Only one other house shares this road and it is invisible from the cottage. A glimpse of a Highland cow in the field way below is a silent but welcome sign of farm life and the hooting owl and fox are the only noises you'll hear as night falls. A blue velvet sofa and wood-burner make the living room the cosy hub of the home and just one glimpse of the kitchen sparks curiosity and appetite. One bathroom is en suite to the master bedroom, the other is off the hall, past the twin room and contains a roll top cast iron tub. Pampering continues with a welcome hamper of local treats and beers. Help yourself to the fishing rods in the hall, bikes in the shed along with two sets of golf clubs and trolleys and even a inflatable kayak. Oh yes, and binoculars and bird book on the window sill, with a bird box within range. Even a leather bound sketch book if you felt artistically inclined. The Loch Awe boatyard is an easy stroll, where you can hire a rowing boat or simply watch the fishermen at work from the jetty. *Garden open space; quiet road behind. Wilds of Argyll & banks of Loch Awe: miles of wonderful walks on the doorstep; books & OS maps. Dog-friendly pub 2-minute walk.*

Rooms	Cabin for 4: from £105 per night. Dogs £15 per dog per stay. Max. 1 medium or 2 small dogs.
Meals	Self-catering.
Closed	Never.

Dog food (James Wellbeloved & Lily's), sometimes local homemade dog biscuits. Poo bags, 'tick' remover tool, dog bed, blankets to cover furniture so you can snuggle up. Outside standing water pipe too.

Canopy & Stars
Blue Cottage, Love Argyll,
Ardbrecknish Dalmally, PA33 1BH

Tel	+44 (0)117 204 7830
Email	enquiries@canopyandstars.co.uk
Web	www.canopyandstars.co.uk/bluecottage

Entry 212 Map 8

The Old House

An extremely comfortable home for a family holiday, or a secret hideaway for two. You feel miles from anywhere (and the night skies are gloriously unpolluted), yet the train from London chugs into the local village. The former sporting lodge has been renovated from top to toe with sensitivity and along green lines with solar panels and a micro hydro powerhouse. On the ground floor is a golden yellow sitting room with a wood-burning stove and a railway-sleeper mantelpiece, and the four-poster bedroom is next door – along with a utility room and a Belfast sink for washing the day's catch; the 'wet room' is so large the whole family could scrub up at once. Upstairs are two light and pleasingly simple twin rooms with valley views. Leave the car behind – delightful Erica or John can pick you up from the village station – and hike to your heart's content. You are spoilt for choice – walk up the hill on the other side of the river for magical woodlands, or climb 2,500 feet up Ben Udlaidh for views to the islands. The pretty garden slopes towards the river, you can relax on the decking and help yourself to home-grown veg. *Secure garden, river to jump in, woodland walks. Working farm – sheep, be careful!*

Rooms	1 house for 6: £570-£1,020 per week. Prices based on 2 people. Additional guests £75 per week each. Dogs £15 per dog per week.
Meals	Pub 4 miles.
Closed	Rarely.

Biscuits, water and blankets. Expert advice on wild, carefree walks and a special welcome from terrier Boris the Arbuthnott.

John & Erica Kerr
The Old House,
Arichastlich, Glen Orchy, PA33 1BD

Tel	+44 (0)1838 200399
Email	glenorchyb8074@gmail.com
Web	www.glen-orchy.co.uk

Entry 213 Map 8

The Airds Hotel & Restaurant

This chic country-house hotel on the Appin peninsular stands above Loch Linnhe with views across the water to the Morvern Mountains. It came to life in 1750, an inn for passengers taking the paddle steamers up to the Caledonian canal. These days, it's one of the loveliest places to stay on the West Coast. Its whitewashed exterior gives no hint of the wonders within. You enter through a small conservatory, then find yourself in a world of smouldering fires, freshly cut flowers, beautiful wallpapers and soft sofas. Bedrooms are divine: beautiful fabrics, warm colours, Frette linen on Vi-Spring beds, sparkling marble bathrooms with robes; in short, the best of everything. Those at the front have the view, bigger rooms have sofas, some at the back have terraces, all spoil you rotten. Best of all is the exceptional food, perhaps West Coast langoustines with pea purée, sea bass with clams and a lemongrass cream, apple terrine with salted caramel and cinnamon doughnuts. There's a garden for croquet and afternoon tea with views to the water. Worth every penny. *Garden & path down to the loch; lovely walks from hotel door – information available. Dogs welcome in conservatory (not unattended in rooms unless in own cage).*

Rooms	8 twin/doubles: £180-£325. 3 suites for 4: £365-£410. 1 cottage for 5: £595-£940; 3-day stays from £210. Dinner, B&B from £145 p.p. Extra bed/sofabed £25 p.p.p.n. Dogs £10 per night. Max. 2 per room.
Meals	Lunch from £7. Dinner, 5 courses £56. Tasting menu £77. Sunday lunch £21.45.
Closed	Monday & Tuesday November – January.
	Dog blankets and water bowls – let us know on booking if you'd like them.

Shaun & Jenny McKivragan
The Airds Hotel & Restaurant,
Port Appin, Appin, PA38 4DF
Tel +44 (0)1631 730236
Email airds@airds-hotel.com
Web www.airds-hotel.com

Entry 214 Map 8

Alton Albany Farm

Discover Ayrshire… pine forests, hills and wild beauty. Alasdair and Andrea (sculptor and garden photographer respectively) are generous hosts who love having you to stay – your visit starts with tea, coffee and cake. There's an arty vibe with their work on display; the dining room brims with gardening books and games; large bedrooms have cosy lamps and more books. Big breakfasts by a log fire are a treat, perhaps with haggis, garden fruit, homemade bread; hearty dinners too. Rich in wildlife and orchids the garden has a rambling charm, the salmon-filled river Stinchar runs past and dogs are welcome – resident Daisy, Clover and Tansy are friendly. *Retreats & guided experiences available. Path round 2-acre garden; burn running through orchard which water-loving dogs are free to romp in; riverside walks; field for exercise & ball throwing (if no livestock).*

Rooms	1 double; 1 double, 1 twin sharing bath (let to same party only): £85-£115. Singles £60-£75. Dogs max. usually 2.
Meals	Dinner £15. Pubs/restaurants 10-12 miles.
Closed	24-29 December.

Treat on arrival. Dog biscuits, cocktail sausages, bowl, hose, towels; toys, balls & launcher.

Andrea & Alasdair Currie
Alton Albany Farm,
Barr, Girvan, KA26 0TL
Tel +44 (0)1465 861148
Mobile +44 (0)7881 908764
Email alasdair@gardenexposures.co.uk
Web www.altonalbanyfarm.com

Entry 215 Map 8

Lochinch Castle Cottages

On an isthmus hugged by freshwater lochs is one of Scotland's finest gardens with the dreamy ruins of Castle Kennedy at one end and Lochinch Castle, the family home of the Stairs (they've been here for generations) at the other. With 75 acres to roam, all ages will be happy here; walks ramble off in all directions. Explore land sculptures built in the 1730s; spot geese, herons, maybe an osprey, red squirrels and otters too. There are mesmerising displays of rhododendrons, azaleas and embothrium, and the ancient Monkey Puzzle Avenue is a treat. Find three charming properties: Chauffeur's, on the top floor of a two-storey Victorian carriage house, has pretty French château-style turrets, an open fire, long views, a large kitchen and three beautifully restful bedrooms; Balker Lodge, originally a gate house, is a cleverly revived bolthole for two; Ice House is a single-storey cottage with two pretty bedrooms, a log-burner in the sitting room and a pristine kitchen. All have their own private outside space, splendid welcome baskets with delicious cakes, and you get the run of the gardens. Why not take a guided tour with head gardener, John, who's worked here for 25 years. *Minimum stay: 3 nights. Great walks in acres of gardens and beautiful countryside,*

Rooms	1 apartment for 6: £400-£825. 1 cottage for 4: £380-£695. 1 house for 2: £360-£550. Prices per week. £15 booking fee per booking; £45 breakages deposit. Dogs £15 per dog per week. Max. 2.
Meals	Cooked or continental breakfast £12-£13. Dinner £12.
Closed	Never.
	Dog baskets, spacious comfortable rooms and advice on walks.

Emily Stair
Lochinch Castle Cottages,
Lochinch Castle, Stranraer, DG9 8RT
Tel +44 (0)1776 702024
Email housekeeping@lochinchcastle.com
Web www.castlekennedygardens.com/holiday-cottages/

Entry 216 Map 5

Trigony House Hotel

A welcoming family-run hotel with good food and nicely priced rooms. There's a small spa in the garden, too, with rather good views from the hot tub. The house dates to 1700 and comes with Japanese oak panelling in the hall, a wood-burner in the sitting room and an open fire in the dining room, where doors open onto the terrace for dinner in summer. Adam cooks lovely rustic fare, perhaps prawns with coconut and coriander, saddle of roe venison, rhubarb and hazelnut crumble; a small, organic kitchen garden provides seasonal veg for the table. Bedrooms – some big, some smaller – have warm colours, crisp linen, good beds and spotless bathrooms. A couple are dog-friendly, those at the back have the view, the suite opens onto a private garden. As for the spa, there's a treatment room, a sauna and a hot tub, so plenty of scope to recuperate after a day walking the Southern Upland Way or discovering the spectacular country between Moniaive and the Galloway Forest, a lost world of huge beauty you'll have to yourself. Don't miss Drumlanrig Castle for its gardens, walking trails and mountain bike tracks. *Beautiful walks. Well-behaved dogs welcome in the lounge and bar area.*

Rooms	4 doubles, 4 twin/doubles: £120-£140. 1 suite for 2: £165. Singles from £90. Extra beds £15. Dogs £9 per dog per night.
Meals	Lunch from £7.50. Dinner £25-£35. Afternoon tea £15.
Closed	24-26 December.
	Poo bag, map of local dog-friendly walks, bag of treats and dog blanket/bed.

Adam & Jan Moore
Trigony House Hotel,
Closeburn, Thornhill, DG3 5EZ

Tel	+44 (0)1848 331211
Email	trigonyhotel@gmail.com
Web	www.trigonyhotel.co.uk

Entry 217 Map 9

Kincaple Stables

The tap-tap of woodpeckers and singsong of birds are the soundtrack to a stay at Kincaple, a quaint hamlet three miles from St Andrews. The cottages, former stables, rest in the pretty, sheltered courtyard of Kincaple House, next to the Coach House where Claudia lives – her friendly terriers and cat sometimes wander over to see you. She has an eye for colour: subtle tones of grey-blue, honey and buttermilk are sparked by vases of flowers; in the living and dining room, a cream sofa curves around a stylish wood-burner and a bleached solid oak table seats four. It's all top quality. Find Villeroy & Bosch, Le Creuset and Siemens in the kitchen – small, square, with a stable door to the courtyard and well-stocked wine cooler – and Molton Brown in the bathroom. The main bedroom is flooded with light; the second bedroom has a zip-link bed. Well-travelled Claudia is passionate about this beautiful area of Scotland where she and her three daughters have settled. There are beaches, birds and golfing to enjoy, as well as ancient St Andrews with its university, vast cathedral and many fine shops and restaurants. *Minimum stay: 3 nights; 7 nights in high season. Plenty of walks for your four-legged friend, including 'Chariots of Fire' beach. Quiet grounds to roam away from traffic, but mind unfenced land.*

Rooms	2 cottages for 4: £625-£825 per week. Short breaks available £95 per night.
Meals	Restaurant within 3 miles.
Closed	Rarely.
	Blankets, and towels to get dry after the sea.

Claudia Daventry
Kincaple Stables,
Coach House, Kincaple,
St Andrews, KY16 9SH
Email cdaventry@me.com
Web www.kincaplestables.com

Entry 218 Map 9

Scourie Hotel

This famous old fishing hotel is a treat from top to toe. It's a quirky place run with great panache by the Campbells, who bought it recently, refurbished it in style and now it shines. It's supremely comfy – smart without being swanky, very much a country hotel. You'll find golden wallpapers, antique furniture, beautifully upholstered armchairs, then an open fire in the sitting room. It's a remarkably friendly place. Fishermen tend to come for the same week each year, re-booking when they leave, so everyone knows everyone but they also go out of their way to welcome interlopers into the fold. There's great tradition, too; a board master allocates fishing beats each morning, a gong announces dinner. Stylish rooms have comfy beds, pretty fabrics, beautiful new bathrooms and no TVs; bliss. Dinner is a treat, perhaps ham hock terrine, fresh local salmon, profiteroles with chocolate sauce. There are two bars, a pretty garden, paths that lead down to the sea. This is a wildly beautiful corner of Scotland: spectacular walking, wildlife tours and golf all wait. You're on the North Coast 500, too. *Plenty of wonderful walks on the beaches and in the hills for your dog to stretch his/her legs.*

Rooms	6 doubles, 6 twins: £135. 2 family rooms for 3: £145-£160. 6 singles: £85. 1 chalet for 4: £200-£250. Dinner, B&B £97 per person. Extra bed £25 p.p. Dogs £10 per night; max. fee £40 for stays over 4 days. Max 2 dogs.
Meals	Lunch from £4.95. Bar meals from £10. Dinner, 3 courses, £32.
Closed	Christmas, 7 October – 1 April.
	Towels for drying off.

Richard, Fiona & Charlotte Campbell
Scourie Hotel,
Scourie, Lairg, IV27 4SX
Tel +44 (0)1971 502396
Email stay@scouriehotel.com
Web www.scouriehotel.com

Entry 219 Map 11

Knoydart Hide

Not content with one gorgeous house high on the hill, Jackie and Ian have put up another and it's every bit as lovely. The only difference is size – this is a magical bolthole for two, perfect for honeymoons or just a blissful time away. Inside, walls of glass open onto a decked terrace, where you can soak in a hot tub while screened from the world by pine trees. Inside, there's a contemporary wood-burner in the sitting room, a kitchen with ample cooking stuff, a lovely big bed that looks out to sea, then a bathroom that's hard to beat with a double-ended bath, a walk-in power shower and an infrared sauna. You'll find all you'd want – fancy TV and DVD player, bath robes to pad about in, a bottle of prosecco on arrival – even the lawn is special, sown with 32 species of wild flower, the same turf as Olympic Park. If you don't want to cook, a chef can do it for you – lazy breakfasts, afternoon tea, seafood barbecues. Further afield, the wonders of Knoydart: wild orchids, sea eagles, mountains to climb. You can kayak, cruise the sea loch or do nothing at all. Stars fill the night sky, the Northern Lights come in winter. *Short breaks available. Forest trails and gorgeous woodland walks on the doorstep, including three Munros. Long sandy beach and coastal shoreline 100m away.*

Rooms	1 house for 2: £1,450-£1,750 per week. Extra beds available £50-£75 per child per night. Dogs £30 per stay. Max. 2.
Meals	Pub/restaurant within 3 miles.
Closed	Never.
	Pet bowls, extra towels for beachy paws, dog treat and advice on walks.

Ian & Jackie Robertson
Knoydart Hide,
Inverie, Knoydart, PH41 4PL
Tel +44 (0)1687 460012
Email stay@knoydarthide.co.uk
Web www.knoydarthide.co.uk

Entry 220 Map 8

Lochan Shepherd's Hut

With spectacular views stretching out over your own lochan, the shoreline and the Sound of Mull it doesn't get much more peaceful than this. All you'll hear are the sheep, the call of the odd eagle and the sound of the waves below you. The area is crammed with history; ancient burial chambers are dotted around and even a Viking boat burial was unearthed in 2011. From this remote vantage point on the coast, with the wild mountains all around, it's not difficult to imagine a real shipload of Vikings sailing past over the sea. Or for more contemporary interest, a short ferry trip will take you to Mull. The hut itself is comfy and functional, with a full-length double bed, wicker chairs and a folding table. As well as a gas ring inside the hut for an evening cocoa, you've got a little kitchenette next to the hut, and there's solar electricity too. There's a private compost loo a few steps away, and good shared showers 200 metres away. Look out across the sea to spot dolphins or stay warm by the wood-burner, with cup of tea in hand, and use the hut as a hide to spot corncrakes and pine martens. *Secure field, plenty of walks, sea, burns and beaches to run in. Countryside all around; cattle & sheep so dogs must be kept under control outside fenced area.*

Rooms	Shepherd's hut for 2: from £65 per night. Dogs £5 per dog per stay. Max. 1.
Meals	Self-catering.
Closed	November – March.

Advice on walks, dog biscuits, fenced field to run in – all to yourself.

Canopy & Stars
Lochan Shepherd's Hut,
Kilchoan, Acharacle, PH36 4LH

Tel	+44 (0)117 204 7830
Email	enquiries@canopyandstars.co.uk
Web	www.canopyandstars.co.uk/lochan

Entry 221 Map 8

Kilcamb Lodge Hotel & Restaurant

Another stunning West Coast setting with Loch Sunart at the end of the garden and Glas Bheinn rising beyond. Kilcamb – a barracks during the Jacobite uprising – is a perfect base. There's a smart drawing room with an open fire, an elegant dining room for super food, a cool little brasserie for a spot of lunch, then a handful of deeply indulging rooms. A 12-acre garden rolls down to the water, where you might spot otters and seals. Ducks and geese fly overhead, if you're lucky you'll see eagles. Back inside, you'll find a whisky bar that also does a good line in gin, then driftwood lamps, fresh flowers, good books and local art. You can eat in the restaurant or the brasserie, either a five-course tasting menu or something simpler, perhaps hand-dived scallops, Highland lamb, raspberry bavarois with champagne sorbet. Bedrooms have a country-house feel, some with a contemporary twist. You'll find warm colours, smart fabrics and excellent beds. One has a balcony, most have the view, all have spotless bathrooms, some with separate showers. Don't miss Ardnamuchan or Senna Bay at the end of the road. *Eleven acres of safe loch front garden.*

Rooms	2 doubles, 6 twin/doubles: £220-£380. 2 suites for 2: £300-£435. 1 family room for 4: £390-£435. Includes dinner. £12 per dog per night; £20 for 2. Dog food from 80p. Dog sitting £12 per hour.
Meals	Lunch from £7.50. Dinner included; non-residents £50. Tasting menu £75. Sunday lunch £25. Afternoon tea £14.
Closed	Jan & first 2 weeks in Dec. Limited opening Nov & Feb.
	Towel, blanket, bowl & mat. Breakfast sausage too!

David & Sally Ruthven-Fox
Kilcamb Lodge Hotel & Restaurant,
Strontian, Acharacle, PH36 4HY
Tel +44 (0)1967 402257
Email enquiries@kilcamblodge.co.uk
Web www.kilcamblodge.co.uk

Entry 222 Map 8

The Inn at Loch Tummel

You weave through the forest, then arrive at this 200-year-old inn to find views of field, hill, loch and sky. It's a magical spot, with a small garden to the front that drinks it all in. As for the inn, Alice and Jade rescued it from neglect, poured in love and money and now it shines. Interiors mix contemporary flair with Highland charm, the very definition of rustic chic. You'll find a cool little bar, painted beams and a wood-burner in the restaurant, then a first-floor sitting room with fat sofas, books and games, goatskin rugs and Jade's guitar. Bedrooms are a treat: chic fabrics, beautiful beds, cool colours, woollen throws. Some are big, none are small, one is dog friendly, most have the view. All have good art, decanters of whisky and spotless bathrooms, some with walk-in showers. By day you explore the hills, whizz down mountain bike trails or climb Schiehallion, the local munro. At night you return for delicious food, perhaps calamari with chilli and lemon, rack of local lamb, an espresso brownie with beetroot meringue. Queen's View, up the road, has one of the best views in Scotland. *Children over 5 welcome. Closed for check in on Sunday & Monday. Lochside walks; Allean Forest, a few minutes' drive away.*

Rooms	2 doubles, 4 twin/doubles: £105-£155. Dogs £10. Max. 2 per room.
Meals	Dinner with wine £27.
Closed	Christmas. January.

Dog biscuits, water bowls, hose pipe for washing off muddy dogs.

Alice & Jade Calliva
The Inn at Loch Tummel,
Queens View,
Strathtummel, PH16 5RP
Tel +44 (0)1882 634317
Email info@theinnatlochtummel.com
Web www.theinnatlochtummel.com

Entry 223 Map 8

Mhor

Monachyle Mhor, boutique hotel run by the Lewis family is also home to two Highland hideouts. Pilot Panther is a classic 1950 showman's wagon originally built by The Coventry Steel Company, once renowned as the finest wagon makers in the country. Off the main living and sleeping area, which also has the oven and grill, is the double bunk room and the views from every window are of the spectacular loch. The Ferry Waiting Room is made up of a lost and found ferry terminal and bothy. Whilst the waiting room has become a cosy bedroom with a double bed and two bunks, the bothy houses a small kitchen – both with incredible views. Hot showers and flushing loos can be found in the courtyard of the hotel, shared with other guests. The great walking and stunning views around the long loch will help you work up an appetite for dinner that's worthy of Monachlye Mhor, an award-winning pilgrimage for Scottish foodies. The family that run the restaurant also manage the farm, which ensures that a good supply of very local produce goes onto the amazing menus – take your pick from take away ingredients or eat-in goodies. *In the middle of a glen with plenty of countryside walks & rivers to jump in. Sheep in some fields where dogs need to be kept on lead.*

Rooms	Wagon for 4: from £125 per night. Ferry Terminal for 2-4: from £140 per night. Dogs £10 per dog per stay, payable on arrival. Max. 2.
Meals	Dinner and breakfast at the hotel must be pre-booked with reception prior to arrival.
Closed	Never.
	Advice on walks.

Canopy & Stars
Mhor,
Mhor, Balquhidder,
Lochearnhead, FK19 8PQ

Tel	+44 (0)117 204 7830
Email	enquiries@canopyandstars.co.uk
Web	www.canopyandstars.co.uk/mhor

Entry 224 Map 8

Cringletie House

Cringletie's splendours are hard to miss. You're wrapped up in 65 acres of beautiful grounds with daffodils that erupt in spring, cows that graze in lush fields and a peaceful walled garden for a game of boules. Pheasants strut, buzzards circle, views roll over nearby hills. As for the house, it dates to 1860, its playful turrets giving it a soft grandeur. Inside, you get the full works: an open fire in the hall, then a fine old staircase that sweeps you up to a striking first-floor dining room that has the feel of an 18th-century gentleman's club; expect panelled walls, vintage wallpapers and a spectacular muralled ceiling. There's a sitting room up here, too – equally grand, with fat sofas in front of the fire. Bedrooms are scattered about. Some downstairs open onto the garden, those at the top have the best views. It doesn't matter which you go for, they're all lovely, with warm colours, crisp linen, comfy beds and excellent bathrooms. Take to the hills, follow the Tweed or scoot up to Edinburgh; it's less than an hour by car. *Walled garden, woodlands and Eddleston river. Sheep and Highland cattle in fields.*

Rooms	12 twin/doubles: £135-£245. 1 suite for 2: £235-£265. 1 cottage for 6: £235-£465.
Meals	Lunch from £9.50. Afternoon tea from £18.50. Dinner, 3 courses, £37.50. Sunday lunch £22.50.
Closed	3-25 January.
	Biscuits, towels, and lots of walks.

Jeremy Osbourne
Cringletie House,
Edinburgh Road,
Peebles, EH45 8PL
Tel +44 (0)1721 725750
Email enquiries@cringletie.com
Web www.cringletie.com

Entry 225 Map 9

Laundry Cottage

Our inspector was reluctant to leave so charming is the conversion and so stunning is the setting. Only the grey stone exterior belies its 19th-century laundry origins; inside all is light and airy in the large open-plan kitchen/diner/living room. The vaulted ceiling soars, original and new beams marry well, thick stone walls set off local art. This is a friendly comfy space: whip up meals in the modern kitchen, dine at the farmhouse table, relax on squashy sofas in front of the wood-burner (first basket of logs free), drink in the hilly views. Bedrooms (all on the ground floor) are calm and uncluttered with deep windows framing more long views; contemporary bathrooms sparkle. Outside there's a terrace for barbecues, a wildflower meadow, and a pond teeming with wildlife (watch small children). Delightful owners – who also let out the farmhouse next door, otherwise you have the place to yourself – leave cake and bubbles in the kitchen; Selkirk is close for supplies. You're in border country so lovers of outdoor pursuits will be in clover: horse-riding, golf, fishing... biking and hiking from the door too. *Minimum stay: 3 nights. Off-road walks with miles of tracks and hills to explore from the doorstep, but watch out for sheep. Ettrick Water (salmon river) for splashing and swimming.*

Rooms	1 cottage for 6: from £545 per week. Dogs £25 per stay.
Meals	Home-cooked meals in the freezer by request.
Closed	Never.
	Towels for drying.

Louisa Marston
Laundry Cottage,
Selkirk, TD7 5HN
Email info@howfordfarm.com
Web www.howfordfarm.com

Fauhope House

Near to Melrose Abbey and the glorious St Cuthbert's Walk, this solid 1890s house is immersed in bucolic bliss. Views soar to the Eildon Hills through wide windows with squashy seats; all is luxurious, elegant, fire-lit and serene with an eclectic mix of art. Bedrooms are warm with deeply coloured walls, pale tartan blankets and soft velvet and linen; bathrooms are modern and pristine. Breakfast is served with smiles at a flower-laden table and overlooking those purple hills. A short walk through the blooming garden and over a footbridge takes you to the interesting town of Melrose, with shops, restaurants and its own theatre. *Parkland in front of house. Fabulous walks up the hill behind; 5-minute walk to a river to jump in. Dogs on leads when the sheep are in lamb and at lambing time.*

Rooms	3 twin/doubles: £140-£160. Singles £98. Dogs charged only if there is damage! Max. 1 dog.
Meals	Pub/restaurant 0.5 miles.
Closed	Rarely.
	Biscuits, pig's ears, good water and advice on walks.

Ian & Sheila Robson
Fauhope House,
Gattonside, Melrose, TD6 9LU
Tel +44 (0)1896 823184
Mobile +44 (0)7816 346768
Email info@fauhopehouse.com
Web www.fauhopehouse.com

Entry 227 Map 9

Ben Lomond

A fusion of Kyrgyz design and local materials, there are three yurts here but Ben Lomond is the only one to welcome your canine friend. All three yurts have a homely, earthy feel, with thick rugs, rough tapestries and wood-burning stoves adding comfort. Ben Ledi and Ben Lomond yurts share the woodland just a little way on from Stuc a'Chroin yurt. In each is a double bed, a double futon, and a single 'sleep over' for a child. From the boardwalk leading to the communal kitchen are impressive views across Flanders Moss National Nature Reserve. Arts and crafts courses aplenty too, from willow crafting to Japanese block printing and yoga. There's an abundance of local produce, including veg from the kitchen garden, steaks for the barbecue, local eggs and homemade bread. With all this and the beauty of the Trossachs National Park to explore, you won't be short of ways to create a memorable stay. And for those furry friends looking to curl up beside the wood-burner, blankets are provided for extra comfort. *Working farm so dogs on leads on farm, but there are no animals in the vicinity of the yurt. Lots of space for a run in the woodland around the yurt.*

Rooms	Yurt for 5: from £100 per night. Dogs £30 per dog per stay. Max. 1.
Meals	Self-catering.
Closed	November – March.
	Water and food bowls, a cosy bed as well as a towel and toothbrush treat! Advice on walks.

Canopy & Stars
Ben Lomond, West Moss-side Organic Farm and Centre, Thornhill, FK8 3QJ

Tel	+44 (0)117 204 7830
Email	enquiries@canopyandstars.co.uk
Web	www.canopyandstars.co.uk/ben-lomond

Entry 228 Map 8

England

Bath & N.E. Somerset

1 'Woof Box' with treats, bowl, Lily's Kitchen dog food, tennis ball and poo bags. Blanket provided overnight too.

2 Advice on walks and a 'Woof Box' that includes dog treats, food and a ball.

3 Dog beds, dog bowls and doggy treats.

4 Dog biscuit tin, dog bed, bowls and towels for drying.

5 Advice on walks, a Bonio and a pat on the back.

Cambridgeshire

6 Water bowls, towels for drying and dog biscuits in the room.

7 Water bowl and hose for washing off muddy paws.

Cheshire

8 Biscuits on the bar, water bowls, Doggie Beer and good walks. Dog basket available for dogs staying in rooms.

9 Dog bowls and towels.

Cornwall

10 Guidance on local walks. Doc Martin's dog Dodger stays here!

11 Jar of Mera Dog pure goody snacks. The Cabin has a 'mud room' for drying off; Pixie Yurt has space for lots of dog beds.

12 Fleecy Chalky's pal blanket, guide to dog walks in Cornwall, personal dog bowls, and 100% natural dog treats from Green & Wilds with selected breaks.

13 Biscuits, bedding and bowls.

14 Bowls, water, biscuits and a leaflet about dogs at the hotel.

15 Underfloor heating, advice on walks and dog poo bags by the door.

16 Dog biscuits, blanket, towels, advice on walks, poo bags and dog bowls. Very friendly staff too.

17 Dog biscuits, blanket, towels, advice on walks, poo bags and dog bowls. Very friendly staff too.

18 Advice on walks, river to swim in, coastal path walks, year-round dog-friendly beaches 5-10 min walk, and lovely dog-friendly pub 5-min walk.

19 Dog-friendly beach map – there are lots of beaches and walks all year round.

20 Coastal, country lane and river walks.

21 Biscuits and blanket.

22 Dog treats, bowls, towel and a collar tag with postcode and phone number. Outside hose for washing dogs off.

23 Private fenced garden for dog to play in; empty field for running free off lead. Throws for furniture. Advice & maps for fantastic dog walks, dog-friendly beaches, pubs and days out.

24 Cosy dog blanket, water bowl and towels.

25 Throws provided, doggy towels and wonderful country walks.
26 Treats, biodegradable poo bags, towels and advice on our favourite walks.

Cumbria

27 Water bowl and perfect walks from the door.
28 Advice on walks and dog-friendly activities and nearby pubs.
29 Outdoor bed, blanket, water bowl and dog lead.
30 Doggy welcome pack including treat, map of local walks and doggy bag.
31 Advice on walks.
32 Wonderful walks from the doorstep up and onto the Cumbrian fells.
33 Welcome dog biscuit, water bowl and spare dog towels.
34 Welcome dog biscuit, water bowl and spare dog towels.
35 Dog treats, toy, bowls, mat and bed.
36 Water bowls and towels for cleaning off muddy dogs.
37 Acres of garden and woodland sniffs; one room has an enclosed garden that's dog-proof for most breeds!

Derbyshire

38 Dog bed, bowls and treats, towels for drying and poo bags. Advice on local dog-friendly cafés, pubs and walks.
39 Dog biscuits at turndown, towels and lots of walking information.
40 Dog treats, bowls and poo bags.
41 Dog treats, water and food bowls and poo bags.
42 Water bowls, towels on request and a hose for washing paws.

Devon

44 Dog biscuits, water bowl, towel, throws for furniture and outside tap with hose.
45 Towels, beds, bowls, treats, poo bags and Dirty Dog shampoo. Also hose and poo bin under the lodges.
46 Pig's ears, and advice on dog walks and local dog-friendly beaches.
47 Blankets and dog biscuits.
48 Woodland walks, maps and dog .
49 Doggy box with towel, blanket, bowls, treats, toys and spare leads.
50 Advice on walks.
51 Bowls, blanket, towels and doggy treats.
52 Dog snacks, 5-acre gardens, loads of great local walks.
53 Towels, bowls and advice on walks. A river to swim in and resident wonder dog Rags to entertain.
54 Maps and advice on walks, towels on request, entertainment and company from resident Labrador Kasper.
55 Organic dog biscuits, dog towels, and acres of private woodland for walks in your pyjamas and wellies.
56 Dog blanket, towels and a welcome treat when booking through Sawday's.
57 Welcome dog treat on arrival and dog towels can be provided.
58 Towels, water bowl, bedding, dog

treats and lovely walks from the door.

59 Advice on walks, dog towels, resident friendly lurchers to play with – and plenty of love and attention!

60 Hose to wash muddy paws, stream running through the garden to splash in. Dog towels on request.

61 Devon-made food, handmade treats; towels, blanket, poo bags, shampoo. Identity tag with local contact details.

Dorset

62 Dog-friendly guide to the area, water bowl, towel and treats. Walking map and dog treats in the bar too.

63 Towels and advice on walks.

64 Dog bowls, homemade dog biscuits (flour, oil, free-range egg, banana, herbs and peppermint oil). Towels are available & hose pipe for muddy dogs.

65 Surprise dog treats in the welcome hamper.

66 Beach runs and towels for drying after splashing in the sea.

67 A little something in the welcome pack and towels for drying.

68 Water bowl, food bowl and a dog treat.

69 Dog treats or pig's ears, doggy wash-down kit with towels & 'pet head' shampoo, poo bags. Long tether so owners can enjoy the hot tub without their dog running off!

70 Advice on walks.

71 Dog treats, towels and comfy bed.

Durham

72 Homemade edible treats and towels for wet dogs.

73 Dog beds, towels for drying and locally made dog treats.

74 Acres of dog-friendly garden and farmland to explore.

Essex

75 Biscuits, blankets, towels and walks.

76 Blankets, towels, advice on walks, doggy dinners, water bowls and treat.

Gloucestershire

77 Dog beds, bowls and treats. Love and fuss for every dog. Snuffle dog beer offered too!

78 Advice on walks.

79 Dog beds in bedrooms, treats and biscuits on request. Towels, water in the gardens and lots of walking maps of the Cotswold Way.

80 Bag of dog biscuits, a collapsible travel dog bowl, a rope toy, mini dog shampoo and a pack of poo bags.

81 Biscuits, a chew, sometimes a piece of ham. Outside bath for dogs who love to roll in fox poo or muddy puddles (candles optional!). Deck to sit on – what better doggy heaven than sharing an evening BBQ with their owners!

82 Dog bowls and dog beds.
83 Bowls, high-quality dog food, beds, hose for washing muddy paws and local ID dog tag.
84 Dog-sitting, towels and advice on walks.
85 Advice on walks and large dog-friendly garden.

Hampshire

86 Lily's Kitchen Bedtime Biscuits, bones, sheepskin rug, water bowl, towels for drying, maps and advice on walks.
87 Doggy treats for tired out hounds.
88 Advice on walks, and river swims!
89 Map showing the best places for walks and advice on days out.

Herefordshire

90 Pond & little stream for doggy paddling in summer; a dog-stop in the workshop where you can snuggle by the fire with them; a veranda where you can wash down muddy hounds.
91 Water bowls, doggy treats and advice on walks.
92 Dog biscuits, basket with a snug blanket and toys.

Hertfordshire

93 Woodland walks from the doorstep.

Kent

94 Towels, blankets, biscuits and water bowls.
95 Dog bed, chews to gnaw on, toys to play with and water bowl.
96 Dog biscuit treats, rugs for the furniture and towels for drying.

Lancashire

97 Dog beds, bowls and towels upon request.

Leicestershire

98 Advice on walks.

Lincolnshire

99 Bowls, biscuits and advice on walks.

Norfolk

100 Dog blanket and bowl with treats in room on arrival. Treats behind the bar and a sausage for breakfast.
101 A dog blanket in the room and a tasty sausage for breakfast. Four-legged guests' gallery on the website.
102 Homemade biscuits, blankets, towels and soft-cushioned bed, water and food bowels, feeding mat, poo bags. Drying room too.
103 Towels for drying.
104 Dog bed, and towels for drying off wet, nicely tired out dogs.
105 Tasty biscuits, bowls for feeding, blankets for snuggling, throws for furniture.
106 Dog treats on arrival and dog bowls.
107 Locally made dog biscuits and wonderful walks.

Northumberland

108 Towels, bowls, and great dog walking from the door.

109 Food and water bowls, and advice on walks through the forest and along the Lakeside Way.

110 Drying room, towels and Bonedrybed dog bed. Advice on walks and hose pipe area. Birthday cakes on request and 37 acres to explore.

111 Leads, bowls, furniture throws and poo bags.

112 Dog bed, towel, bowl and advice on walks.

Oxfordshire

113 A box of dog treats, water bowls and a beer garden to sit in.

114 Four-legged friends are offered a selection box of tasty treats, comfy bed, water bowl, a towel to dry muddy paws after country walks and poo bags.

Rutland

115 Advice on walks.

116 Leads, bedding, poo bags, bowls, food and biscuits. Crates, cuddly toys, waterproof coats and towelling for muddy paws.

Shropshire

117 Advice on walks.

118 Doggy box in every pet owner's bedroom with towels and cloths, dog mat, lead, bowl, treats and poo bags.

119 Dog biscuits, medium-sized dog bed, 2 bowls and towels for drying.

120 Dog Welcome Box in the room for your pet which includes a feeding mat, food bowl, towel, lead, treats and poo bags.

121 Walks, lots of space and many dog-loving staff!

122 Dog treats, blankets and advice on walks.

123 A Bonio at bedtime.

124 Throws, dog bowls, towels and advice on walks and places to eat. Downstairs room has direct access to enclosed garden.

Somerset

125 Doggy treat tin: anything from pig's ears/pizzle sticks & cow's hooves to dried banana & sweet potato; bowls aplenty. And ultimate treat: book your dog in for bath, brush & pamper, with a blueberry & vanilla facial!

126 Dog bed & bowl, towel to dry paws & small pack of doggy treats. Hose outside room for washing off, or wet room ideal for showering them. Dog biscuits on the bar.

127 Dog biscuits, water bowls, hose for washing muddy dogs after after walks.

128 Maps and advice on local walks.

Suffolk

129 Dog biscuits, water bowls and maps with local walks.

130 Homemade treats, towels, walks, and a bookable "doggie table" in the restaurant.

131 Blankets, towels, walks, bowls and doggy dinners.

132 Dog's own welcome letter, biscuits, water and food bowls, walking lead and spare poo bags. Underfloor heated boot room for dogs to sleep in.

133 Dog treats, water bowl and towel (any items owners might have forgotten can be supplied too: leads, spare bed, food).

134 Doggy towels and poo bags.

Sussex

135 Dog bowls and towels for drying.

136 Advice on walks and dog-friendly pubs nearby.

137 Dog beds and bowls in rooms. Free dog biscuits at bar; 'dog beer' for sale!

138 Towels, advice on walking and walks from the door. Dog sitting if you want to go out without your dog.

139 Poo bags, dog biscuits and towels.

140 Woodland walks straight from the door and dog bowls.

141 Homemade dogs biscuits, towels and drying room.

142 Advice on walks.

Sussex

143 Treats, poo bags and advice on walks.

Warwickshire

144 Dog biscuits in the bar area and dog bowls available.

145 Dog biscuits, pig's ears, water, dog beds, blankets and advice on walks.

146 Dog bed, water bowls, a hose for washing off muddy paws – and a sausage for breakfast.

Wiltshire

147 Maps and advice on walks – and towels if required.

148 Dog treats, water bowls, towels, advice on walks – and dog bed if required.

Worcestershire

149 Cosy blankets to snuggle up in, towels; dog bowls and poo bags provided.

150 Towels, water bowls and dog treats.

151 Towels, dog bowl and dog treats.

152 Cosy basket and box of dog treat biscuits.

153 Doggy bed/basket, bowls, hose pipe & towels. 2 butchers within 10 minutes' drive for meaty dog treats (pig's ears & bones can be ordered, by prior arrangement).

Yorkshire

154 Towels for drying and advice on great walks.

155 A lake for dog swimming, lovely walks on site, and a contained two-acre bamboo garden for comfort and safety.

156 Advice on walks and suggestions of local dog-friendly pubs.

157 A guide to local dog-friendly pubs and beaches.

158 Dog bowl.

159 Advice on walks, and a lovely nature reserve just 2 minutes from cottages.

160 Dog treats upon arrival.

161 Blankets, throws, treats and bowls. Dog tags with our phone number; hose for cleaning muddy paws and towels for drying off.

162 Towels for drying and advice on walks.

163 Raw beef bones from the butcher, great dog walks, and towels.

England – pubs

Bedfordshire

163.1 Dog biscuits on the bar, beef bone and pig's ears, water bowls and hose for washing off muddy paws.

Brighton & Hove

164 Water bowls and treats, and a warm open fire in the winter months which dogs love.

Bristol

165 Dog bowls available at all times.

Buckinghamshire

166 A huge garden to run around in. Dog biscuits on the bar, fresh water bowls outside and a large OS map by the front door. Lovely circular walk on iFootpath.

167 Dog biscuits, bowls of water and open fires to snooze by.

Cambridgeshire

168 A dogs welcome sign at the front of the pub, dog biscuits behind the bar and bowls at the front door and in the back garden.

Cheshire

169 Dog biscuits, dogs' dinner menu, Doggie Beer and water bowls. Shakerley Mere bird nature reserve walks, and a play in enclosed extensive gardens.

170 Biscuits on the bar, water bowls and Doggie Beer. A good pub walk between The Bull's Head and The Church Inn.

171 Dog bowls, dog biscuits and Doggie Beer too. A great pub walk, extensive gardens and terrace to play in.

Cornwall

172 Dog treats and water bowls.

Gloucestershire

173 Homemade biscuit in room. Water bowls, advice on walks, poo bags. Hose for mucky paws, towels after a good shake. Lounge bar & snug area for doggy dining – gluten-free breakfast sausages sometimes!

174 Dog treats and a water bowl.

Hertfordshire

175 Dog biscuits on the bar, fresh water bowls outside and a large OS map by the front door. Lovely circular walk on iFootpath.

Northamptonshire

176 Water bowls inside and out. Solid floors throughout the pub so we are never fazed by muddy paws.

Somerset

177 Dog bowls available at all times.

Staffordshire

178 Dog biscuit, water bowls and Doggie Beer.

Suffolk

179 Dog treats, water bowls, dog breakfast, blanket, map with local walks, dog wash and towels.

Sussex

180 Dog treats on the bar; water bowls throughout the pub. Book a table with dogs and there will be a plate of dog biscuits waiting when you arrive. Great walks around the village too.

181 Water bowl and dog bed in the bar, and doggy menu featuring biscuits and treats.

182 Dog biscuits, water bowls – and a friendly welcome!

Wiltshire

182.1 Dog biscuits for our four-legged guests and a bowl outside. Their owners get mints with their bills.

Wales

Anglesey

183 Advice on dog-friendly pubs, beaches and days out.

Cardiff

184 Towels, and advice on walks and local dog-friendly pubs.

Carmarthenshire

185 Advice on walks.

186 Dog biscuits, beds, bowls, towels, leads and advice on walks.

Ceredigion

187 Advice on walks and dog-friendly beaches.

188 Dogs truly welcome! Lovely gardens and lots of advice on beaches, local pubs and days out.

189 Towels for drying, feeding and water bowls, poo bags, nice dog biscuits and guided walks.

190 Water bowl and advice on walks.

191 Homemade biscuits, doggy guide with vet details, walks, dog-friendly pubs. Towels, blankets for the sofa, poo bags and scoop.

Conwy

192 Advice on walks, a dog bowl, treats and a warm welcome.

Gwynedd

193 Advice on dog-friendly dining, dog biscuits, dog towel, poo bags and suggestions for walks.

194 Bonios and tap in downstairs loo for

washing off muddy dogs.

195 Advice on walks and seven acres of garden to play in.

196 Advice on walks, lots of private space and a river on the doorstep.

197 Treats, towels and throws for muddy paws, and wonderful walks from the doorstep.

198 Dog bed, dog blankets, biscuits, outside hot water shower, dog shampoo and towels.

Monmouthshire

199 Dog welcome pack with biscuits or gravy bones. Dog blanket and throws for protecting furniture so you can cuddle up.

200 Outside tap for cleaning muddy paws & blankets for drying off. Dog bed & crate available if needed. Sue & Nick have 2 active collies and are always happy to advise.

201 Towels for drying off after lake swimming.

202 Dog parlour and towels. Dog treats for well-behaved dogs.

Pembrokeshire

203 Dog bowls and outside hose for washing off muddy paws. There is always a sausage at breakfast too.

204 Dog biscuits, towels, walking advice and 3 acres of woodland where dogs can run around off the lead.

Powys

205 Water bowl and tether. Maps and routes for walks around the farm and local footpaths and bridleways.

206 Dog biscuits, blanket, towels, advice on walks, poo bags, dog bowls – and very friendly staff.

207 Biscuits, dog leads, bowls and advice on walks.

208 Great walks from the house.

209 Sausages for breakfast, towels, dog bowls and walks.

Scotland

Aberdeenshire

210 Dog sleepover pack! Includes gravy bones, towel, blanket to put on the sofa, dog bed, bowls and lead. (Must keep off the beds!)

Argyll & Bute

211 Dog biscuit.

212 Dog food (James Wellbeloved & Lily's), sometimes local homemade dog biscuits. Poo bags, 'tick' remover tool, dog bed, blankets to cover furniture so you can snuggle up. Outside standing water pipe too.

213 Biscuits, water and blankets. Expert advice on wild, carefree walks and a special welcome from terrier Boris the Arbuthnott.

214 Dog blankets and water bowls – let us know on booking if you'd like them.

Ayrshire

215 Treat on arrival. Dog biscuits, cocktail sausages, bowl, hose, towels; toys, balls & launcher.

Dumfries & Galloway

216 Dog baskets, spacious comfortable rooms and advice on walks.

217 Poo bag, map of local dog-friendly walks, bag of treats and dog blanket/bed.

Fife

218 Blankets, and towels to get dry after the sea.

Highland

219 Towels for drying off.

220 Pet bowls, extra towels for beachy paws, dog treat and advice on walks.

221 Advice on walks, dog biscuits, fenced field to run in – all to yourself.

222 Doggy towel, blanket (covers the bed for those moments when they need a cuddle), water bowl & mat. All in a package on the bed with a welcome letter. Breakfast sausage too!

Perthshire

223 Dog biscuits, water bowls, hose pipe for washing off muddy dogs.

224 Advice on walks.

Scottish Borders

225 Biscuits, towels, and lots of walks.

226 Towels for drying.

227 Biscuits, pig's ears, good water and advice on walks.

Stirling

228 Water and food bowls, a cosy bed as well as a towel and toothbrush treat! Advice on walks.

Photo: Dave (Maisy Richardson)

1. Ask yourself, is your human going to enjoy the destination and its surroundings? Do they like a buzzing city or the quiet countryside? It's important to keep them safe and happy in an unfamiliar environment. Make sure you stick to their routine as much as possible – it seems humans are terrible at handling changes!

2. "Sniffing" the place out before you get there is a great idea, as is learning the difference between a place merely 'welcoming' humans and those which are truly human-friendly. Always check there's a place for you to dine with your human in harmony. If you're lucky, the waiters won't be able to resist those sad baby eyes and will bring them an extra sausage at breakfast. This is obviously yours as a reward for organising everything.

3. Pack the essentials! Make sure to snoopervise the preparations. These humans are barking. While they'll obviously pack spare collars, treats, tags, leads and poo bags, you should make sure they have plenty of games to play otherwise they get grumpy. Also remember that they're saying, "wine" and not "whine". It seems to be very important to them.

4. Always check the house rules. You'll have a cover or bag so you can sit in a lovely armchair, but do you have everything you need to stop your human making a mess? Watch out for their feet especially. For some people, a dog on a seat and a human putting their feet up are much the same. Even on holiday don't forget your etiquette.

5. Finally, the most important thing is to have fun! Find the best smells and views, get off the beaten path (but be careful that your human doesn't chase livestock), and be sure to share stories with your pawtners!

Best Woofs,

Marcel @lecorgi
Food Critic and Corguide Extraordinaire

BREAD
PETERS
& SONS.
81 QUEENS PARK
BRIGHTON
PHONE: 68233

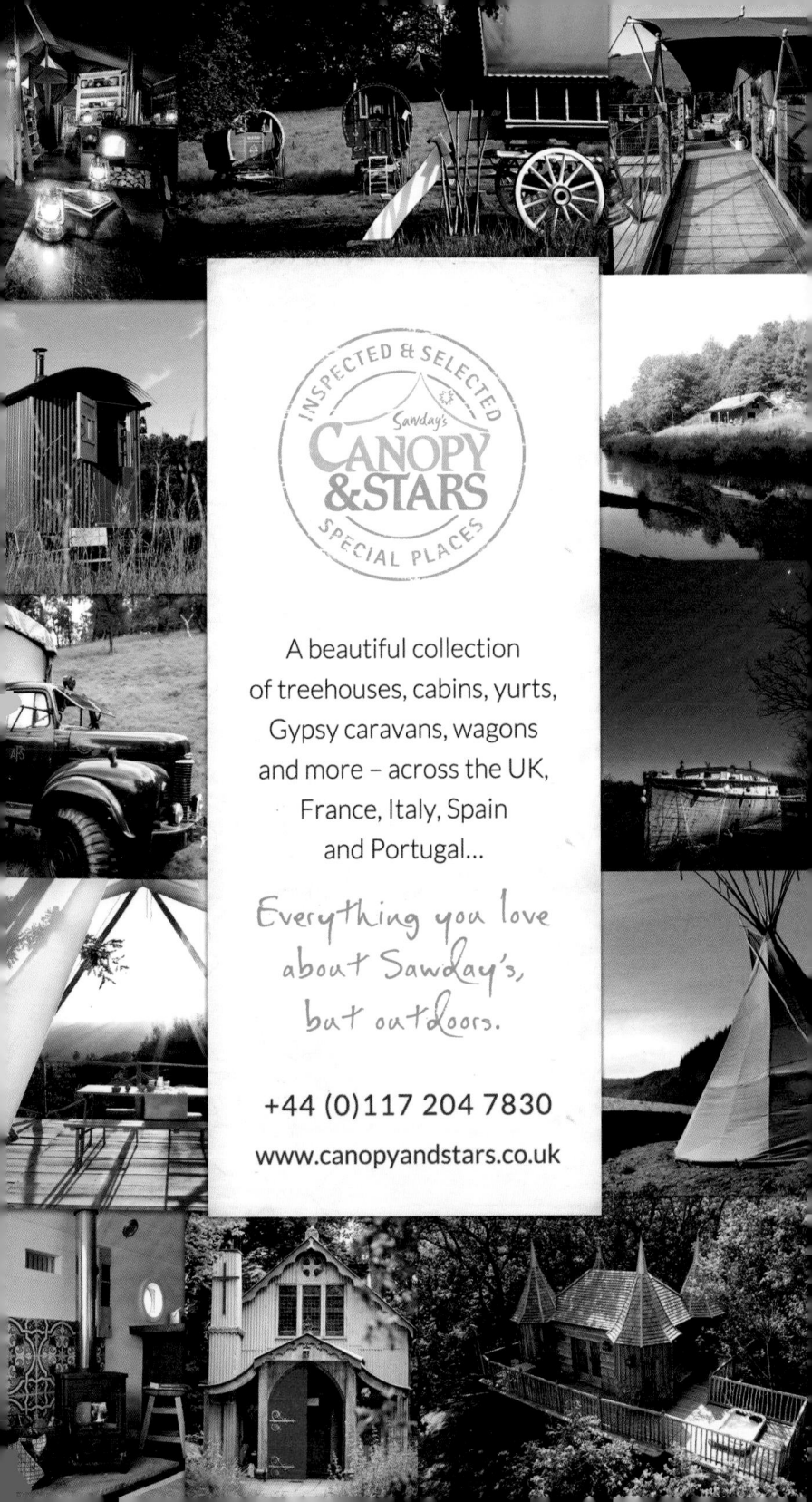
INSPECTED & SELECTED
Sawday's
CANOPY
&STARS
SPECIAL PLACES
A beautiful collection
of treehouses, cabins, yurts,
Gypsy caravans, wagons
and more – across the UK,
France, Italy, Spain
and Portugal...
Everything you love
about Sawday's,
but outdoors.
+44 (0)117 204 7830
www.canopyandstars.co.uk

Sawday's has been publishing books for over 20 years, finding Special Places to Stay in Britain and abroad. All our properties are inspected by us and are chosen for their charm and individuality. And there are many more to explore on our perennially popular website: www.sawdays.co.uk. You can buy any of our books at a reader discount of 25%* on the RRP.

List of titles:	RRP	Discount price
British Bed & Breakfast	£15.99	£11.99
British Hotels and Inns	£15.99	£11.99
Pubs & Inns of England & Wales	£15.99	£11.99
Dog-friendly Breaks in Britain	£14.99	£11.24
French Bed & Breakfast	£15.99	£11.99
French Châteaux & Hotels	£15.99	£11.99
Italy	£15.99	£11.99

*postage and packaging is added to each order

How to order:

Call us on: **+44 (0)117 204 7810**

Photo opposite: Bugsy (Bethan Walker)

DON'T FOLLOW THE CROWD

Find hundreds of inspiring alternatives to boring motorway service stations. Amazing food, stunning settings & lovely people.

ESCAPE THE CROWDS & ENJOY YOUR JOURNEY

£12.99

WWW.THEEXTRAMILE.GUIDE

Abergavenny 202
Abermaw 198
Acharacle 221, 222
Adhurst 88
Alfrick 153
Appin 214
Ardbrecknish Dalmally 212
Arthog 197
Ashbourne 40, 41
Badminton 77
Barnard Castle 72, 73
Barnstaple 60
Bath 1-5
Baughurst 86
Beaumaris 183
Beckley 140
Berkhamsted 93
Betws-y-Coed 192
Bishop's Castle 119, 120
Blakeney 82
Blanchland 112
Blandford Forum 68
Bonvilston 184
Brechfa 186
Brecon 206, 207
Bridport 63, 64
Brockweir 81
Bromyard 90
Brynhoffnant 189
Builth Wells 208
Buxton 38
Caernarfon 193
Calstock 25
Canterbury 96
Cardigan 187
Carlisle 27
Cheltenham 79
Chepstow 199
Chipping Norton 113
Chulmleigh 48
Cirencester 84
Clearwell 80
Cleobury Mortimer 122
Clifton Upon Teme 152
Clitheroe 97
Colchester 75
Combe Martin 45
Craven Arms 124
Crediton 49
Crickhowell 209
Cullompton 57
Dartmouth 59
Derby 42, 98
Dingestow 201
Dolgellau 195
Dorchester 62
Dulverton 128
East Dean 136
East Grinstead 139
Fairford 78
Fowey 20
Frampton on Severn 83
Girvan 215
Glen Orchy 213
Hambledon 89
Hartland 46
Harwich 76
Helston 18, 19
Hereford 91
Hexham 109-111
Hindringham 103
Horsham 138
Huntingdon 6
Huntly 210
Ipswich 131, 132
Isle of Mull 211

Kincaple 218
Kingsbridge 54, 55
Kirkby Stephen 32-34, 36
Knoydart 220
Lairg 219
Lampeter 190
Lanchester 74
Leyburn 163
Lifton 51
Liskeard 23
Llanbedr 194
Llandeilo 185
Llandysul 188
Llanon 191
Lochearnhead 224
Looe 21, 22, 24
Luckington 148
Ludlow 123
Lydbury 121
Lyme Regis 65
Lynton 44
Machynlleth 205
Malpas 8, 9
Matlock 39
Mawgan Porth 14
Melrose 227
Milford Haven 204
Morpeth 108
Newport 203
Newquay 13, 15
Newton Abbot 61
Norwich 104
Oakham 115, 116
Okehampton 50
Oswestry 117, 118
Padstow 12
Pateley Bridge 160
Peebles 225
Penrith 28-31, 37
Penzance 17
Petworth 137
Polegate 143
Puckshipton 147
Radstock 125
Ramsgate 95
Rezare, Launceston 26
Richmond 154
Ridlington 107
Ross-on-Wye 92
Rye 141
Saxmundham 129, 134
Selkirk 226
Settle 162
Sherborne 71, 126
Shipston-on-Stour 144
Sinnington 158
Southam 146
Southrepps 105
St Ives 16
Stamford 7
Stape 157
Staveley 159
Stranraer 216
Stratford-upon-Avon 145
Strathtummel 223
Stroud 85
Sturminster Newton 69
Sturminster Newton 70
Sudbury 133
Swanage 67
Taunton 127
Tavistock 52
Tenbury Wells 149-151
Thimbleby 156
Thornham 100, 101
Thornhill 217, 228

Tiverton	58
Torrington	47
Totnes	56
Trebarwith	10
Trellech	200
Tunstall	155
Tywyn	196
Wadebridge	11
Wantage	114
Washingborough	99
Wealden	142
Wells-Next-The-Sea	102
West Bexington	66
West Wittering	135
Whitstable	94
Wigglesworth	161
Winchester	87
Windermere	35
Winterton-on-Sea	106
Woodbridge	130
Yelverton	53

Town index for Dog-friendly Pubs

Allostock	169
Amberley	173
Berwick St James	182.1
Brighton	164
Bristol	165
Cambridge	168
Everdon	176
Frithsden	175
Halestown	172
Hastings	182
Hedgerley	167
Long Ashton	177
Lurgashall	180
Marlow	166
Maulden	163.1
Mobberley	170, 171
Saxmundham	179
Swynnerton	178
Tetbury	174
Wisborough Green	181

Photo: The Amberley Inn, entry 173

Join us

TIME AWAY IS FAR TOO PRECIOUS TO SPEND IN THE WRONG PLACE. THAT'S WHY, BACK IN 1994, WE STARTED SAWDAY'S.

Twenty years on, we're still a family concern – and still on a crusade to stamp out the bland and predictable, and help our guests find truly special places to stay.

If you have one, we do hope you'll decide to take the plunge and join us.

ALASTAIR & TOBY SAWDAY

"Trustworthy, friendly and helpful – with a reputation for offering wonderful places and discerning visitors."

JULIA NAISMITH, HOLLYTREE COTTAGE

"Sawday's. Is there any other?"

SONIA HODGSON, HORRY MILL

1 Inn

Warwickshire 2

3 The Fuzzy Duck

4 Nestled in the rolling folds of the Cotswold countryside, close to Stratford-upon-Avon, is this 18th-century coaching inn, polished to perfection by Tania, Adrian and their team. Beautiful fireplaces and gleaming tables, fine china and big sprays of wild flowers tell a tale of comfort and luxury, while the smiling staff are rightly proud of this gem of a pub. You dine like kings and queens in the sparkling bar, or in the clever conversion at the back, overlooking grounds that are part-orchard, part-walled-garden. Try Cotswold chicken breast with slow-cooked chorizo and white bean stew, or a splendid ploughman's with warm Scotch quail's egg. For pudding, try the zingy lemon posset, or treacle tart with orange scented milk ice. If you over-indulge, borrow wellies in your size for a bracing walk then back to your beautiful bed above the bar; rooms are sound-proofed and two have double loft beds (up very vertical ladders) for families. Best of all, the generous team has provided indulgent treats: lovely slippers; a nightcap tipple – come prepared to be spoiled. Bliss. *Secure outside garden; lots of walks on the doorstep. Some livestock nearby.*

5 Rooms 2 doubles: £110–£140.
2 family rooms for 4: £180–£200.

6 Meals Starters from £4.50. Mains from £9.95.

7 Closed Never.

8 Dog biscuits, pig's ears, water, dog beds, blankets and advice on walks.

The Manager
The Fuzzy Duck,
Ilmington Road, Armscote,
Stratford-upon-Avon, CV37 8DD
Tel +44 (0)1608 682 635
Email info@fuzzyduckarmscote.com
Web www.fuzzyduckarmscote.com

9 Entry 145 Map 3

10

WHY BECOME A MEMBER?

Becoming a part of our 'family' of Special Places is like being awarded a Michelin star. Our stamp of approval will tell guests that you offer a truly special experience and you will benefit from our experience, reputation and support.

A CURATED COLLECTION

Our site presents a relatively small and careful selection of Special Places which helps us to stand out like a brilliantly shining beacon.

INSPECT AND RE-INSPECT

Our inspectors have an eagle-eye for the special, but absolutely no check-lists. They visit every member, see every bedroom and bathroom and, on the lucky days, eat the food.

QUALITY, NOT QUANTITY

We don't pretend (or want) to be in the same business as the sites that handle zillions of bookings a day. Using our name ensures that you attract the right kind of guests for you.

VARIETY

From country-house hotels to city pads and funky fincas to blissful B&Bs, we genuinely delight in the individuality of our Special Places.

LOYALTY

Nearly half of our members have been with us for five years or more. We must be doing something right!

The friendly crew

GET IN TOUCH WITH OUR MEMBERSHIP TEAM...

+44 (0)117 204 7810

members@sawdays.co.uk

...OR APPLY ONLINE

sawdays.co.uk/join-us